Liedeke Plate, László Munteán, Airin Farahmand (eds.)
Materials of Culture

Culture & Theory | Volume 285

Liedeke Plate is professor of culture and inclusivity at Radboud University, where she researches the relationship between art, culture and inclusion. A cultural theorist at heart, she focuses on literature, gender and cultural memory and publishes internationally on the subject of women, reading and rewriting, forgetting, the material turn in literary and cultural studies, cultural memory, and gender and urban space. The red thread throughout her research is an inquiry into in the mechanisms in art and culture that foster or hinder inclusive thinking.

László Munteán is assistant professor of cultural studies and American studies at Radboud University. His publications have focused on the memorialization of 9/11 in literature and the visual arts, American cities and architecture, as well as the architectural heritage of Budapest. In a broader sense, his scholarly work revolves around the juncture of literature, visual culture, and cultural memory in American and Eastern European contexts.

Airin Farahmand is a Ph.D. candidate at Radboud University, where she also obtained her B.A. in arts and culture studies (cum laude) and her research master's in art and visual culture. Her dissertation project focuses on artworks engaging with the plastic crisis. Before moving to the Netherlands, she completed a B.Sc. in mechanical engineering at Tabriz University. In a broader sense, her research interests include questions of agency, representation, body politics, and feminist future-making.

Liedeke Plate, László Munteán, Airin Farahmand (eds.)

Materials of Culture

Approaches to Materials in Cultural Studies

[transcript]

The Editors wish to thank the Radboud Institute for Culture and History (RICH), the Literary and Cultural Studies Chair Group, and the Department of Modern Languages and Cultures of Radboud University for their financial support for this project.

Bibliographic information published by the Deutsche Nationalbibliothek
The Deutsche Nationalbibliothek lists this publication in the Deutsche Nationalbibliografie; detailed bibliographic data are available in the Internet at http://dnb.d-nb.de

This work is licensed under the Creative Commons Attribution 4.0 (BY) license, which means that the text may be remixed, transformed and built upon and be copied and redistributed in any medium or format even commercially, provided credit is given to the author.
Creative Commons license terms for re-use do not apply to any content (such as graphs, figures, photos, excerpts, etc.) not original to the Open Access publication and further permission may be required from the rights holder. The obligation to research and clear permission lies solely with the party re-using the material.

First published in 2023 by transcript Verlag, Bielefeld
© Liedeke Plate, László Munteán, Airin Farahmand (eds.)

Cover layout: Kordula Röckenhaus, Bielefeld
Cover illustration: Detail of façade, 15 Síp utca, Budapest, photo by László Munteán
Printed by: Majuskel Medienproduktion GmbH, Wetzlar
https://doi.org/10.14361/9783839466971
Print-ISBN 978-3-8376-6697-7
PDF-ISBN 978-3-8394-6697-1
ISSN of series: 2702-8968
eISSN of series: 2702-8976

Printed on permanent acid-free text paper.

For Anneke Smelik

Contents

Preface 11

Introduction: Materials Matter
László Munteán and Liedeke Plate 13

Part I: Materials of Art

1. **Stitched into Material: On the Makeability of Shells**
   Hanneke Grootenboer.. 37

2. **Celluloid**
   Wilco Versteeg 45

Part II: Materials of Empire

3. **Roman Concrete**
   Astrid Van Oyen 55

4. **Postclassical Marble: Reclaiming Flux in the Reception of Marble in Contemporary Art**
   Maarten De Pourcq 61

Part III: Extractivism and Toxic Colonialism

5. **Asbestos: The Fallout of Shipbreaking in the Global South**
   László Munteán... 75

6. Copper's Suppressed History Unearthed in Otobong Nkanga's Sensual and Embodied Art Practice
   Mette Gieskes 83

7. The Coloniality of Materiality: Brazilwood, or Unlearning with Anton de Kom in the Mauritshuis
   Oscar Ekkelboom 93

Part IV: Energyscapes of the Future

8. Lithium for the Metaverse: Myths of Nuclear and Digital Fusion
   Niels Niessen 103

9. Harnessing the Sun in Tech-on-Climate Discourse
   Rianne Riemens 113

Part V: Materials of the Nation

10. Dutch Peat
    Tom Sintobin 123

11. Milk: Material Entwinements and the Making and Unmaking of Healthy Bodies
    Tess J. Post 133

12. Wool
    Michiel Scheffer 143

Part VI: Affordances of Edible Matter

13. Yes, There Are No Bananas
    Timotheus Vermeulen 151

14. Coca(ine)
    Brigitte Adriaensen 157

Part VII: Material Practices in Digital Culture

15. The Ephemeral Materiality of Sound
    Vincent Meelberg 169

16. Tracing the Voice's Digital Materiality
    Nuno Atalaia 173

17. Interface
    Nishant Shah 181

Part VIII: Enfolding the Body

18. Becoming-*with*: On Textile Companions and Fungi Friends
    Daniëlle Bruggeman and Lianne Toussaint 189

19. Clothing For/Against Walking
    Anna P.H. Geurts 197

20. Mylar Foil: Blankets of Silver and Gold
    Jeroen Boom 207

Part IX: Touching Texts

21. An Archive of the Future: Wood in Thomas Pitfield's *The Poetry of Trees*
    Frederik Van Dam and Ghidy de Koning 215

22. Soft Leather, Wounded Buttons, and a Silk Ribbon: Clothing a Birgittine Rule Manuscript
    Kathryn M. Rudy 223

Part X: Materials of Scholarly Performance

23. The Arts Classroom
    Edwin van Meerkerk 237

24. Ink on Paper
    Carlijn Cober 245

25. The Scholar's Coffee
Liedeke Plate 255

List of Contributors 263

Preface

This book appears on the occasion of our colleague and friend Anneke Smelik's retirement as Professor of Visual Culture. It is meant to honor her pioneering work as a cultural studies scholar and to thank her for her intellectual leadership and companionship.

Anneke's vast oeuvre encompasses visual culture in the broadest sense of the term. Following her dissertation on feminist cinema, *And the Mirror Cracked: Feminist Cinema and Film Theory* (1998), she wrote engagingly about a wide range of topics, including multiculturalism in film and television adaptations of Shakespeare's *Romeo and Juliet*, the (hairless) body, the cyborg, Dutch fashion, techno-fashion, the scientific imaginary in visual culture, new media and education, fashion and memory, and, most recently, fashion, sustainability, and materiality. Anneke always sought ways to share her innovative and thought-provoking insights with colleagues in the field of cultural studies, her students, and the larger public.

In recent years, Anneke's interest in fashion shifted from the visual to the material culture of fashion, particularly to the material dimensions of the clothing we wear and toward the cultural conditions that would allow a more sustainable practice of fashion in an age of technological innovation. Without letting go of her concerns with matters of representation, Anneke's critical thinking about materials and materiality in fashion in her articles and as co-editor of the journal *Critical Studies in Fashion and Beauty* sets the agenda for the next generation of fashion scholars.

It is this critical legacy that we wish to celebrate with this volume. Together with twenty-five colleagues and friends of hers from Radboud University and around the world, we have collected a variety of case studies showing how important it is to give materials more attention than we have done in the past. Demonstrating the entangled relationship between materials and meaning in culture, as Anneke's work on fashion does, *Materials of Culture* advocates for a materials-based approach in cultural studies and thereby honors her invaluable contribution to the field.

Nijmegen, January 2023
The Editors

Introduction: Materials Matter

László Munteán and Liedeke Plate

> But why should people think with the artifacts of material culture alone? Why not also with the air, the ground, mountains and streams, and other living beings? Why not with materials? (Ingold, "Toward an Ecology" 438)

> All things . . . are only momentary aggregations of material. (Appadurai, "The Thing Itself" 15)

In August 2017, anti-racist activists pulled down a Confederate monument in Durham, North Carolina. Making for spectacular photographs, the fallen metal soldier is a clear reminder that materials matter. The statue, indeed, was not merely toppled; it was "crumpled like a beer can," as anthropologist Robin Kirk wrote in an opinion piece. The reason for the relative ease with which the statue was discarded is precisely the same that, throughout the first decades of the twentieth century, allowed for the erection of thousands of similar monuments across the United States: mass-produced, it was made of zinc, a low-cost material that manufacturers dubbed "white bronze" (Fisher; Giaimo) and that allowed for thin wall casting. Ironically, most of these manufacturers were initially based in the industrial North, where both Union and Confederate statues were cast from the same molds (Grissom).

How materials matter can further be illustrated by the so-called Golden Coach (*Gouden Koets*), the Dutch royal carriage gifted by the people of Amsterdam to Queen Wilhelmina of the Netherlands on the occasion of her coronation in 1898. Used throughout the twentieth century to carry the monarch on festive occasions, the Golden Coach had become subject to controversy due to one of its wooden panels called "Tribute of the Colonies," which depicts Black people stooping down in front of the monarch and presenting her with a variety of colonial goods, including sugarcane and cocoa. This representation of the Kingdom of the Netherlands extended to the materials used to make the coach. Modeled after carriages used by Javanese rulers such as the Sultan of Yogyakarta, the coach was made of teak from Java, while the ivory for the handles originated from Sumatra. The gold leaf to which it owes its name was mined in Suriname. Other materials came from different places in the Netherlands: the red woolen cloth from Leiden and the leather from Brabant.

Displaying the entanglement of material and symbolic production, these two examples illustrate the relevance of materials for studying culture. Indeed, if much of the public discussion and scholarly debate revolves around their symbolic meaning, a more material approach reveals that the materials from which the monument and the coach were made are integral, not only to their material constitution, but also to how and what they signify and to whom. In this book, we offer over twenty-five case studies of materials of culture, ranging from marble and concrete to copper, lithium, and asbestos to wool, peat, milk, coffee, ink, bacteria, and mycelium. Together, these case studies illustrate the argument that materials matter if we are to formulate a clear understanding of culture today.

This book brings materials back into the fold of cultural studies. Focusing on dimensions of cultural objects, lives, and practices long taken for granted and therefore largely left unexamined, the "materials turn" we propose here echoes with paradigmatic shifts in scholarship and resonates with a more general trend in culture and society, which has much to do with the present anthropocenic condition—climate catastrophe, mass extinction, planetary exhaustion, and energy transition. Awakening to the depletion of the Earth and its natural resources and confronted with the very material consequences of our way of life, we find ourselves lacking knowledge about materials and material life, ignorant of how they work, act, react, and interact with other materials, including those that make up our bodies. By calling for a "materials turn" within the larger sweep of the material turn in the humanities and the social sciences, we propose to adopt a materials-based perspective on culture, which has so far been lacking in cultural studies scholarship.

Toward a Materials-Based Perspective

As consumers living in the Global North, we may be aware that the stuff with which we surround ourselves is predominantly made and assembled in Asia, yet we seldom know what materials they are made from, nor do we know whence those materials have been retrieved, how, by whom, and at what cost. This "genesis amnesia," as Pierre Bourdieu termed the cultural obliviousness to how things are made (*Outline of a Theory* 79), including their commoditization and the outsourcing and offshoring of their production, applies in particular to the food we eat and the clothes we wear—the stuff we put in and on our bodies, and disperse in our surroundings (through the excretion of metabolic waste and the microfibers that detach from the clothes, among others). We hardly know what our processed foods are made of, under what conditions the foodstuffs are produced, or how they come to us prior to reaching the supermarket or web shop. Even if care labels in clothes inform us about their place of manufacture and the materials they contain, we rarely know how those materials were produced and what journeys they underwent before reaching the garment manufacturing factories, workshops, or sweatshops. Often, we prefer to remain oblivious to how our clothes are made and the human and environmental cost of the global garment industry, even after the 2013 collapse of the Rana Plaza building in Bangladesh and the 2015 documentary *The True Cost* that revealed its devasting effects, including death, disease, and river and soil pollution.

Materials have long been used as temporal landmarks for human technological advances, as in the Stone, Bronze, and Iron Ages (Miodownik 6). Although artificial materials such as paper, glass, and textiles have existed for millennia, the recent onset of what anthropologist Adam Drazin calls a "materials revolution" ("Materials Transformations" xvi) has led to the proliferation of a variety of synthetic materials, alloys, and superalloys that are too difficult to trace in the gadgets we use, the clothes we wear, the food we eat, the air we breathe, and the bodies we have. Inscriptions such as "Designed by Apple in California. Manufactured in China" offer little help in identifying the materials used for manufacturing a MacBook, not to mention their histories and places of origin. Such blind spots in our knowledge of materials apply to almost everything that we take for granted in our lives and without which the curing of illnesses, telecommunication, the Internet, and air travel, to name only a few, would be unimaginable.

With growing awareness of the irreversible trajectory of an unfolding environmental crisis and its unequal effects across the globe, sustainability has become the order of the day. Increasingly, the drive to buy, consume, and discard is met with calls to buy less, buy consciously and ethically, and reuse, recycle, exchange, and donate. These incentives urge us to look at the things around us with new eyes. Selective garbage collection, to take a mundane example, compels us to think about the objects we want to dispose of in terms of the materials they have been made from. Used to the comfort of encountering objects as commodities ready to be used and discarded, this relatively new prominence afforded to materials is symptomatic of a shift toward a materials-based perspective in both public and academic discourse.

Materials science has been spearheading the study of the properties of materials in the service of industry, design, and engineering that have provided us with the technological feats of the Silicon Age, indispensable for twenty-first-century life (Fratzl et al.). In response to the proliferation of materials from which to choose and with which to work, so-called materials libraries have emerged, raising awareness of new innovative and sustainable materials and facilitating the transfer of knowledge about them between materials producers and users (Wilkes; Wilkes and Miodownik).

The need to become familiar with the world of materials also extends to the general public. In recent years, several books have appeared that aim to (re-)educate us about the materials that constitute our lives. A manifesto denouncing the paucity of materials education in schools and aiming to reclaim material culture from the sphere of consumption, French designer David Enon's recent publication *La vie matérielle: Mode d'emploi* (*Material Life: User's Manual*) challenges its readers to re-acquaint themselves with the material world through a series of practical exercises. In the same vein, in *Stuff Matters: Exploring the Marvelous Materials That Shape Our Man-made World*, London-based materials scientist Mark Miodownik takes us on a tour of the materials in his immediate vicinity while drinking coffee on his rooftop and groups them according to qualities such as indomitable, trusted, fundamental, and delicious to foreground the sensuous ways in which we encounter them as parts of objects. For instance, explaining how a range of volatile organic molecules are responsible for the peculiar smell of old books, he mentions how research into the chemistry of book smell can help libraries to monitor and preserve extensive collections (Miodownik 37).

Recently, claims for increased material literacy have been made outside materials science. Evoking László Moholy-Nagy's injunction to incorporate sensory experiences in education, art historian Ann-Sophie Lehmann defines material literacy as "a broad sensitivity to materials and their diverse meanings," which differs from the in-depth knowledge of materials scientists and the specialized skills of craftspeople ("Material Literacy" 22). Seetal Solanki, founder and director of the relational practice called Ma-tt-er and author of *Why Materials Matter: Responsible Design for a Better World*, advocates for a similar kind of material literacy—one that would make the academic knowledge production of materials accessible beyond university campuses and research laboratories ("Material Literacy"). A related term with a slightly different emphasis is "material intelligence," coined by Glenn Adamson, author of *Fewer, Better Things: The Hidden Wisdom of Objects*. Adamson defines material intelligence as "a deep understanding of the material world around us, an ability to read that material environment, and the know-how required to give it new form" (4). While material literacy foregrounds the importance of sensorial exposure to materials, material intelligence emphasizes the hands-on knowledge of working with them—a largely instinctive faculty "that can flourish or fade depending on how it is nurtured" (Adamson 4). Finding ways, methods, and a language to reconnect—and literally get in touch—with the world of materials is also the aim of the recently launched online journal *Material Intelligence*, which Adamson coedits with Carolyn Herrera-Perez. Each issue is dedicated to a specific material—thus far including copper, rubber, linen, and oak—approached from a variety of disciplinary, artistic, and craft-related perspectives.

Material literacy should also include materials that we mostly perceive as nuisances, such as dust and pollution. A closer look at dust reveals it as "a gathering place, a random community of what has been and what is yet to be, a catalog of traces and a set of promises: dead skin cells and plant pollen, hair and paper fibers, not to mention dust mites who make it their home" (Marder xi–xii). In his 2009 project "The Ethics of Dust," preservation architect Jorge Otero-Pailos used innovative technology to clean a wall surface of the Doge's Palace in Venice and preserve the pollution removed from the wall in a layer of latex, which he exhibited in the palace. Revealing the pervasiveness of pollution as a civilizational product, Otero-Pailos's project configures dust as a material of culture (Ebersberger and Zyman).

Energy is also material and should not remain in the background when thinking of materials of culture. As a subset of the Environmental Humanities—a developing interdisciplinary field that brings Humanities perspectives to pressing environmental problems—"Energy Humanities" (Szeman and Boyer) draws attention to the role of energy in modern societies and examines the cultural, political, and ethical aspects of their current reliance on fossil fuels. What matters is not only the amount of extracted gas and oil burnt but also their properties and affordances. In *Art and Energy: How Culture Changes*, Barry Lord argues that human creativity is deeply linked to the resources available on Earth and that each new source of energy, from the ancient mastery of fire through the exploitation of coal, oil, and gas, to the development of today's renewable solar and wind energy sources, fundamentally transforms art and culture. Similarly, in "The Problem of Energy," sociologist John Urry calls for social thought to engage with energy, pointing out how curious it is that Zygmunt Bauman's famed analysis of modern life as "liquid" did not include a consideration of how the "literal liquid" oil enabled this modernity (6). This oversight of social thought derives from its roots in the Enlightenment and modern thought. Urry writes: "Energy especially shows what we can call the 'hubris of the modern'. The human and physical/material worlds are utterly intertwined and the dichotomy between the two is a construct that mystifies understanding of the problem of energy" (7). A decade later, the energy crisis in Europe in the wake of the war in Ukraine and the global energy transition have further underscored the need to theorize energy and address it as a material of culture, as some of the chapters in this book do.

Whereas the recent material turn in the humanities and social sciences has yielded an upsurge of interest in objects, things, commodities, and the materiality of the body (Attala and Steel; Bogost and Schaberg; Cornish and Saunders; Del Val; Salamon), materials have, thus far, remained a largely uncharted terrain in these fields. Arjun Appadurai's influential 1986 volume, *The Social Life of Things: Commodities in Cultural Perspective*, inspired a reevaluation of commodities through the lens of the cultural practices whereby they are invested with value and meaning in the longue durée of what he terms their "social life" (e.g., Boscagli; Miller). In response to the spate of such inquiries, fellow anthropologist Tim Ingold proposes that studies in material culture focus less on materiality in the abstract and more on the properties of the materials that things are made of, their "fluxes," as he writes in "Materials against Materiality," and their movement and lines of flow, as he discusses in "Toward an Ecology of Materials." In his 2006 essay "The Thing Itself," Appadurai had already conceded that "[i]n some way, all things are congealed moments in a longer social trajectory. All things are brief deposits of this or that property . . . they are only momentary aggregations of material" (15). In the face of a materials revolution and concomitant concerns about sustainability, we believe it is high time that Appadurai's temporary approach to things, as moments in a longer trajectory, is updated to encompass the lives of materials in a critical and socially engaged manner. This update would recognize that materials are emergent and the product or result of historical relations; and that, "birthless and deathless as materials are," their trajectories are more about transformation than biographies (Drazin, "To Live in a Material World" 14).

The proposed update, moreover, is made all the more pertinent by the circulation of an unprecedented diversity of materials that, as Drazin contends, are extracted from sources that are often scarce or located in conflict zones ("Materials Transformations" xvi). The use and circulation of materials, he adds, is therefore "not politically or economically neutral" (xvii). In addition, legislation regulating the use of materials also affects their use and presence in culture. A case in point is asbestos, which is the subject of Chapter 8. Long valued for its fire-resistant properties, its toxicity (leading, among others, to lung cancer) led to an asbestos ban in many countries of the Global North. However, due to the high cost of its safe removal and recycling, the dismantling of cargo ships owned by Western corporations and containing large amounts of asbestos is outsourced to the Global South, where safety and environmental regulations are often unenforced, attesting to the persistence of lingering colonial and imperial fault lines. Other examples discussed in this book include the effects of legislation on the material proliferation of the banana and its cultural uses and significance as a material of popular film culture in Chapter 18 and those of legislation facilitating the commodification of cocaine in Chapter 19. By adopting a materials-based perspective within the interdisciplinary field of cultural studies, the essays in the present volume set out to respond to this call.

Materials of Culture

The approaches featured in this book are centered on "materials of culture"—a notion that we employ to account for the ways in which materials enable the emergence and transformation of cultural practices or evince a life of their own that may thwart such practices through their combinations, affordances, and agency. We use this notion in two interrelated senses. First, "materials of culture" denotes the material foundations of cultural and artistic practices, namely that our corporeal existence and day-to-day actions in life are entangled in, and facilitated or hampered by, materials of all sorts. Second, "materials of culture" also highlights the ways in which materials are invested with meaning once encountered in the form of objects, things, commodities, and bodies. Culture, in this sense, refers to the ways in which materials are negotiated, both physically and discursively, as well as sensorily and affectively. While enacting different approaches—from the material to the cultural and vice versa—the essays in this book demonstrate that these two senses are inextricably entwined.

A case in point is the gold leaf covering the above-mentioned Golden Coach, the origin of which had been the subject of some speculation until recently. Ultrasensitive analysis of gold samples retrieved from the carriage allowed researchers to examine lead isotopes formed by the radioactive decay of uranium and thorium that vary by geographical region. The analysis provided conclusive evidence that the gold had been extracted in the former Dutch colony of Suriname. From the perspective of the present publication, the methods employed in this research and the discourse that its results have engendered calls for the recognition of materials as "actants" in Bruno Latour's sense, rather than merely the inert constituents of objects. The gold used for the carriage can be visualized as a rotating vortex generating both centripetal and centrifugal forces that illustrate the two senses that we ascribe to materials of culture. The former pulls us into the spectroscopic realm, to analyze the very fabric of the gold and its chemical properties that supplied scientists with information on its geographical origin, while the latter highlights the widening gyre of cultural practices, networks, discourses, and emotions attached to the material. The inward- and outward-directed currents of this vortex delineate the contours of an affectively charged material-discursive forcefield within which material evidence of the gold's colonial origins is negotiated through cultural practices, including King Willem-Alexander's decision to refrain from using the carriage.

A materials-based perspective on culture, therefore, requires that we attend to the operations of such forcefields around materials in cultural practices. In order to do so, however, we need to learn about materials just as much as we need to unlearn our inclination to think of them as less important than the objects made from them. It is only by way of releasing the world of materials from the hold of objects that we are able to follow materials, as Ingold insists in "Bringing Things to Life" (8). Representing a wide range of theoretical and methodological traditions within cultural studies scholarship, each of the chapters in this volume is centered on a particular material and leads readers through their transformations in a variety of artistic and cultural practices. The following section maps the trajectory of scholarship that provides the theoretical backbone for the present volume.

Materials in Cultural Studies

Much of the thrust of the material turn in Western academia has been geared toward unsettling the deeply entrenched precepts and methodological instincts of the linguistic turn that dominated scholarly inquiry in the humanities and the social sciences for the bulk of the twentieth century. Reacting to the linguistic turn's propensity to interpret culture in terms of texts, signs, and signification, the material turn entails a vast body of interdisciplinary scholarship that constitutes a paradigm shift in conceptualizing materiality, material agency, human-nonhuman relations, and the life of things in general. Challenging such foundational binaries of modern Western thought as nature versus culture, object versus subject, and human versus thing, the theories of the material turn have sought to redress implicit anthropocentric biases, which are seen to have led to the current ecological and civilizational crises. One of the ways in which these biases can be challenged is through the strategic mobilization of a terminology originating in a variety of philosophical traditions, including (but in no way limited to) Merleau-Ponty's phenomenology, the philosophy of Heidegger, Spinoza, Deleuze, and Guattari, as well as in recent feminist, non-representational, new materialist, and environmentalist thought. A bird's-eye view on the terminology emerging in the wake of these diverse trends reveals a discursive shift: from essences to flows; from meanings to forces, becomings, and assemblages; from inert objects and human agency to actants and material agency; and from apparatuses of interpretation toward the sensorial and the affective. While the conceptual paradigm shift that such changes in terminology indicate has affected cultural studies in a variety of ways, thinking with and from materials (rather than things, objects, and materiality in general) is still an unexplored path in the field. It is, therefore, necessary to assess preexisting approaches that can facilitate a "materials turn" in the field.

One of the nodal points in the debate concerning materiality has been the question of agency. In this regard, Bill Brown's "Thing Theory" has been an often-quoted reference for the distinction it draws between objects and things. According to Brown, objects are easily recognizable, nameable, and usable, while things undermine schemes of categorization and control. We usually encounter the "thingness" of objects, he argues, when they stop functioning in ways that we expect them to do. The distinction between objects and things is not based on ontological differences between those categories, but on the different ways in which we experience the material world around us. Brown distinguishes between three manifestations of thingness that are helpful when trying to discern material agency: first, "the amorphousness out of which objects are materialized by the (ap)perceiving subject;" second, "as what exceeds their mere materialization as objects or their mere utilization as objects—their force as a sensuous presence or as a metaphysical presence;" and, third, "as the before and after of the object" in the form of latency, or, its counterpart, excess (5). Although Brown says little about materials themselves, these conceptualizations of thingness gesture toward a form of material agency that manifests itself in the experience of excess that transgresses physical, temporal, linguistic, and conceptual borders.

The interdisciplinary field of material culture studies more broadly, and the work of Daniel Miller in particular, conceive of agency as the potential of material things in the formation of social relations (*Materiality* 11–15). Preexisting work on the analyses of patterns of consumption (Bourdieu) and practices of everyday life (Barthes; De Certeau; Lefebvre), on material production vis-à-vis systems of signification and symbolization (Williams), as well as the notion of object biographies (Appadurai, *The Social Life*; Kopytoff) have been instrumental to this conceptualization of agency. Although material culture studies have drawn heavily on science studies, particularly Bruno Latour's Actor-Network Theory, as well as social anthropology, for example, through Alfred Gell's work on the agency of art objects, its focus on social relations is predicated on the human and thus reinforces the human/nonhuman binary. Edited by Tony Bennett and Patrick Joyce, the contributions to the 2010 volume *Material Powers: Cultural Studies, History, and the Material Turn* constitute a pioneering interdisciplinary effort in thinking through the problem of material agency and state power in relation to, among other themes, colonial infrastructures.

A significant movement in philosophy that challenges this binary is new materialism, a multifaceted area of inquiry associated with the work of, among others, Rosi Braidotti, Karen Barad, Jane Bennett, and Manuel DeLanda. New materialist conceptualizations of material agency shift the focus from human-nonhuman relations toward the ontology of things. In her *Vibrant Matter: A Political Ecology of Things*, Bennett presents the notion of thing-power as a political and ethical category that "gestures toward the strange ability of ordinary, man-made items to exceed their status as objects and to manifest traces of independence or aliveness, constituting the outside of our own experience" (xvi). Drawing on Spinozist understandings of affect, she regards the intensity of impersonal affect as the catalyst of thing-power and goes as far as equating affect with materiality (xiii). While Bennett admits to the necessity of a modicum of anthropomorphism to ensure the political force of thing-power in language, Karen Barad's theory of agential realism destabilizes the material/discursive binary ("Posthumanist Performativity"; *Meeting the Universe Halfway*). Drawing on quantum physics and Judith Butler's theory of performativity, Barad introduces the term "intra-action" to relocate agency in the dynamic forces in which things are constituted. Replacing "interaction," which presupposes the existence of preexisting entities exercising their agencies, intra-action also entails that discourse is not imposed on, but rather is co-constitutive of, material relations, engendering what Barad calls material-discursive phenomena ("Posthumanist Performativity" 825).

Archaeology and anthropology have yielded significant contributions to the debate on material agency. Like in material culture studies, the influence of Actor-

Network Theory makes itself felt in both fields. The archaeologist Bjørnar Olsen, for instance, criticizes preexisting approaches to material culture in archaeology as a "mediating window" (25) onto social relations, while the anthropologist Tim Ingold takes a fundamentally different angle on agency. Ingold takes issue with proponents of agency by emphasizing its counterproductive tendency to "re-animate a world of things already deadened or rendered inert by arresting the flows of substance that give them life" ("Bringing Things" 7). Ingold relegates this approach to what he calls the hylomorphic model of the world, in which "[c]ulture furnishes the forms, nature the materials" ("Toward an Ecology" 432). Drawing on Deleuze and Guattari's idea of forces and Heidegger's understanding of things as gatherings, Ingold redefines things as a "gathering of materials in movement" (439) and advocates abandoning the concept of agency for what he describes as "life"—a "generative capacity of that encompassing field of relations within which forms arise and are held in place" ("Bringing Things" 3). Thinking of materiality as raw and situated in relation to human agency ("Toward an Ecology" 432) is, as Ingold reminds us, one of the pitfalls of the hylomorphic model. Instead, he makes a plea for materials as "matter considered in respect of its occurrence in processes of flow and transformation" (439). This is akin to Barad's understanding of matter as "ongoing historicity" ("Posthumanist Performativity" 810). To underline the co-constitutive power of such transformations in Barad's sense, Ingold upgrades Actor-Network Theory's focus on networks by introducing the term meshwork instead. He does so in order to highlight "the fluid character of the life process, wherein boundaries are sustained only thanks to the flow of materials across them" ("Bringing Things" 12). Rather than capturing or pinning down such relations, Ingold defines the task of the researcher as following these lines (8).

Adam Drazin and Susanne Küchler's 2015 edited volume entitled *The Social Life of Materials* represents a significant shift of interest from objects and material culture toward materials in the field of anthropology. Challenging views that associate materials with nature yet are devoid of a social component, their volume sets out to relocate materials in society, asking: "what is it that materials actually do?" (Drazin, "Materials Transformations" xviii). While our project on "materials of culture" has clear affinities with their "anthropology of materials," our focus nonetheless differs fundamentally, inquiring instead into what happens when we think of culture as materially constituted and "follow" such materials in artistic and cultural practices. In doing so, we build on earlier work, notably *Materializing Memory in Art and Popular Culture*, in which we explored the materiality of memory, inquiring into the previously overlooked material dimensions of "technologies" and "performances" of cultural memory (Munteán, Plate, and Smelik; Plate and Smelik). Discussing a wide range of memory objects, things, and practices, from miniatures, monumental books, and souvenirs, to ruins, techno-fashion, the Internet of Things, and traumatic reenactment, *Materializing Memory in Art and Popular Culture* sought to account for the material form and substance of acts of memory while illuminating the agency of objects and things in remembrance.

Yet our turn to materials in cultural studies does not stand in isolation. Rather, it is accompanied by parallel inquiries, notably in art history and fashion studies. Let us return for a moment to art historian Ann-Sophie Lehmann's call for material literacy. Discussing the role of education and the legacy of the Bauhaus school in promoting material literacy, Lehmann underlines that material literacy entails unlearning the impulse of privileging form over material: "Increasingly, therefore, material—long perceived as merely a dull prerequisite to the far more important notion of 'form'—is returning to creative curricula as a meaningful agent" ("Material Literacy" 26). In a similar vein, fellow art historian Edward S. Cooke Jr. emphasizes the role of the sensorial in giving a fuller account of the world of materials in scholarship:

> When we privilege sight and visual analysis alone, we fail to use a full battery of analytical tools deploying our eyes, touch, *and* embodied experiences to understand the material world. How might we link visual, haptic, and tacit knowledge of the material world when we have become distant from *making* and are more comfortable with approximations? ("The Need for Material Literacy")

Anneke Smelik's work in critical fashion studies, bringing new materialism and posthumanism to a domain long dominated by visual analyses, is crucial here. Smelik shifts the emphasis to materials, examining non-human factors in the field of fashion, ranging from so-called raw materials (cotton) to so-called smart materials (solar cells), and from the texture of the garment to the tactility of the human body ("New Materialism"). Introducing the notion of material agency, which "helps to understand fashion as materially embedded in a network of human and non-human actors . . ., expanding fashion beyond the frame of the human body and human identity to the non-human world of technology and ecology" (34), Smelik discusses the intertwinement of human bodies with the non-human—fibers, silicones, garments, and technologies—in the fashion of Dutch designer Iris van Herpen in the light of posthumanist theory ("Fractal Folds"). It parallels work in literary studies, for example Kiene Brillenburg Wurth's work on "book presence" and the materiality of the book (*Book Presence*), and Liedeke Plate's efforts to (re-)materialize literary studies, discussing the lack of a language to speak of the materiality of reading, the resulting impoverishment of sense experience, the reduction of a multisensory experience to a mental activity, and the ensuing neglect of the act of reading's many and diverse social and cultural meanings ("Doing Things with Literature"). Similarly relevant is the work of anthropologist Birgit Meyer in materializing the study of religion, building on the precept that the dimension of the material, including the sensing body, is integral, rather than supplemental, to religion (Meyer and Houtman).

A parallel track of inquiry concerns space and the built environment. In "Bringing Things to Life," Ingold refers to the theoretical works of Finnish architect Juhani Pallasmaa, who conceives of buildings not as fixed structures, but as ongoing processes laden with life that entail all the materials used for their construction being exposed to, and transformed by, their inhabitants and elements (5). In order to follow this meshwork of processes, one needs to practice haptic vision, which "seeks not to freeze the surface corrugations in some momentary form, so that they may be modeled in the mind through a one-to-one mapping of data points on the surface and in the model, but to join with the currents and with the wind" (Ingold, "Surface Visions" 103). Although working toward different ends, a similar disposition toward materials can be traced in the work of Eyal Weizman, founder of forensic architecture. In Weizman's view, "[d]eterioration and erosion continue the builders' processes of form-making. Cracks make their way from geologic formations across city surfaces to buildings and architectural details. Moving within and across inert matter and built structures, they connect mineral formations and artificial constructions" (7). A similarly materials-based perspective can be traced in anthropologist Gastón Gordillo's notion of rubble (in relation to ruin) as a process of disintegration imbued with colonial histories unclaimed by the heritage industry in his native Argentina. Drawing on these ideas, László Munteán's work on plaster archaeology has attempted to engage with architectural façades as layered surfaces holding information about the urban past unintentionally preserved in plaster.

Material Vocabularies and Methodologies

To think of culture as materially constituted, and to propose to follow these materials of culture as they gather in artistic and cultural practices, entails rethinking what the object of cultural studies is and how it works. Such a reframing, moreover, calls for alternative approaches, and we will need to acquaint ourselves with material vocabularies, methods, and methodologies if we are to pursue cultural studies in a way that gives materials their due.

As Drazin explains, materials "may be distinguished in a number of different ways: by chemical atomic composition, chemical or crystalline structure, origins, or the ways they are used in a particular place" ("Materials Transformations" xxvi). Depending on how one frames the material, one will follow different things. The differences are disciplinary, of course, although part of the present argument is that the study of materials should not continue to be confined to a separate area of the natural sciences but that more knowledge of materials should be integrated with cultural studies scholarship. Following Sophie Woodward in her practical guide to doing materiality studies, *Material Methods: Researching and Thinking with Things*, we might say that a material understanding of culture requires two initial steps: first, to frame an issue, object, or practice as material; and second, to frame the material in a particular way (24). All of the authors in this book took a discrete material as their point of departure, framing it from the onset as material. However, how they framed the material depended on their understanding of how art and culture are constituted in materials. The chapters, therefore, present an array of material understandings, with authors sometimes discussing the chemical composition or structure of their selected material, and other times focusing on the latter's material properties or material effects.

However, how does one "follow" materials of culture as they gather in artistic and cultural practices and in processes of flow and transformation? To pose the question is to raise the issue of method. With the shift of perspective from text, sign, and meaning to materials in flux come serious methodological and terminological challenges for cultural studies.

To begin with the latter: a focus on materials requires a vocabulary to talk about them—a "jargon" that is often the preserve of the professionals that work with them. Robert Macfarlane's acclaimed *Landmarks* brought to the attention of the wider public the disappearance of words to speak of landscape, nature, and the weather from our lexicons. This impoverishment of language is also an attrition of our empirical, phenomenological, and material experience—the words falling into disuse being on a par with a lack of need for them. Such linguistic attrition we find reflected in the chapters on peat and wool, whose respective authors both observe how the words used to talk about the materials are better known in proverbs and metaphorical uses than in their literal meanings denoting material condition, property, or use. However, wielding specialized vocabularies as they write about materials, the authors in this book also unlock these terminologies for the benefit of a more material understanding of art and culture.

Method, which etymologically means "mode of proceeding" or "mode of investigation," can be defined as "the way in which research is done." And surely, this way is different when one's research centers on materials. While there is no shortage of methods in cultural studies to research art objects or cultural things, materials of culture require new methods and experimentation. In the above-mentioned *Material Methods*, alongside methods for researching (with) objects and things, Woodward outlines some methodological possibilities (and implications) for researching materials. Here we limit ourselves to those most pertinent to the study of materials of culture as we have defined them, thus focusing on methods for researching materials as they gather in cultural things (and leaving aside methods that are more focused on, or using, objects, such as object interviews, object elicitations, and object biographies).

The methods for researching materials outlined by Woodward are derived from the field of archaeology, for instance, excavation, but also methods exploring surface assemblages and depositional practices, which can provide insight into how an assemblage came into being, as well as into the effects of things being drawn or placed together (77–79). They are adapted from anthropology, for instance, ethnography, observation, and participation, which allow "for different ways of knowing—the embodied, multi-sensory, material, and kinaesthetic" (139). Furthermore, they are borrowed from creative material practices, for instance, arts-based and design-led methods such as model building and prototyping, which, as methods that foreground materials and their transformations as part of a creative and embodied multi-sensory process, can be reframed as a material method (67).

Finally, there is the method of "follow-the-thing" or "follow-the-materials," which may or may not concur, not least, as "things can endure when materials decay or things fall apart yet their materials endure" (Woodward 110). Akin to, yet different from, Appadurai's and Kopytoff's "cultural biography of objects," this method may involve following the trajectories of things and of materials but differs, as Drazin points out, insofar as "[m]aterials have no births and deaths but emergences and re-emergences in reconfigurations of matter" ("To Live in a Materials World" 27). Whereas the Life Cycle Assessment (LCA) or cradle-to-grave analysis, which follow a product through its different phases, from the extraction of materials to manufacture to use and disposal, have become standard methods of measuring the environmental impact of products for companies, governmental institutes, and NGOs in all sectors and around the world, following the thing in the opposite direction—in "reverse commodity flow," that is—"opens up the possibilities for seeing things as just assemblages of materials that come together or are disassembled" (Woodward 113).

Of course, one can follow materials in many different ways. For instance, the essays in a 2013 edited volume, *Meaning in Materials, 1400–1800*, are predicated on the tripartite criteria of interaction, attribution, and comparison in their approximations of the relation between materials and meaning-making in art (Lehmann, "How Materials Make Meaning"). In contrast, in his recent book, *Global Objects: Toward a Connected Art History*, Edward S. Cooke Jr. takes a different path by dedicating the first part of his book to an extensive survey of materials, focusing both on their entangled histories and global circulation, and on their movement across continents and cultures, in order to provide a more holistic—and indeed alternative—understanding of the interrelation of materials, craft, artistry, and culture that only a materials-based perspective on objects can disclose. Discussing the agency of materials in relation to their properties and affordances and the way in which they have been extracted, processed, and worked on, Cooke lays bare the hidden histories they hold and suggests that scholars "resist the tendency to become medium specialists which precludes an understanding of material flows and a fuller sense of artistic, social, and historical context" (25).

While few of the essays in this volume explicitly address the question of method, all of them, in one way or another, engage with it through the framing of their "object" of study as material and their chosen mode of proceeding to do research. In the section that follows, we describe these material approaches to materials of culture.

The Content of This Book

The first part of the book, "Materials of Art," focuses on the materials of which art is made and discusses the performative power of art in relation to the ontology of its materials. It opens with Hanneke Grootenboer's "Stitched into Material: On the Makeability of Shells," which argues that shells, as hybrid things—part nature, part artifice—assume a particular position as materials of culture. A thrill to the senses, shells have been mysterious and awe-inspiring objects of nature ever since they flooded the exotica markets of early modern Amsterdam. Grootenboer uses this early modern fascination for shells to rethink "materiality" and "the material." In "Celluloid," Wilco Versteeg discusses Jean-Luc Godard's practice of filmmaking as *"penser avec les mains"* ("thinking with the hands") as a material practice of resistance foregrounding the material of film—celluloid—against domineering Hollywood-modes of filmmaking predicated on plot, characters, and visual effects. Focusing on *Le livre d'image* [*The Image Book*] (2018), the culmination of Godard's sixty-plus years of cinematic experimentations with film, Versteeg demonstrates how Godard "thinks film" through his material practice as a filmmaker, seeking to understand the possibilities and limits of celluloid through radical montage.

The second part of the book, "Materials of Empire," explores materials that have been central to the expression and manifestation of Ancient Rome's imperial power. In "Roman Concrete," by tracing its material histories, Astrid Van Oyen discusses how *opus caementicium*—Roman concrete—helped produce the imperial Roman world. Rather than tracing a Roman cultural revolution via proxy evidence, such as the shape of pots or styles of wall painting that effectively leave matter and materials silent, Van Oyen explores how a more fundamental rethinking of concrete's historical role can lead to new historical insights. In "Postclassical Marble: Reclaiming Flux in the Reception of Marble in Contemporary Art," Maarten De Pourcq takes materials as his starting point for his postclassical inquiry into the reception of Greco-Roman antiquity. Concentrating on Kara Walker's installation *Fons Americanus* (2019), his chapter takes a materials-based postclassical stance, first, on the way in which white marble became a central element of the art-historical paradigm of classicism and, second, on the role played by white marble in contemporary artworks that question classicist paradigms by calling attention to their materials and the contingency of their presence, monumentality, and social use.

The third part, "Extractivism and Toxic Colonialism," highlights lingering colonial routines in practices of material extraction and the disposal of toxic materials. In "Asbestos: The Fallout of Shipbreaking in the Global South," László Munteán focuses on asbestos, a carcinogenic material once used extensively for fireproofing and insulation. Munteán's chapter explores how the high costs of recycling asbestos in the Global North have led to the outsourcing of this task to the shipbreaking yards of Bangladesh, India, and Pakistan, where lenient environmental, safety, and health regulations allow for the recycling and reselling of asbestos stripped from ships built in the 1970s and 1980s. The chapter highlights the damage caused by asbestos in these countries as one engrained in lingering colonial and imperial power dynamics that continue to ravage and exploit human lives, the environment, and the economies of the Global South. In her chapter "Copper's Suppressed History Unearthed in Otobong Nkanga's Sensual and Embodied Art Practice," Mette Gieskes discusses the Belgian-Nigerian artist's work exploring the ecological damage and human suffering caused by the extraction of materials such as copper. Her chapter highlights the uneven distribution of resources in the circulation of materials in the globalized world via an analysis of a number of Nkanga's installation, sculptural, and performance works, which critically explore the scarred landscape of a former Nigerian copper mine, but also poetically articulate the metal's sensory qualities and potential to connect people through the soil. This part is concluded by Oscar Ekkelboom's "The Coloniality of Materiality: Brazilwood, or, Unlearning with Anton de Kom in the Mauritshuis," which provides a powerful critique of "materials" as a concept that is predicated on an extractivist practice that reinforces the logic of coloniality. Using the wooden interior paneling of The Hague's Mauritshuis as a case study and taking into account that the original brazilwood paneling has been lost to fire, Ekkelboom's decolonial approach opens up thinking about the afterlives of things in the absence of their materiality, underlining how slavery's history often hides in intangible legacies.

The essays in the fourth part of the book, "Energyscapes of the Future," delve into the ethical dimensions of cultural discourses on energy resources supplying new technologies. In "Lithium for the Metaverse: Myths of Nuclear and Digital Fusion," Niels Niessen argues that lithium may prove essential in the development of virtual worlds and the virtualization of the material world, destroying natural and human ecosystems in the process. The lightest metal and the least solid of all solid elements, lithium is used in batteries, but it is also essential to nuclear fusion, potentially introducing humankind to a new space-time currently imagined as the "Metaverse." Rianne Riemens' chapter, "Harnessing the Sun in Tech-On Climate Discourse," focuses on representations of the Sun in promotional materials by Big Tech companies, examining the energy imaginaries created by Apple's "Better" (2014) and Amazon's "The Future of Energy" (2020) commercials, both of which propose solar energy and technological innovation as critical solutions for a green future. Riemens argues that these discursive texts harness the Sun as a limitless and immaterial source of energy, just as "the cloud" metaphor is used to frame the Internet as limitless and immaterial.

"Materials of the Nation," the fifth part of the book, discusses the role of certain materials in imaginaries of national identity. Tom Sintobin focuses on the peat and bogs that once played a vital role in the production of fuel and, even after their replacement with charcoal fuel, remained nostalgic reference points for regional, national, and even transnational identities and memory in Dutch literature and regional museums after 1950. Sintobin's chapter explores contemporary discourses on peat and bogs in the Netherlands facilitated by, and woven around, a range of site-specific artworks. In her chapter on milk, Tess Post examines the ways in which cow's milk has been construed as a material domain for the negotiation of Dutch national identity from colonial times to the ongoing farmers' demonstrations. Discussing the recent upheaval about the waste of Dutch wool, Michiel Scheffer argues that the commotion is misplaced, the result of a misunderstanding of the materiality of wool. Whereas the recent shift toward sustainability is revitalizing a European wool industry on the verge of extinction, any rebirth of the industry, Scheffer contends, is dependent upon a thorough knowledge of the material intricacies of wool and of the physical and chemical processes required to produce an acceptable woolen product.

The sixth part is dedicated to "Affordances of Edible Matter." Timotheus Vermeulen's chapter considers the life of the banana in art and popular culture to both problematize and instantiate the relationship between object and thing in Heidegger's sense (i.e., a thing understood exclusively in relation to a subject, which is to say, as use or value) and between metaphor and materiality in twenty-first-century discourse. Tracing how the banana's diverse cultural narratives are afforded by the berry's qualities and properties, Vermeulen proposes that the banana may always be the actualization of one or more of its material affordances in a specific interaction. In her chapter "Coca(ine)," Brigitte Adriaensen discusses a variety of perspectives on the ontological categorization of the coca leaf and examines their relationships with indigenous cultural perceptions of coca(ine). Challenging the tendency to discuss coca and its derived alkaloid, cocaine, mainly from the perspective of commodity studies, Adriaensen argues for the recognition of their material agency and invites us to think of them as semi-subjects.

Part seven explores "Material Practices in Digital Culture." In his contribution, "The Ephemeral Materiality of Sound," Vincent Meelberg highlights the material and agentive qualities of sound. Taking the Tasty Chips GR-1 granular synthesizer as a case study, his chapter explores how digital technology has changed the affordances of sound for composers, performers, and sound artists. Centering his argument on interface, movement, and affect, Meelberg demonstrates how digital technologies have turned sound from an intangible thing into a tangible object and, in doing so, radically changed the material nature of sound. In his chapter "Tracing the Voice's Digital Materiality," Nuno Atalaia takes Amazon's voice assistant Alexa and its devices as a case study and undertakes a technical analysis of voice-user-interface systems, focusing on their mechanisms of vocal digitization. These, he claims, impose on the voice a condition of "brute materiality" available for human commodification. Atalaia demonstrates that this newfound posthuman materiality opposes the historical framing of the voice as a human-exclusive vehicle of subjectivity. In "Interface," Nishant Shah proposes that the Graphical User Interface (GUI) was the cornerstone by which the ephemerality of computation could be understood as a material, embodied, and techno-cultural practice. The emerging AI-driven, self-learning, computational networks, however, produce a machine intimacy that does not need the mediation of an interface. Drawing on feminist and queer interventions in digital cultures, Shah's chapter considers how, in a post-GUI world, the interface enables us to think about the materiality of ephemeral digital practices and the methodologies that we need to rescue them from the realm of the ineffable.

The eighth part of the book, "Enfolding the Body," focuses on materials used for covering human bodies. In their essay "Becoming-with: On Textile Companions and Fungi Friends," Daniëlle Bruggeman and Lianne Toussaint focus on textile design practices that reinvent the aesthetics, matter, and meaning of fashion, and on the emotional connections between human subjects and the new material "things" they can wear. Using innovative Dutch design practices as a source of inspiration, the authors think through their new materialist and posthuman theoretical and methodological implications. In the essay "Clothing For/Against Walking," Anna Geurts explores how shoes, coats, skirts, and the materials of which they were made impacted past cultures of mobility, in particular walking. In doing so, Geurts examines their own walking experiences as part of their methodological approach. In his chapter "Mylar Foil: Blankets of Silver and Gold," Jeroen Boom attends to the materiality of the mylar foil used as a protective cover for shipwrecked or freshly arrived migrants. Apart from its compression of different plastic and metallic materials, the reflective thermal material, Boom argues, also produces, and is imbued with, conflicting layers of signification replete with tensions between various connotations and affects that stick to this material, from its hopeful humanitarian promises to its dehumanizing threats.

The contributions in the ninth part, "Touching Texts," delve into materials that influence practices of reading, writing, and engaging with texts in general. Frederik Van Dam and Ghidy de Koning examine Thomas Pitfield's *The Poetry of Trees*, a handbound booklet from 1942, the carved oak cover of which encloses a series of linocuts of trees that are accompanied by hand-calligraphed prose-poem descriptions. Van Dam and De Koning highlight the political and ecocritical implications in Pitfield's work: absorbing the fleeting presence of each human generation they outlive, the multiple trees of which the book is made, and which it depicts, ask that readers pay attention to the natural world in an age of nuclear war. In her chapter "Soft Leather, Wounded Buttons, and a Silk Ribbon: Clothing a Birgittine Rule Manuscript," Kathryn Rudy analyzes the chemise binding of a medieval rule for Birgittine nuns.

Considering the various skills and crafts required to manufacture, such a binding and relating those skills to those required for manufacturing clothing, Rudy's chapter explores how the nuns' clothing of the Rule contributed to asserting their Birgittine identity.

The book concludes with "Materials of Scholarly Performance," containing three essays that ponder some of the material dimensions of academic life. In "The Arts Classroom," Edwin van Meerkerk sketches new directions for research on arts education. Focusing on the materiality of the classroom (the art objects, chairs, and tables, the smells and the sounds that direct the artistic and teaching practice in school) and taking a Post-Qualitative Inquiry (PQI) approach, van Meerkerk analyzes two case studies to bring the art classroom to the fore as a space and a terrain of non-human actors, without a pre-determined, neo-positivist methodological framework. In her chapter "Ink on Paper," Carlijn Cober considers ink as an emblem of academic material culture by looking into the history and connotations of different types of ink pens. Mobilizing Barthes's notion of *tangibilia*, she goes on to examine ink as the point of connection between material and affective elements of academic culture. In "The Scholar's Coffee," Liedeke Plate breaks a lance for materializing theories of embodied subjectivity by discussing the relationship between food and the performing body of the (cultural studies) scholar, focusing on coffee. Given the colonial roots and neocolonial dimensions of this foodstuff in the context of the academic culture of the Global North, her chapter addresses the material and biochemical dimensions of the embodied subject of academic scholarship, and inquires into the coloniality of academic scholarship understood as a competitive, high-performance sport.

Works Cited

Adamson, Glenn. *Fewer, Better Things: The Hidden Wisdom of Objects*. Bloomsbury, 2018.
Adamson, Glenn and Carolyn Herrera-Perez, editors. *Material Intelligence*, https://www.materialintelligencemag.org/.
Appadurai, Arjun, editor. *The Social Life of Things: Commodities in Cultural Perspective*. Cambridge UP, 1986.
———. "The Thing Itself." *Public Culture*, vol. 18, no. 1, 2006, pp. 15–22.
Attala, Luci, and Louise Steel. *Body Matters: Exploring the Materiality of the Human Body*. U of Wales P, 2019.
Barad, Karen. *Meeting the Universe Halfway: Quantum Physics and the Entanglement of Matter and Meaning*. Duke UP, 2007.
———. "Posthumanist Performativity: Toward an Understanding of How Matter Comes to Matter." *Signs*, vol. 28, no. 3, 2003, pp. 801–31.
Barthes, Roland. *Mythologies*. Seuil, 1957.

Bennett, Jane. *Vibrant Matter: A Political Ecology of Things*. Duke UP, 2010.
Bennett, Tony, and Patrick Joyce, editors. *Material Powers: Cultural Studies, History and the Material Turn*. Routledge, 2013.
Bogost, Ian, and Christopher Schaberg, editors. *Object Lessons*. Bloomsbury, 2015.
Boscagli, Maurizia. *Stuff Theory: Everyday Objects, Radical Materialism*. Bloomsbury, 2014.
Bourdieu, Pierre. *Distinction: A Social Critique of the Judgement of Taste*. Translated by Richard Nice, Harvard UP, 1984.
———. *Outline of a Theory of Practice*. Translated by Richard Nice, Cambridge UP, 1977.
Braidotti, Rosi. *The Posthuman*. Polity Press, 2013.
Brillenburg Wurth, Kiene, et al., editors. *Book Presence in a Digital Age*. Bloomsbury, 2018.
Brown, Bill. "Thing Theory." *Critical Inquiry*, vol. 28, no. 1, 2001, pp. 1–22.
Certeau, Michel de. *The Practice of Everyday Life*. Translated by Steven Rendall, U of California P, 1984.
Cooke, Edward S. *Global Objects: Toward a Connected Art History*. Princeton UP, 2022.
———. "The Need for Material Literacy." *Princeton UP*, 3 Oct. 2022, https://press.princeton.edu/ideas/the-need-for-material-literacy.
Cornish, Paul, and Nicholas J. Saunders, editors. *Bodies in Conflict: Corporeality, Materiality, and Transformation*. Routledge, 2019.
DeLanda, Manuel. *Assemblage Theory*. Edinburgh UP, 2016.
Del Val, Nasheli Jiménez. *Body between Materiality and Power: Essays in Visual Studies*. Cambridge Scholars Publishing, 2016.
Drazin, Adam. "Materials Transformations." Preface. *The Social Life of Materials: Studies in Materials and Society*, edited by Adam Drazin and Susanne Küchler, Bloomsbury Academic, 2015, pp. xvi–xxviii.
———. "To Live in a Materials World." Introduction. *The Social Life of Materials: Studies in Materials and Society*, edited by Adam Drazin and Susanne Küchler, Bloomsbury Academic, 2015, pp. 3–28.
Drazin, Adam, and Susanne Küchler, editors. *The Social Life of Materials: Studies in Materials and Society*. Bloomsbury Academic, 2015.
Ebersberger, Eva, and Daniela Zyman, editors. *Jorge Otero-Pailos: The Ethics of Dust*. Thyssen-Bornemisza Art Contemporary/ Verlag der Buchhandlung Walther König, 2009.
Enon, David. *La vie matérielle : Mode d'emploi [Material Life : User's Manual]*. Premier Parallèle, 2021.
Fisher, Marc. "Why those Confederate Soldier Statues Look a Lot Like Their Union Counterparts." *Washington Post*, 18 Aug. 2017, https://www.washingtonpost.com/politics/why-those-confederate-soldier-statues-look-a-lot-like-their-union-counterparts/2017/08/18/cefcc1bc-8394-11e7-ab27-1a21a8e006ab_story.html.
Fratzl, Peter, et al., editors. *Active Materials*. De Gruyter, 2022.

Gell, Alfred. *Art and Agency: An Anthropological Theory*. Oxford UP, 1998.
Giaimo, Cara. "Those Mass-Produced Civil War Statues Were Meant to Stand Forever." *Atlas Obscura*, 25 Aug. 2017, https://www.atlasobscura.com/articles/white-bronze-civil-war-statues.
Gordillo, Gastón R. *Rubble: The Afterlife of Destruction*. Duke UP, 2014.
Grissom, Carol A. *Zinc Sculpture in America, 1850–1950*. U of Delaware P, 2009.
Ingold, Tim. "Bringing Things to Life: Creative Entanglements in a World of Materials." *Realities / Morgan Centre, U. of Manchester*, 2010. NCRM working paper. https://eprints.ncrm.ac.uk/id/eprint/1306.
———. "Materials Against Materiality." *Archaeological Dialogues*, vol. 14, no. 1, 2007, pp. 1–16.
———. "Surface Visions." *Theory, Culture and Society*, vol. 34, no. 7–8, 2017, pp. 99–108.
———. "Toward an Ecology of Materials." *Annual Review of Anthropology*, vol. 41, 2012, pp. 427–42.
Kirk, Robin. "Reflections on a Silent Soldier: After the Television Cameras Went Away, a North Carolina City Debated the Future of Its Toppled Confederate Statue." *The American Scholar*, 3 Sept. 2019, https://theamericanscholar.org/reflections-on-a-silent-soldier/.
Kopytoff, Igor. "The Cultural Biography of Things: Commoditization as Process." *The Social Life of Things: Commodities in Cultural Perspective*, edited by Arjun Appadurai, Cambridge UP, 1986, pp. 64–92.
Latour, Bruno. *Reassembling the Social: An Introduction to Actor-Network-Theory*. Oxford UP, 2005.
Lefebvre, Henri. *The Production of Space*. Translated by Donald Nicholson-Smith, Wiley-Blackwell, 1992.
Lehmann, Ann-Sophie. "How Materials Make Meaning." *Netherlands Yearbook for History of Art / Nederlands Kunsthistorisch Jaarboek Online*, vol. 62, no. 1, 2012, pp. 6–27.
———. "Material Literacy." *Bauhaus Zeitschrift*, vol. 9, 2017, pp. 20–27.
Lord, Barry. *Art and Energy: How Culture Changes*. The AAM Press, 2014.
Macfarlane, Robert. *Landmarks*. Penguin Books, 2015.
Marder, Michael. *Dust*. Bloomsbury Academic, 2016.
Meyer, Birgit, and Dick Houtman. "Material Religion: How Things Matter." Introduction. *Things: Religion and the Question of Materiality*, edited by Dick Houtman and Birgit Meyer, Fordham UP, 2012, pp. 1–24.
Miller, Daniel. *The Comfort of Things*. Polity Press, 2008.
———, editor. *Materiality*. Duke UP, 2005.
———. *Stuff*. Polity Press, 2010.
Miodownik, Mark. *Stuff Matters: Exploring the Marvelous Materials That Shape Our Manmade World*. Houghton Mifflin Harcourt, 2014.
Munteán, László. "Plaster Archeology in Budapest's Seventh District: Toward a Mode of Engagement with Architectural Surfaces." *Hungarian Cultural Studies: E-Jour-*

nal of the American Hungarian Educators Association [AHEA], vol. 11, 2018, https://doi.org/10.5195/ahea.2018.319

Munteán, László, Liedeke Plate, and Anneke Smelik, editors. *Materializing Memory in Art and Popular Culture*. Routledge, 2017.

Olsen, Bjørnar. *In Defense of Things: Archaeology and the Ontology of Objects*. AltaMira Press, 2010.

Plate, Liedeke. "Doing Things with Literature in the Digital Age: Italo Calvino's *If on a Winter's Night a Traveller* and the Material Turn in Literary Studies." *Book Presence in a Digital Age*, edited by Kiene Brillenburg Wurth et al., Bloomsbury Academic, 2018, pp. 109–26.

Plate, Liedeke, and Anneke Smelik, editors. *Performing Memory in Art and Popular Culture*. Routledge, 2015.

———. *Technologies of Memory in the Arts*. Palgrave Macmillan, 2009.

Salamon, Gayle. *Assuming a Body: Transgender and Rhetorics of Materiality*. Columbia UP, 2010.

Smelik, Anneke. "Fractal Folds: The Posthuman Fashion of Iris van Herpen." *Fashion Theory*, vol. 26, no.1, 2022, pp. 5–26.

———. "New Materialism: A Theoretical Framework for Fashion in the Age of Technological Innovation." *International Journal of Fashion Studies*, vol. 5, no.1, 2018, p. 33–54.

Solanki, Seetal. "Material Literacy: Why We Need to Rethink Language to Survive the Climate Crisis." *It's Nice That*, 26 June 2019, https://www.itsnicethat.com/features/response-and-responsibility-seetal-solanki-material-literacy-product-design-260619.

———. *Why Materials Matter: Responsible Design for a Better World*. Prestel, 2018.

Szeman, Imre, and Dominic Boyer, editors. *Energy Humanities: An Anthology*. Johns Hopkins UP, 2017.

Urry, John. "The Problem of Energy." *Theory, Culture and Society*, vol. 31, no. 5, 2014, pp. 3–20.

Weizman, Eyal. *Forensic Architecture: Violence at the Threshold of Detectability*. Zone Books, 2017.

Wilkes, Sarah. "Materials Libraries as Vehicles for Knowledge Transfer." *Anthropology Matters*, vol. 13, no.1, 2011, https://doi.org/10.22582/am.v13i1.233

Wilkes, Sarah, and Mark Miodownik. "Materials Library Collections as Tools for Interdisciplinary Research." *Interdisciplinary Science Reviews*, vol. 43, no. 1, 2018, pp. 3–23.

Williams, Raymond. *Marxism and Literature*. Oxford UP, 1977.

Woodward, Sophie. *Material Methods: Researching and Thinking with Things*. SAGE Publications, 2019.

Part I: Materials of Art

Fig. 1: Dora Maar, Hand-Shell, 1934. London, Tate Modern.

1. Stitched into Material: On the Makeability of Shells

Hanneke Grootenboer

> ...her life roared in her ear like an empty shell.
> (Deborah Eisenberg, Under the 82nd Airborne)

In 1934, Dora Maar (1907–1997) created *Sans Titre*, also entitled *Hand-Shell* (fig. 1). It displays a photograph of a large nautilus shell out of which a mannequin's severed hand is crawling, as if it were a hermit crab. The nautilus lies on a sandy beach, but the composition has obviously been staged in an artist's studio. Its dramatic sky reinforces a sense of creation, even revelation. What exactly has been conceived here? Is it Maar's absurdist invention of a hand that seems to have been born from a mollusk? Is the elegant, plastic hand a reference to Maar's practice as a woman artist? Or is Maar musing about the hand as a reference to handicraft, in contrast to the shape of the nautilus, which is not made by hands but has grown organically?

Maar's photograph resonates with Paul Valéry's beautiful essay "The Man and the Sea Shell," written around the same time that Maar created her surrealist photographs. In this poetic essay, Valéry compares the way that human beings make things to the slow, continuous process by which nature fashions its forms. For Valéry, a shell is an enigma. The curiously ornamented object troubles him so much that he becomes almost obsessed with the question, "Who made this?" (117). Though it is one of nature's creations, a shell (such as Maar's nautilus) looks, Valéry writes, as if it had been *made for someone*. It appears as if some mind has chosen its patterns and colors. Shells seem to be disguised as artworks, tricking us to appear as if they have been made by the human hand—a quality that Maar keenly explores as well. A shell, like a work of art, is conspicuous for its total lack of utility, Valéry reasons. It is a hybrid entity comprising a union of contrary ideas "of order and fantasy, invention and necessity, law and exception" (112). By what sign, Valéry wonders, do we recognize that a given object "is or is not *made by a man?*" (118).

On the basis of Valéry's text and Maar's photograph, I argue that a shell is a fitting object with which we can rethink recent concerns raised in the debate on material culture studies regarding the confusion around the terms "material" and "materiality." In his essay "Materials against Materiality" (2007), Tim Ingold observes that in discussions around materiality there is a lack of attention to actual materials. The slippage from material to materiality is a result of the rigid mind/matter separation or the gap between, as Ingold writes, "the tangible stuff of craftsmen and manufacturers" and "the abstract ruminations of philosophers and theorists" (2). The notion of "material" has largely been replaced by materiality, Ingold suggests, due to the ever-dominant subject/object divide that places human beings on one side and the world of objects on the other. This split reinforces the idea that material seems somehow locked up in things, considered not to be part of our lived environment.

Unlike what is generally assumed, it is not that people live in their houses "inside" the material world and are able to step away from it when going outdoors. We always are in touch with material surfaces, whether inside or outside our houses: there is always the earth under our feet and the air around us. We should not distinguish between what is material and what is not, Ingold argues, but rather we should differentiate between *different* materials. Materials touch. Objects and humans alike are surrounded not by a void but by other materials. Actually, Ingold writes, we should imagine humans to be moving *through* the material world like moles, carving out pathways *in* materials rather than building constructions *from* them. Arguing against the subject-object divide, he insists that there is no separation that would somehow situate humans on one side and materials on the other. Living as we do in an all-encompassing ecology, we are always in touch with stuff. We "swim in an ocean of materials," Ingold writes, poetically (7).

This beautiful metaphor seems to make a lot of sense. However, Ingold appears to apply his conception exclusively to raw materials such as earth, water, beeswax, or stone. At the beginning of the essay, he invites his reader to pick up a stone outside, get it wet and then observe how it changes when it dries. The exercise is meant to demonstrate that the stoniness of the stone is not part of the stone's nature but emerges from its interaction with its environment. The example of the stone indicates that Ingold is less interested in *our* interaction with *it*. Our involvement is limited to observation: we on the one side, the object on the other. The classic subject-object divide that he argues against is, in this particular instance, still firmly in place. He continues his line of argument in "Toward an Ecology of Materials," an essay written a few years later arguing that we should think not *about* materials but *from* them. This is a fascinating proposal, but he does not really explain how this works. He refers to the phenomenology of Maurice Merleau-Ponty, arguing that humans are "stitched" into the fabric of the world as an integral part of matter's flow, but it remains unclear exactly how we are enveloped by materials as if having been woven into their texture. What remains equally unclear is how we should reflect on how we are in touch, how we might theorize that position.

I suggest that one particular term is missing from his general theory on materials (based on the list of concepts that he provides, 439): the artwork. In the classic *Art and Evidence: Writing on Art and Material Culture* (2001), Jules Prown lays out the very first steps in the study of material culture, steps that have remained relevant up through today. Prown distinguishes among various categories of objects (of adornment, diversion, applied arts, devices and modification of the landscape), making a special case for works of art, which possess "considerable underlying theoretical complexity as opposed to technical or mechanical complexity" (87). It is precisely this kind of theoretical complexity that is needed to reflect on how humans and materials, and as a consequence body and surface, are knotted together.

Certain things such as art works are capable of inviting us to reflect on the nature of the "stitches" that have sewn us into the fabric of the world. The key issue here is touch. I suggest that only if we take touch into account can we start thinking *from* materials. And, to go one step further: if we start thinking from materials, we will see that mind and matter are not in fact opposed but are actually quite similar in formation. Thought, I argue, is not an abstract rumination, but is partly shaped by the things and materials with which it is concerned.

For the remainder of this essay, I will take the nautilus shell as the point of contact between a human individual and the "ocean of materials" that Ingold has in mind. It is a theoretically complex entity, which foregrounds its material even as it defies its materiality. Whereas feathers can be plucked from a bird, wool can be shorn from a sheep, and stone can be cut from rock, "shell" cannot quite be taken from a shell. It is hard to unlock the shell's materiality—the shell stubbornly remains, first and foremost, a material *thing*. A shell's properties (what is out there) and its qualities (what we ascribe to them) are intricately intertwined, much like the spiral form that constitutes its core.

Mimicking Ingold's experiment with the stone, I would like to ask the reader to pick up a shell from a beach and embrace it as a thing to think from. When you let it slowly move through your fingers, you will see that it is a perfect model for understanding the way humans are enveloped in the world of materials. You will almost automatically lift it to your nose to breathe in its scent or press it against your cheek for a moment so as to feel its wobbly surface. You may even stick out your tongue to taste its pearly, salty interior. Without much consideration, you will probably put it up against your ear. Valéry was fascinated by the set of automatic responses elicited by shells, which are distinct from those reactions prompted by other things such as stones. He describes these responses to the shell as instances of wonder. Every time we pick up a shell, it is as if we are seeing it for the first time. It awakens the oft-forgotten child in you, Valéry writes. As far back as antiquity, Cicero knew about the special effect that shells exert on human beings. In *The Orator* (46 BCE), he recommends that city officials who are worn out by worldly duties should start gathering shells on the beach, as it will, he claims, refresh their minds and free them from sorrow. He keenly observes that shell-gathering somehow allows grown-ups "to become boys again" (*repuerascere*, 213–15). For Cicero, shells have a healing effect as they generate, quite literally, a different mindset.

Fig. 2: The Dolls' House of Petronella Oortman, 1685–1710. Amsterdam, Rijksmuseum.

The effect of shells on the body (through the senses) and the mind (through relief of what we would now call stress), undoubtedly played a role in the collective passion for shell collecting that emerged in seventeenth-century Netherlands. Trade with the West and East Indies made shells sought-after luxury commodities. The collective passion for shells was part of a larger fascination among Dutch merchants for exotica: rare, curious items that flowed into the harbor of Amsterdam from the colonized corners of the world. Most well-to-do households owned a curiosity cabinet, which would have contained a mixture of objects and artifacts including minerals, butterflies, coins, small sculptures, and shells. Shell collecting was a social pastime. Images produced in the Dutch Republic show men in conversation while interacting with shells and handing them to one another. Women, too, collected shells and placed them in so-called table cabinets; the assemblages of small shells gathered here would correspond to the larger, older shells their husbands owned. Miniaturization, it seems, was a pathway to collecting for women. Petronella Oortman's dolls' house (fig. 2), one such collection of curiosities, comprising banal household objects rendered in exactly the same fashion as their life-size models, contains a Japanese lacquer cabinet filled with tiny shells, the baby versions of shell species.[1] Amid seven hundred handmade objects, these baby shells are the only items that have not been fabricated. We also see a female hand evident in the preservation of one of the largest collections of natural history items in the Netherlands, which was owned by the merchant Levinus Vincent (fig. 3). Open to the public, if one paid a small entrance fee, the collection attracted many visitors who could then admire the huge collection of shells laid out in colorful designs by Vincent's wife, Johanna van Breda, a gifted embroiderer known for her complicated patterns. Her skillful hands transformed shells into a kind of fabric, akin to decorative textiles.

Fig. 3: Johanna van Breda, Shell Arrangement, from Levinus Vincent, Het Wondertooneel der nature, 1706.

Curiosity cabinets were meant to represent a microcosm: the world in a box. Variety was considered the key to the acquisition of knowledge. The main organizing

---

1   For more on Oortman's dollhouse and shells, see Grootenboer.

principle of such eclectic collections was the distinction between *artificialia*, artifacts made by the human hand such as coins and ivory figures, and *naturalia*, such as minerals or insects. Due to its hybrid nature, the shell occupied a unique position in this rudimentary classification system. It belonged to both categories, or so it seemed to seventeenth-century eyes. Baffled by shells' otherworldly forms, shell enthusiasts initially did not fully understand how they were "made." First interested primarily in the mollusk's exterior, they had been long ignorant of the sea creature that produced it as its form of shelter. Some still thought, following Aristotle, that shells were born from mud that had been dried by the sun. In early modern inventories, shells are listed as objects within curiosity collections, but they are also found in studies, among papers and books, which indicates that for seventeenth-century scholars, shells were literally things to think with. Erasmus is said to have owned one of the first shell collections in Europe. They were often exchanged among likeminded thinkers. Margaretha van Godewijck received, from her friend and mentor Colvijn in Dordrecht, a shell that she probably kept in her little "museum," which also served as her study.

This widespread scholarly interest yielded considerations of its fascinating shape and form as metaphors for creation. In his long ode to shell-collecting entitled "The Beach" (1612), Philibert van Borsselen compares the human being, God's ultimate creation, to a shell's almost perfect spiral form. Referring to a species called "spiral staircase," he calls out to the Almighty: "Let your Creature be a spiral staircase" ("Laet dyne Schepsel zijn een cromme wendel-trap") (137). In philosophical discourses, the shell became the example par excellence for God's meticulousness when creating the natural world. In a long poem on the benefits of keeping a cabinet of curiosities published in 1748, Christoffel Beudeker uses a shell as evidence that God is the divine mechanical engineer who has designed and created the world:

> Behold [this shell], to which no other kind compares, and tell me whose intellect is able to make a judgment, as to how she is stitched together, her circles chained together, forged by nature's links. Who has invented this art work? you disbeliever! He alone who created all. (160–61; my trans.)

Here it is as if Beudeker has taken a shell from a cabinet and is holding it up to his reader's face: "behold this shell." The word "invented" indicates, significantly, the shell's status as a technological marvel, paradoxically "stitched together" as if by human hands, or more precisely by women's hands, which traditionally stitched linens together as one of the tasks of housework (as so many paintings of the time demonstrate).[2] Declaring a shell to be a stitched-together work of art, Beudeker uses it as an example against the claim of the controversial philosopher Baruch Spinoza (1632–1677) that nature's beautiful patterns (of flowers or trees, or shells) have not

---

2   See, for instance, van Asperen.

been created by God but are generated by their own "conception." Nature designs itself, Spinoza claims, and the cause for its existence, rather than being explained away through the existence of a transcendental God, must be found within nature as such. While Aristotle's view that shells were formed by dried mud had, by that time, been largely rejected, it was not yet clear that tiny mollusks build their own shelters around themselves, bit by bit—and indeed according to *their* own design.

Beudeker's stitches are best perceived when holding a shell in your hand. They can be felt on the shell's surface in relief as rims and wobbles, where chalk substances come together. These patterns are visible as well as tangible. I argue that the experience of simultaneously seeing and feeling the material of a shell as something stitched together is a perfect correlative for Merleau-Ponty's concept that humans are "stitched into" the fabric of the world. Touching a shell also involves being touched *by it*, feeling it also involves letting *us* feel *it*. We share visibility and tangibility with our surroundings, Merleau-Ponty insists. That is how we merge into the world: both as perceiving subjects and as other-perceived objects. By letting a shell go through our hands, skin upon mother-of-pearl, our flesh against the "flesh" of the shell, we share surfaces. Unlike what Ingold demonstrated with the stone, our experience with a shell is not that of an observant but rather of a participant, experiencing the oceanic feel of this diminutive vessel from the sea. The intertwining of vision and touch is further articulated by the nautilus' spiral curves, which fold and unfold so that the inside is also the outside and the exterior turns seamlessly into the interior. Only if we understand materiality to be the intertwining of materials, human flesh included, can we overcome the subject-object divide. The thought of the shell as such bridges that gap.

Works Cited

Asperen, Hanneke van. "Praying, Threading, and Adorning: Sewn-in Prints in a Rosary Prayer Book (London, British Library, Add. MS 14042)." *Weaving, Veiling, and Dressing: Textiles and their Metaphors in the Late Middle Ages*, edited by Kathryn M. Rudy and Barbara Baert, Brepols, 2007, pp. 81–120.
Borsselen, Philibert van. *Strande oft ghedichte van de schelpen, kinck-hornen, ende andere wonderlicke zee-schepselen, tot lof van den Schepper aller dinghen.* [*The Beach, or Poems of Shells, Horns and other Curious Creatures of the Sea, in Praise of the Creator of all Things*] Haarlem, by Adriaen Rooman, 1611.
Beudeker, Christoffel. *De Sprekende Konstkamer, Vertoonende het regte Gebruik der Boeken, Konsten en natuurkundige Wetenschappen in zedige Gedachten*, 1748.
Cicero. *On the Orator.* Translated by E. W. Sutton, Harvard UP, 2014.
Eisenberg, Deborah. *Under the 82nd Airborne*. Farrar, Straus, and Giroux, 1992.

Grootenboer, Hanneke. "Thinking with Shells in Petronella Oortman's Dollhouse." *Conchophilia: Shells, Art and Curiosity in Early Modern Europe*, edited by Marisa Anne Bass et al., Princeton UP, 2021, pp. 103–26.

Ingold, Tim. "Materials against Materiality." *Archaeological Dialogues*, vol. 14, no. 1, 2007, pp. 1–16.

———. "Toward an Ecology of Materials." *Annual Review of Anthropology*, vol. 41, no. 1, 2012, pp. 427–42.

Prown, Jules David. *Art as Evidence: Writings on Art and Material Culture*. Yale UP, 2001.

Valéry, Paul. "Man and the Sea Shell." Translated by Ralph Manheim. *Paul Valéry: An Anthology*, selected, with an introduction by James R. Lawler, Princeton UP, 1977, pp. 108–35.

Vincent, Levinus. *Wondertooneel der nature, geopent in eene korte beschryvinge*. Amsterdam, François Halma, 1706.

2. Celluloid

Wilco Versteeg

Celluloid cracks, tears, disintegrates, and spontaneously combusts without proper care. Exposed to heat, sparks, flames, or friction, it might ignite with explosive violence. Contact with celluloid may cause burns to the skin and eyes. Its chemical formula—$C6H7O2(ONO2)3$ approximatively—denotes, through the added "approximation," the instability and impurity of the combination of cellulose nitrate and camphor. Filmmakers have metaphorized these material properties to describe their practices. For instance, Pier Paolo Pasolini famously called making films "writing on burning paper" (109). While the Italian master deployed this metaphor to describe the political and aesthetic potential of narrative cinema, Jean-Luc Godard (1930–2022) took these material properties as a call to arms in exploring political filmmaking as manipulative labor. This essay focuses on his understanding of film as a material of art and of filmmaking as material labor. He describes filmmaking as "thinking with hands," which in his late-style-essay films takes the form of unrelenting work with film plastics through cutting and rearranging disparate fragments of visual, textual, and sonic material (fig. 1). The ubiquitous presence of hands throughout his last film *Le livre d'image* [*The Image Book*] (2018) reinforces the notion that thinking for Godard is a physical, even violent, activity. As Beugnet and Ravetto-Biagioli argued, "Godard associates the hand with mastery and potential to destroy or act violently" (12). Through this thinking with hands, Godard wishes to make of cinema "a form that thinks" and to emancipate the medium and its audience from dialogue, plot, and spectacle; in short, from being a mere object to be consumed and then discarded.

As a form that thinks, film is intimately tied to the material existence of moving images in institutional and personal archives, in forgotten corners of attics, on tape, and in digital repositories. While curatorial practices of film preservation are one way to safeguard material cinematic culture from disappearing, the active reuse of celluloid and other film stock in new works seems more in line with the malleable nature of these sturdy thermoplastics and the moving-image culture it made possible. To Godard, cultures of cinephilia can only survive if something is done with these materials: the musealization of cinema is the death of the art as a living, revolving, and revolutionary practice. He takes his inspiration from Chris Marker and

Alain Resnais's warning in *Les statues meurent aussi* [*Statues Also Die*] (1953) that "when people die, they become history. When images die, they become art. This botany of death we call culture." To prevent cinema from becoming culture, Godard keeps images in constant movement through montage and collage. This implies a radical appropriation of other people's images on a variety of materials: he cuts up celluloid, other plastics such as VHS, and paper to create image-clashes that serve to define and demarcate what can be considered cinematic or not: racial stereotypes, cultural or artistic clichés, and unethical camera movements should be excised from its original context and be re-exposed in a new work. These uncinematic elements can be considered forms of pollution, turning Godard's act of appropriation into a cinematic ecology (Aubon 12). This critical gesture should not be confused with striving for cinematic purity: like the chemical compounds of celluloid, cinema itself thrives on the impurity of form in its mix of sights, sounds, movements, stills, colors, and its necessarily collaborative nature as a creative medium.

Fig. 1: Jean-Luc Godard, Le livre d'image, 2018. Casa Azul Films.

While celluloid has long been replaced by digital formats as the main aesthetic and economic choice in shooting and showing films, it is anything but obsolete. Things, it seems, are never past: the near obsolescence of celluloid is exaggerated. Celluloid attracts attention for at least two reasons: as a material of culture, it fails to call attention to itself. In painting or sculpture, one cannot separate the visual object and the material from which it is made. The same cannot be said for cinema: one does not look at a strip of celluloid in the hope of encountering a cinematic experience. The carrier of film is not the experience of film; the material existence of film is not film itself. Raymond Bellour calls this the "irreducibility of the filmic substance" that "serves to limit analysis" (54). Moreover, experiments with celluloid in the narrow confines of the contemporary art space contribute to what Kim Knowles describes as an interest in "the aesthetic and potential of celluloid as it shifts . . . from the dominant to the residual" in an art economy of "recuperation, re-use, and recycling of old matter" (Knowles), which can be said to provide an alternative to disposability but could also be seen as an act of appropriative preservation. This calls attention to the deep ties between obsolescence and medium specificity, specifically in practices that are now retrospectively labeled "analog."

Experiments with celluloid in art cinema seem to be motivated by a search for the physical breaking point of the material. In the case of celluloid, this might be the point of combustion or disintegration. Developing celluloid in bodily fluids, such as spit or urine, scratching the photosensitive surface, or long-term exposure of the film plastics to earth are examples of radical acts that have taken place within a highly artistic discourse. Many of these experiments are in reaction to digitization and the fear of the dematerialization of culture in cinema as well as in other arts, such as literature and painting. Godard's practice takes place outside the white cube and is engaged with digital and technological developments rather than being dismissive of them: *Le livre d'image* was first shown in 2018 in a Swiss theater on the flattest available state-of-the-art HD screen chosen for its exquisite rendition of black. To him, the digital serves as a promise that needs to be creatively developed in practices of filmmaking and showing: Godard has explored the function and possibilities of 3D as well as played with varying screen sizes of phones and tablets. Digitization, to Godard, offers new possibilities for current cinema and visual culture.

Le livre d'image is Godard's most radical experiment with film material. One of the first images is of a filmmaker's hands behind an editing table, moving around spools of film. While Godard has always experimented with montage, his collaging using the archives of visual culture took flight in his monumental *Histoire(s) du cinéma* [*Histories of Cinema*] (1988–1998) and (essay) films such as in *Les enfants jouent à la russie* [*Children Play Russia*] (1993) and *Allemagne année 90 neuf zéro* [*Germany year 90 nine zero*] (1991), *De l'origine du XXI siècle* [*Origins of the XXI Century*] (2000), and narrative works such as *Film socialisme* (2010) and *Adieu au langage* [*Goodbye to Language*] (2014). In a commemorative text after Godard's passing in September 2022, Jean Narboni describes Godard's artistic development as removing from films what seemed, at first, essential to cinema: story, characters, narrative unity, dramatic development, closure, and, finally, the originality and integrity of the visual material (10). *Le livre d'image* is an archaeology of our visual culture and is at times so tightly sealed that it seems impossible to glean any meaning from it. Whereas the montage form itself asks the utmost of the viewer, Godard's reworkings of the celluloid, VHS, or digital file add another difficulty to understanding even the intention of the auteur. At times, the image is pure white, hermetically black, noisy, or pushed to the utmost limits of color saturation (fig. 2). The viewer is also invited to engage actively and creatively with the object, in an insistent need to continuously reflect on the necessity and ethics of images. Although tempting, this active viewing cannot take the form of an intellectualized game of identification: knowing that a certain fragment is extracted from, for example, *The Night of the Hunter*, is unproductive in making sense of *Le livre d'image*. The fragments do not want a reconstructive reading to function. Rather, it is the loss of original context that releases meaning potentialities, foregrounds the fluidity of interpretative processes, and creates a space that enables cinema to become a form that thinks. This carving out of a literal and metaphorical space within and between images is at once the emancipation of the medium, the viewer, and the academic vis-à-vis their object.[1]

Throughout his oeuvre, Godard tried to emancipate the image, saving it from the repressive hands of a culture that infantilizes (cinematic) images by limiting their polyphonous potential. Famously, in *Le gai savoir* [*Joy of Learning*] (1969) Godard integrates a minute of image-silence in commemoration of "absent images, censured images, prostituted images, criticized images, delinquent images, fucked images, images beaten down by all governments, by television and all westernized cinemas that make rhyme information with repression, ordure with culture." The references to these forms of wasted potential call to mind the material properties of celluloid: as a plastic it can easily be considered trash, like other plastics. Reusing these physical remains is a recycling of ideas as much as of materials and serves as the foundation upon which to construct a new world.

Godard's ideology of montage needs further elucidation and contextualization, as here the actual labor with film plastics takes cinematic form. Montage—the only feature that distinguishes cinema from its ancestors, photography, and theater—is deeply political for Godard. While his intellectual father André Bazin defines montage as nothing other than the organization of images in time, Godard would add that it is also the laborious (re-)organization of material in space. He shows a fundamental revision of ideas on cinematic organization: images are not only edited sequentially in time but are overlaid, juxtaposed, and intercut and have undergone other such material interventions. This is all to show that the image is flat (Godard, "Candide" 13), just as the screen on which *Le livre d'image* was shown was the flattest available at the time. He rejects perspective, or the original sin of Western art as Bazin so eloquently called it ("Ontology" 7) as well as the "fantasy of referentiality" derided by Didi-Huberman ("Index" 74). The possibility of critique is not inherent in individual images but can be brought out by montage. An image needs a counter-image to speak beyond words: $1 + 1 = 3$ is Godard's didactic formula for explaining how a third image is born from two separate ones ("Candide" 13). Unlike Bazin's "montage interdit" or prohibited montage ("Montage"), Godard is inspired by Serge

---

1   For various approaches to art as a form of thinking, see Grootenboer; Warner; and Rancière.

Daney's ideas of "obligatory montage" as the sine qua non of critical thinking and as the ultimate resistance against a society at war with polyphonous meaning (fig. 3).

Fig. 2: Jean-Luc Godard, Le livre d'image.

Fig. 3: Jean-Luc Godard, Le livre d'image.

Godard's material labor should not be seen as a purely formalistic practice similar to the above-mentioned contemporary art practices. By naming his last film *The Book of Images*, he calls attention to materials and objects in the transfer and survival of forms and ideas. For him, montage always stands in the service of ideas. The essence of history, to Godard, is montage. Both connect elements that were not connected before: "Like when Cocteau said: had Rimbaud lived longer, then he would have died in the same year as Pétain" (Godard, "Geschiedenis" ["History"] 181; my trans.) (fig. 4). Through material labor, Godard is "à la recherche du siècle perdu" ("in search of the lost century") (fig. 5). This, without doubt, is the twentieth century, with cinema's complicity in genocide and mass murder. Cinema was not only unable to show the Shoah, let alone prevent or stop it to prevent. In fact, it even helped prepare the world for genocidal murder by perpetuating stereotypes and spectacularizing violence. Godard's relationship with images is complexly related to that of Georges Didi-Huberman, who in his critical study of the former *Passés cités par JLG* (2015), writes that history is an assemblage, a montage. Images do not resurrect the past but are material remains of the past that imperfectly and incompletely witness a foregone age. They are a *survivance*, like archaeological remains that are incompletely recovered from layers of earth and debris, and that only come to mean connection with other ideas and materials.

Fig. 4: Jean-Luc Godard, Le livre d'image; Fig. 5. Jean-Luc Godard and Anne-Marie Miéville, De l'origine du XXIe siècle, 2000.

Godard's work cannot be enjoyed from the position of pseudo-passivity usually summed up as the willing suspension of disbelief, which in the final analysis is nothing but a form of bad faith. His work demands an active, cinephilic attitude. This attitude at its most extreme calls for iconoclasm not as the destruction of all images but as a critical gesture that questions the ethics of visuality, reflects on visibilities, and resists uniform, repressive meaning. Through acts of material destruction, one rids the loved object of anything wrong and harmful. Celluloid and film plastics are an integral part of this attitude, as they ground not only the creation but also the critique of films in materiality and, therefore, in history. For Godard, working with material, hands-on, is physical labor that ensures the survival of cinematic cultures. His work, in which engaged making and reflecting are inseparable, is all that remains after his death in 2022. The strength of his oeuvre is precisely that it does not speak for itself but that it provides the methodological and theoretical tools to pry open its potential and approximate meanings and that of cinema and visual culture as a whole. The end of cinema as a cultural form and practice haunted Godard. Now that he is gone, we should listen, again or for the first time, to his words in the film essay *Lettre à Freddy Buache* [*A Letter to Freddy Buache*] (1982): "Cinema is going to die soon, too young, without having been able to give what it could have. So, we must go quickly to the heart of the matter. There's an urgency to do so." This call for action is no less relevant today than it was in 1982.

Works Cited

Aubron, Hervé. "Cavaliers de l'apocalypse." ["Horsemen of the Apocalypse"]. *Cahiers du cinéma*, July 2022, pp. 10–14.
Bazin, André. "Montage interdit." *Qu'est-ce que le cinéma? [What is Cinema?]* Les éditions du Cerf, 1958.
———. "The Ontology of the Photographic Image." *Film Quarterly*, vol. 13, no. 4, 1960, pp. 4–9.
Bellour, Raymond. "Analysis in Flames." *Diacritics*, vol. 15, no. 1, 1985, pp. 52–56.
Beugnet, Martine, and Kriss Ravetto-Biagioli. "The Image Book: or Penser avec les mains." *Alphaville: Journal of Film and Screen Media*, no. 23, 2022, pp. 10–31.
Daney, Serge. "Montage Verplicht" ["Obligatory Montage"]. *Een ruimte om in te bewegen*. Octavo, 2011.
Didi-Huberman, Georges. "The Index of the Absent Wound." *October*, vol. 29, 1984, pp. 63–81.
———. *Passés cités par JLG [Cited Pasts]*. Paris, Les Éditions de Minuit, 2015.
Godard, Jean-Luc. "Fidèle Candide: Propos à partir du *Livre d'image*" ["Faithful Candide : On *Livre d'image*"]. *Traffic*, Winter 2019, pp. 13–20.
———. "Over cinema en geschiedenis" ["On Cinema and History"]. *Een ruimte om in te bewegen*. Octavo, 2011.
———, director. *Le gai savoir* [*Joy of Learning*], 1969.
———, director. *Histoire(s) du cinéma* [*Histories of cinema*]. Canal +, 1998.
———, director. *Lettre à Freddy Buache* [*A Letter to Freddy Buache*], 1982.
———, director. *Le livre d'image* [*The Image Book*]. Casa Azul Films, 2018.
Godard, Jean-Luc, and Anne-Marie Miéville, directors. *De l'origine du XXIe siècle* [*Origins of the XXI Century*], Véga films, 2000.
Grootenboer, Hanneke. *The Pensive Image: Art as a Form of Thinking*. U of Chicago P, 2021.
Knowles, Kim. "Blood, Sweat, and Tears: Bodily Inscriptions in Contemporary Experimental Film." *NECUS*, Autumn 2013, https://necsus-ejms.org/blood-sweat-and-tears-bodily-inscriptions-in-contemporary-experimental-film/.

Narboni, Jean. "Dormir...Rêver peut-être" ["To Sleep... Perchance to Dream"]. *Cahiers du cinéma*, October 2022, pp. 10–11.
Pasolini, Pier Paolo. "Is bestaan iets natuurlijks?" ["Is Existing Natural?"]. *De Ketterse Ervaring*. Wfilm, 1981, pp. 106–12.
Rancière, Jacques. *Le spectateur émancipé [The Emancipated Spectator]*. La Fabrique, 2008.
Resnais, Alain, and Chris Marker, directors. *Les statues meurent aussi [Statues Also Die]*. Tadié Cinéma, 1953.
Warner, Rick. *Godard and the Essay Film: A Form That Thinks*. Northwestern UP, 2018.

Part II: Materials of Empire

3. Roman Concrete

Astrid Van Oyen

Archaeology writes human history based on material traces.[1] Yet it has been surprisingly reluctant to write truly *material* histories. Instead, form has featured as the signifier of historical change: changing mentalities are read from new tableware shapes; altered political relations from novel building types; shifts in socio-economic cycles from new styles of packaging. Material changes, instead, are relegated to the timespace of geological epochs, as in the debate surrounding the Anthropocene and the role of plastic as one of its guiding fossils in geological stratigraphies (Harris; Waters et al.). Within the more fine-grained timespace of human history, materials similarly feature as delimiting broad eras, a legacy that can be traced back to Thomsen's Three-Age system separating the (Eurocentric) human past into Stone, Bronze, and Iron Ages. According to such models, once discovered or invented, materials are simply part of the stock of human resources, passively waiting to be formed, shaped, modeled, and thus given a historical role.

The consequences of placing materials outside of history have been dire. This epistemological move has fostered a denial of coevalness (Fabian): if stone tools are of a different epoch altogether, then so are their users. It has also been complicit in colonial resource-grabbing: severing mute matter from its historical entanglements paves the way for capitalist alienability (Irvine). Finally—and this is the issue tackled in this chapter—it skews the human histories we write, slanting them in favor of the drama of human agency.

Concrete offers a productive case study to destabilize the role of matter in history-writing. Concrete as a structural component rather than a surface or a bonding agent first appeared in Late Republican Italy, probably around the second half of the second century BC (Coarelli; Mogetta). It is thus one of the rare pre-industrial examples of a material whose invention is historically anchored. Yet invention narratives are at danger of activating the distinct moment of invention and development, only to have the rest of a material's history slide back into a mass of mute matter at the whim of human instrumentalism (e.g., Blake and Van Deman 327; Jackson

---

1   This chapter revisits and deepens parts of an argument made earlier in Van Oyen, *Finding the Material*.

and Kosso 283; Quenemoen 65). This chapter explores two alternative material histories: one following Tim Ingold's organicism and "generative fluxes" (12); the other inspired by Karen Barad's notion of performativity and "material-discursive phenomena."

Matter is in constant flux. The multivalent rhythm of its pulse blurs the analytical distinctions between geological and historical timespaces. Roman concrete is a composite material consisting of a core of rubble bonded with mortar, often contained by a facing of stone or brick. The material histories of these components stretch far back in time: the fine aggregate used for the mortar in Roman Italy, for instance, consisted of volcanic ashes or so-called "pozzolana" from various formations along Tyrrhenian Central Italy (Lancaster, "Concrete Vaulted Construction" chapter 2). Volcanic ash reacted with lime to create an exceptionally strong and durable conglomerate; yet this chemical reaction needed water and was therefore not possible when hot temperatures caused rapid evaporation (Lechtman and Hobbs 99; Lancaster, "Concrete Vaulted Construction" 52). The mortar's longevity that resulted in the preservation of such things as Roman harbor infrastructure up to today was thus the product of a highly specific and fickle confluence of "currents of the lifeworld" (Ingold 12): millennia-old geological processes responded to contingent conditions of temperature and humidity at the time of construction.

Mixed in with the mortar were *caementa*, heterogeneous fragments of stone or tile that formed the core of concrete walls (Lancaster, "Innovative Vaulting" 19). The ability to reuse the rubble from previous buildings without having to carve each individual piece was a boon amidst a bustling building industry in Late Republican Rome. In what was effectively a form of recycling (Duckworth et al.), each fragment carried with it its own history and the concrete wall, vault, or building that resulted became a temporary halting point of meshworks knotting together different buildings, projects, and fabrics. In contrast to its modern counterpart, Roman concrete was not poured but layered: the facing of walls arose in tandem with layers of mortar in which the *caementa* were placed (Blake 160; Lechtman and Hobbs 102). From the perspective of crafting, this technique did not require a radical break with previous modes of stone-built construction. Vaults and domes, instead, necessitated that form was conceived before matter. Indeed, their negative space would be modeled in wooden formwork, resulting in close collaboration between architects, carpenters, and construction workers (Lancaster, "Concrete Vaulted Construction" 22–50).

This shift from matter growing to form being modeled through matter identifies an important lacuna in the material history of concrete sketched so far. Absent from an Ingoldian narrative of growth, flux, and flow are politics, economics, and inequalities. These only enter when we acknowledge the ruptures within the flow, the stopping points, the fractures, and the boundaries—an epistemic move guided by Barad's question of how concrete "comes to matter."

"Roman concrete" was not an undifferentiated category. *Caementa*, for instance, became gradually more standardized. Concrete buildings of the second century BC employ coarse *caementa*, often forty centimeters in size or larger, and randomly laid (Blake 160; Jackson and Kosso 280). From the Augustan period onwards, the size of individual components decreased to about ten to thirty centimeters, now regularly ordered in layers. In addition, from imperial times onwards, the properties of *caementa* became increasingly adjusted to their position and role in the building. Heavier components were placed at the base of vaults and domes, while lightweight materials occupied positions higher up.[2] As a result, higher-end construction projects would import specially sourced stones to serve as *caementa*. Whereas *caementa* had been a key component in fostering the Ingoldian flow of recycling in the initial phases of concrete construction, they now actively halted, interrupted, and redirected those flows, creating additional costs and demands.

The volcanic ash that formed the fine aggregate of the mortar-mix was also subject to an increasing process of differentiation and categorization. The greyish ash from the Bay of Naples, *pulvis puteolanus*, was preferentially selected for underwater construction and exported across the Mediterranean for use in harbor facilities (Jackson and Kosso 273; Jackson).[3] Trajanic monuments on land in the city of Rome, instead, favored the reddish ash (*pozzolane rosse*) over the black variants from distinct geological horizons around the city (Bianchi et al. 77).

The process of sorting and categorization erected new boundaries between materials and between their users. The widened palette of choice generated distinctions as one choice excluded the other, and choices became ranked (Bourdieu). Not importing special lightweight pumice for use in high vaults, for instance, would place building, builders, and commissioners in an inferior position to those able to do so. Not everyone's concrete was the same, and concrete became one more differentiator in a Roman game of inequality and consumption.

The semantics of concrete extended beyond the city of Rome. For instance, at the small rural site of Podere Marzuolo, Tuscany, an early first-century AD builder chose to break with the local building tradition of employing earthen walls on low, stone socles. Instead, they designed a large-scale building with concrete walls, one-meter-deep foundations, and a facing of diamond-shaped stones, so-called *opus reticulatum* (Van Oyen, *Innovation and Investment*). A longstanding argument reads these diamond-shaped stones as a narrative of efficiency: by front-loading the labor of cutting, the carved blocks could easily be assembled by an unskilled labor force that flooded the city of Rome as a result of war and urban pull (Coarelli 18; Torelli 155;

---

2   See Lechtman and Hobbs 102; Lancaster, "Concrete Vaulted Construction" 59–62 for examples of this strategy as applied in individual buildings; Lancaster et al.; Quenemoen 65; Wilson Jones 187, for the second-century AD Pantheon.
3   On export, see Hohlfelder and Oleson 224–25; Oleson et al. 206.

Mogetta). In Rome and environs, such *opus reticulatum* stones were carved from relatively soft tufa stone. In the stone-poor region of Marzuolo, instead, rounded, hard calcareous river stones were used, making carving rather more difficult and creating imperfectly fitting stones. The result was a huge investment of labor both at the carving and the assembling stages. Instead of an instrument of expediency, building in concrete at Marzuolo was a spectacle and a statement that paraded form *despite* matter: its aim was to stake a claim of differentiation and power.

If it seems like we have now returned to a model of passive matter waiting to be formed in the pursuit of human drama, we should quickly re-center concrete's own material logics. Early concrete buildings mimic the forms of preceding stone architecture or "trabeated" architecture, with its posts, lintels, plinths, and sharp angles (Wilson Jones). It took several centuries of experimentation and confidence-building for builders to release concrete's structural and spatial affordances. In particular, the lateral thrust of concrete structures made the traditional load-bearing walls, piers, and columns redundant. Stronger still, it was structurally impossible to create flat ceilings in concrete; the material demanded to be curved. As a result, spaces became newly opened up, with sequences of vaults creating uninterrupted vistas and axiality and with domes aspiring to a new sense of centrality and verticality. Buildings increased in scale (Quenemoen 68–9) and focused on interaction inside of their impressively shaped volumes rather than on integration in a broader landscape (MacDonald 31–41; Ball). Concrete thus generated a wholly novel architectural language, facilitating large gatherings of people yet severing their connection with any outside world. This language translated into—and reinforced—the new social and political concerns of the Roman imperial order, an order in which citizens barely partook in politics, and in which even the elites had limited maneuver space in the face of an all-powerful emperor and imperial court. As anything but passive matter, concrete, then, actively dazzled, muting an increasingly muzzled body (im)politic.

Works Cited

Ball, Larry F. *The Domus Aurea and the Roman Architectural Revolution*. Cambridge UP, 2003.

Barad, Karen. "Posthumanist Performativity: Toward an Understanding of How Matter Comes to Matter." *Signs*, vol. 28, no. 3, 2003, pp. 801–31.

Bianchi, Elisabetta, et al. "Archaeological, Structural, and Compositional Observations of the Concrete Architecture of the Basilica Ulpia and Trajan's Forum." *Commentationes Humanarum Litterarum*, vol. 128, 2011, pp. 73–95.

Blake, Marion E., and Esther B. Van Deman. *Ancient Roman Construction in Italy from the Prehistoric Period to Augustus*. Carnegie Institution of Washington, 1947.

Blake, Marion E. *Roman Construction in Italy from Tiberius through the Flavians*. Carnegie Institution of Washington, 1959.
Bourdieu, Pierre. *Distinction: A Social Critique of the Judgement of Taste*. Routledge, 2010.
Coarelli, Filippo. "Public Building in Rome between the Second Punic War and Sulla." *Papers of the British School at Rome*, vol. 45, 1977, pp. 1–23.
Duckworth, Chloë N., et al. "When the Statue is Both Marble and Lime." *Recycling and the Ancient Economy*, edited by Chloë N Duckworth and Andrew Wilson, Oxford UP, 2020, pp. 449–59.
Fabian, Johannes. *Time and the Other*. Columbia UP, 1983.
Harris, Edward C. "Archaeological Stratigraphy: A Paradigm for the Anthropocene." *Journal of Contemporary Archaeology*, vol. 1, no. 1, 2014, pp. 105–09. http://dx.doi.org/10.1558/jca.v1i1.105
Hohlfelder, Robert L., and John Peter Oleson. "Roman Maritime Concrete Technology in Its Mediterranean Context." *Building for Eternity: The History and Technology of Roman Concrete Engineering in the Sea*, edited by John Peter Oleson, Oxbow, 2014, pp. 223–35.
Ingold, Tim. "Materials against Materiality." *Archaeological Dialogues*, vol. 14, no. 1, 2007, pp. 1–16.
Irvine, Richard. *An Anthropology of Deep Time*. Cambridge UP, 2020.
Jackson, Marie D., and Cynthia K. Kosso. "Scientia in Republican Era Stone and Concrete Masonry." *A Companion to the Archaeology of the Roman Republic*, edited by Jane DeRose Evans, Wiley Blackwell, 2013, pp. 268–84.
Jackson, Marie D. "Sea-Water Concretes and Their Material Characteristics." *Building for Eternity: The History and Technology of Roman Concrete Engineering in the Sea*, edited by John Peter Oleson, Oxbow, 2014, pp. 141–87.
Lancaster, Lynne C. *Concrete Vaulted Construction in Imperial Rome: Innovations in Context*. Cambridge UP, 2005.
———. *Innovative Vaulting in the Architecture of the Roman Empire: 1st to 4th Centuries CE*. Cambridge UP, 2015.
———, et al. "Provenancing of Lightweight Volcanic Stones Used in Ancient Roman Concrete Vaulting: Evidence from Rome." *Archaeometry*, vol. 53, no. 4, 2011, pp. 707–27.
Lechtman, Heather and Linn Hobbs. "Roman Concrete and the Roman Architectural Revolution." *High-Technology Ceramics: Past, Present, and Future: The Nature of Innovation and Change in Ceramic Technology (Ceramics and Civilization 3)*, edited by William David Kingery, The American Ceramic Society, 1986, pp. 81–128.
MacDonald, William. L. *The Architecture of the Roman Empire. I. An Introductory Study*, 2nd ed., Yale UP, 1982.
Mogetta, Marcello. *The Origins of Concrete Construction in Roman Architecture: Technology and Society in Republican Italy*. Cambridge UP, 2021.

Oleson, John Peter, et al. "The ROMACONS Project: A Contribution to the Historical and Engineering Analysis of Hydraulic Concrete in Roman Maritime Structures." *International Journal of Nautical Archaeology*, vol. 33, no. 2, 2004, pp. 199–229.

Quenemoen, Caroline K. "Columns and Concrete: Architecture from Nero to Hadrian." *A Companion to Roman Architecture*, edited by Roger B. Ulrich and Caroline K. Wiley, Blackwell, 2014, pp. 63–81.

Torelli, Mario. "Innovazioni nelle tecniche edilizie romane tra il I sec. a.C. e il I sec. d.C. *Tecnologia, economia e società nel mondo romano. Atti del convegno di Como, 27–29 settembre 1979*, Banca popolare commercio e industria, 1980, pp. 139–62.

Van Oyen, Astrid. "Finding the Material in 'Material Culture': Form and Matter in Roman Concrete." *Materialising Roman Histories*, edited by Astrid Van Oyen and Martin Pitts, Oxbow, 2017, pp. 133–52.

———. "Innovation and Investment in the Roman Rural Economy Through the Lens of Marzuolo (Tuscany, Italy)." *Past and Present*, vol. 248, no. 1, 2020, pp. 3–40.

Waters, Colin N., et al. "The Anthropocene is Functionally and Stratigraphically Distinct from the Holocene." *Science*, vol. 351, no. 6269, 2016, https://doi.org/10.1126/science.aad2622

Wilson Jones, Mark. *Principles of Roman Architecture*. Yale UP, 2000.

4. Postclassical Marble: Reclaiming Flux in the Reception of Marble in Contemporary Art

Maarten De Pourcq

Classicizing Marble

Perhaps no other material has been more closely associated with ancient Greco-Roman culture than marble. One can even argue that marble is a prime material connector between the Greek and Roman worlds, instantiating the hyphen used to bind Greco to Roman. Only sparingly used in earlier ancient worlds, like Mesopotamia or Egypt (Waelkens et al. 14–15),[1] it was in archaic Greece that marble became a privileged material, first for sculpture and later for architecture. The figurines of Cycladic sculpture, dating from 3000 to 2000 BC and among the earliest examples of Greek art, were made from marble. The stone was a natural resource relatively easy to quarry on the Cycladic islands of the Aegean Sea (Marthari et al., esp. 468–82). The perfectly white marble from the island of Paros later became in high demand for sculptures from archaic Greek to Roman times. The so-called Pentelic marble, from Mount Pentelicon near Athens, was used from the sixth century BC onwards, for instance, for buildings in Athens as well as for triumphal monuments in Rome (Bernard), when Greece had fallen into the hands of Roman imperialism. At the same time, Rome, according to the Roman poet Horace's famous saying, was captured by Greek culture.[2] That marble connects Greek and Roman material culture is also because many of the Greek statues that we know of today are Roman marble copies or adaptations, usually from Greek originals in bronze (Anguissola). Nearly all of these bronzes have been lost since bronze decays faster and is more easily recycled than the crystalline limestone that is marble. Along with the fact that it is relatively easy

---

1   According to Hochscheid (117–19), the Greeks adopted not so much the use of marble but most probably the use of monumental stone and the quarrying and carving techniques of stones from the Egyptians and the Hittites. See also Rohleder; Spier et al. 107.
2   The saying is from Horace's *Epistles* (II.1). It goes as follows: "Graecia capta ferum victorem cepit" ("Captive Greece conquered in its turn its savage victor"), meaning not by military force but with its culture.

to carve, marble's durability is an important reason why it became a mnemonic device par excellence. In a sense, the age of classical marble began with this material used by people to make monuments that could outlast their generation and do their specific cultural work: temples, busts, palaces, votives, fountains, churches, gravestones, and political buildings.

Marble also plays a central role in the imagination of what Greco-Roman culture looked like, both during and after antiquity. Marble became one of its most imitated aspects, a paradigm to be followed. There is a dual mnemonics at play here: as a material, marble helped to stand the test of time; as matter used in and for an object, marble also became a cultural marker, a visual and material reference to Greco-Roman culture and the classical tradition anchored in that culture, especially in Europe. Among the more iconic statues in European art history is Michelangelo's *David*, a classicizing sculpture from around 1500 made in white Carrara marble. As of the Early Modern period, marble and marble imitation became in vogue outside Europe and the Mediterranean. This was partly due to the use of marble in Byzantine and Islamic art and partly because Europeans decided to stretch their wings and claws to other parts of the world (Barry 1–2). Among the more iconic buildings in world history is the White House in Washington DC from around 1800, which has the classicist look of a temple and is painted white to give it the semblance of classical marble, a tactic of *faux marble* that was already in use in antiquity.

Revisioning Marble

Given this longstanding status of privileged material, it is a surprise that a history of marble as a material of culture has not yet been written.[3] Such a study of marble would be all the more welcome since the cultural work of marble as a privileged material is currently being questioned and reconfigured by contemporary artists. The Barcelona-born artist Sergio Roger, for one, produced an extensive series of what he termed "soft statuary," which was on show during the 2021 Milan Design Week.[4] Roger's statuary plays with the imaginary of classical marble: his busts look like white marble, some mimicking the style of Cycladic sculpture, but they are made from recycled natural textile fiber. These soft statues elicit a markedly different feeling from the robust marble meant to cross the ages in an immutable form. The American artist Kara Walker made a similarly subversive gesture to marble in

---

3 It has been done for many other materials and resources, like steel (Fry et al.), porcelain (Marchand), and nutmeg (Ghosh). Barry comes closest with his history of the poetics of marble in architecture from antiquity to the Enlightenment. See also Rohleder; Goldhill, "Marmoreal."

4 For Roger's portfolio, see https://www.sergioroger.com/augusto-1.

Fons Americanus (2019), a commissioned art installation for the Turbine Hall at the London Tate Modern (fig. 1) that takes the marble Queen Victoria Memorial (1911) in London as its point of reference. Continuing the memorial's nautical theme, it highlights its imperialist background as it commemorates the naval power of the British Empire. Walker radically changes the narrative as well as the material of the memorial. Instead of Queen Victoria and the personifications of her virtues and imperial achievements, Walker's working fountain commemorates the people involved in the transatlantic slave trade, linking Great Britain and Europe with Africa, America, and Asia. She does so through running water and the depiction of emblematic slavery scenes, such as the racist practice of lynching, which persisted in the USA after the abolition of slavery until deep into the twentieth century.

Fig. 1: Kara Walker, Fons Americanus, Sculpture, 2019, Tate Modern, Hyundai Commission, London, UK, Main: 73.5 x 50 x 43 feet, Grotto: 10.2 x 10.5 x 10.8 feet, Artwork © Kara Walker, courtesy of Sikkema Jenkins and Co. and Sprüth Magers. Photograph: © Tate (Matt Greenwood)

On top of the memorial stands not a winged Victory like in the Victoria Memorial, but the large figure of a black woman from whose breasts and a slit in her throat burst piercing streams of water. Whereas the Victoria Memorial uses 2,300 tons of white Carrara marble, nicely polished, Walker's memorial consists of heaps of non-glazed white clay of officially unknown weight. The clay gives the semblance of marble from a distance. However, closer inspection reveals a rough and unwrought material, prone to wear and transformation, less refined in its finish but sensually much more present, also in its earthly odor. The whiteness of the clay makes the bursting streams of water look like milk, turning the female figure on top into a revision of both the Victory figure and the mother figure, also featured in the Victoria Memorial. Walker's revision raises the question of who gave life to whom and who gave her life for which victories.

The soft statuary and the fountain invite spectators to see marble even if it is not there. The objects are "anchored" (Sluiter) in marble in that these works draw upon the expectation that this type of artwork—white statuary with a classicizing look—is, as a rule, made from marble. In a second gesture, as the audience sees the marble replacement, it is invited to reflect upon why the marble has been suggested in the first place and why a different material replaces it. Marble here is as much a material as a code, a relatively established set of experiential features that makes these objects meaningful and valuable to those expected to be familiar, and perhaps also to agree, with this code.[5] From a material-discursive point of view, these artworks attempt to reconfigure the experience of marble. They work with and intervene in the material-discursive practice of boundary-drawing (e.g., marble means civilized culture as opposed to primitive cultures, which typically do not (know how to) use marble) and meaning-making (e.g., marble mimics human skin) that is produced by the use of marble through the apparatus of an artwork. By artistically rewriting this code (i.e., by reiterating, differentiating, and redrawing recog-

---

5   See Brown: "As they circulate through our lives, we look through objects (to see what they disclose about history, society, nature, or culture—above all, what they disclose about us), but we only catch a glimpse of things. We look through objects because there are codes by which our interpretive attention makes them meaningful, because there is a discourse of objectivity that allows us to use them as facts" (4). Precisely this "discourse of objectivity" and its universalist pretensions are what is being questioned today, for instance in colonial cultural studies: "Such a system of knowledge, referred to here as the 'Western code', serves not all humanity, but only a small portion of it that benefits from the belief that in terms of epistemology, there is only one game in town. The 'code' has been preserved in the security box since the Renaissance" (Mignolo xii). In this essay, I adopt a material-discursive approach to the concept of code, partly by drawing upon the work of Karen Barad. This means that "codes," as I tentatively and heuristically envision them here, are not imposed upon marble by (Western) humans; rather, marble co-produces this code: "Matter is always already an ongoing historicity ... [Matter is] not a thing but a doing, a congealing of agency" (Barad 151).

nizable boundaries made by prior art), contemporary artists are reviewing marble as a cultural marker, raising different sorts of issues, including questions about materiality, aesthetics, tactility, provenance, history, and memory. In what follows, I will succinctly discuss these questions by highlighting two of marble's distinct but interrelated features that are part of its transhistorical code: luminosity and luxury. These features share a duplicity that is aesthetic and political: marble's luminosity involves the social issues of whiteness and monoculturalism, and marble's luxury recalls colonialism and imperialism. These questions are timely: they are part of an ongoing reparation work between and within present-day social groups and individuals that urges us to reconsider the role of classical traditions in global history and to attend to the material, aesthetic, social, and ethical effects and relationships that the use of marble may establish.

Marble's Luminosity

One distinct feature of marble is that it can reflect light. According to ancient popular etymology, the Greek word for marble, *marmaros*, goes back to the verb *marmairein*, which means to shine, gleam, and twinkle (Chantraine 643). Marble owes this capacity to its crystalline structure, making it more luminous than limestone, which is also used to construct buildings. Marble is a type of limestone in which the calcite has been transformed by intense heat or extreme pressure. This has changed the texture of the original porous rock into a dense network of crystals. Possible sediments like clay minerals, fossils, or iron oxides rend flashes of color to the stone. These sediments are called "impurities," qualifying the monochrome white marble as the "pure," telluric product. Especially when polished and waxed, the stone, of whatsoever color, adds luminosity and depth to an object by reflecting and refracting the light in its crystals. No wonder, then, that architects of buildings that were to express a sacred connection with the world started to deploy this natural feature of marble. The importance given to luminosity can already be found in the white-washed limestone temple in Uruk, dedicated to Anu, the Mesopotamian god of the sky, and built around 3000 BC. This so-called White Temple stood on a platform similar to how ancient Greek temples or the Roman-Jewish Temple of Jerusalem, for instance, were constructed in marble and located on heights, seeking to express their intimate connection with the cosmos (Goldhill, "Temple" 71; Stewart 1). Alongside marble's capacity to reflect light, marble in antiquity was also believed to add cosmic force to an artefact because of its provenance, being quarried from Mother Earth.[6] Marble connects the below and the above, which can explain why the translucent

---

6   E.g., Pliny 33.1.

stone was used to materialize, or generate experiences of, transcendence. It connects across time and space.

Alongside white marble, many types of colored marble were in use, too, such as the popular *rosso antico* (red marble) and *giallo antico* (yellow marble) in Roman culture. Ancient marble does not necessarily equal whiteness, even more so since marble temples and statuary were usually lavishly painted in different colors and covered with precious metals. The strong emphasis on whiteness as part of marble's classical code characterizes European classicism much more than Greco-Roman antiquity, even though the latter was believed to be classicism's paradigm. Today, we know that the whiteness of the remnants of Greco-Roman buildings and statues was not an aesthetic choice of ancient artists and architects but has been accidentally caused by external conditions that have worn off the colors over time. This means that the paradigmatic whiteness of marble is the result of a process of material flux. Rather than a cultural idea, for instance, the presumed "noble simplicity and quiet grandeur" of ancient Greek civilization, an often-quoted dictum from the German art historian Johann Joachim Winckelmann (21),[7] it was the impact of weathering and erosion that has established the white image of Greco-Roman culture. This cultural debt to nature is seldom acknowledged as such.

In place of the historical polychromy of the ancient marbles, whiteness became, in the words of Philippe Jockey, a *rêve occidental* ("Western dream") in the reception of Greco-Roman culture until today. Alt-right meme culture, for instance, still uses pictures of white ancient and Renaissance marble torsos to propagate masculinist and white supremacist ideals of beauty (Jockey). Although people have been aware of the original polychromy for centuries, some of them, like Winckelmann (Manfrini 24), have refused to accept it. Interestingly, specialist scholarship on ancient color use began to grow only at the end of the twentieth century (Ostergaard and Nielsen; Brinkmann and Koch-Brinkmann), as if correcting the monochrome white image of ancient Greco-Roman culture was no priority for a very long time. Already in the nineteenth century, Nietzsche capitalized on ancient polychromy to criticize the mindset of his time (Babich). He took the historically mistaken white monochromy of classicism as a telling example of the dominant mode of monotheist and monocultural thinking among his contemporaries that his philosophy strove to counteract by mobilizing the idea of *poikilia* ("variegation," also used for colors) of the ancient Greeks (Grand-Clément). The British artist Sonia Boyce vented a similar critique of white monoculturalism as she perceived it in the Victorian imagination of classical mythology that dominates various British museum collections. Her video installation *Six Acts* (2018) captures a performance in which she introduced various cross-cultural and cross-gender mythological characters replete with color and glitter into

---

7   For Winckelmann's legacy on classicist thinking, see Harloe; Moormann.

the Manchester Art Gallery. As a guest curator, Boyce explicitly questioned the museum's collection by temporarily removing A.W. Waterhouse's popular painting *Hylas and the Nymphs* (1896). By doing so, she called attention to its representation of the heterosexual gaze on the marble-white bodies of the nymphs. Her intervention confronts the audience with how museums' historical collections continue normalizing white monoculturalism. Marble here is a cultural reference that links whiteness to idealization, like in the idealized white bodies of the nymphs. Color has been given value, and therefore, it can also be used, as Walker does, to reassess traditions and question underlying power structures.

Marble's Luxury

Augustus is said to have boasted that he had found Rome a city of bricks and left it of marble (Suetonius 28.3). The ruler who transformed the Roman Republic into the Roman Empire made no secret of what symbolized wealth and power best: marble. As Clayton Fant explains: "Marble made a particularly appropriate symbol of wealth and power because it was expensive, imported, and unnecessary (especially in a land endowed with good building stones like perperino and travertine)" (149). Although Roman Italy had its own resources (the Carrara marble quarries, for example, were opened just before August's reign), a special imperial quarry system delivered marble from conquered regions all over the Empire to Rome. Of different colors, these marbles represented the vastness, diversity, and opulence of the Roman Empire, as viewers were expected to recognize that the yellow giallo antico, for instance, came from Numidia in Northern Africa, and the white Pentelic marble from Greece.[8] It has even been claimed that "colored marble from conquered lands was especially popular for thresholds, enabling the Romans to walk over the territory of their defeated enemies each time they entered their houses" (Stewart 34). The symbolism of imperial power was thus firmly anchored in marble's use, both in its colored and white versions. As to the latter, it has been argued that it was not so much the hue of the white color as its luminance that defined white marble's capacity to evoke wealth and luxury (Sassi).

The global marble trade also had its critics in antiquity. Pliny the Elder famously described the Roman marble craze as an ecological and moral daze. He regarded the removal of the marble support from below the earth's crust and the shipping of the quarried marble "mountains" across the sea as profoundly contranatural. Marble trade brings the Earth and people's lives out of balance: people would live happier

---

8 "The employment of colored marbles from Africa and Asia Minor as well as the expensive white marble from Mount Pentelicon in Greece . . . reflects the Roman supremacy over the Mediterranean world in the early imperial period" (Van de Liefvoort 66).

without this luxury, so he claimed (Pliny 36.1–3). In a gripping essay on Walker's *Fons Americanus*, Zadie Smith points to a saying that she attributes to the Athenian ruler Pericles in Thucydides' *History of the Peloponnesian War*: "What you leave behind is not what is engraved in stone monuments, but what is woven into the lives of others" (Smith 33). In other words, the Augustan rhetoric of the shining Eternal City, which, it should be mentioned, is not unlike the rhetoric—and the use of marble, for that matter—of Pericles' building programs in his metropole, is not adequate to the historical bloodshed, the abused lives, and the social violence, as enacted by Walker's *Fons Americanus*. Walker's use of clay rather than marble recalls the creation myths in which clay is the primary matter from which the world was molded. Walker's material selection turns the depicted scene into a primary scene, showing "the lives of others" that were violently used to harvest natural resources that have produced a world of luxury for those living in the shining white classicist metropoles which emulated Rome and Athens. It is a sidenote but a telling irony of history that there has been a discussion about whether the ancient Greek term *lychnites* for the most refined white marbles of Paros has to be interpreted as a testimony to its luminosity or as a reference to the lamplight in which the enslaved worked in the marble mines (Barry 44). In Roger's soft statuary, the act of replacing marble with textile also involves a reference to labor. His textiles are recycled historical linen and silk that the artist collected from antique shops. The work foregrounds re-use rather than use, and in so doing, it also honors the quality of the historical craftwork, usually done by anonymous women. Roger's techniques to create his statuary merge the world of sculpture with the world of fashion, two worlds that have been strongly gendered throughout history. Rewriting the code of marble, Roger tries to position the old world of masculine monumental stone against his new world of gender-inclusive fabric by making his soft statuary "perform" memory (Plate and Smelik) rather than monumentality. Recalling past and neglected historical moments of labor, Roger and Walker replace marble to introduce flux and highlight its social significance.

Postclassical Marble

The Swiss artist Urs Fisher recently explained why he finds it difficult to create new art with marble: "The problem is that it [marble] is very dominant—there's a lot of history there that weighs things down. . . . [T]o bring your voice into that conversation you have to have a very clear way of expressing yourself" (Holmes 68). Fisher captured the spotlight during the 2011 Venice Biennale with an untitled sculpture that copied Giambologna's sixteenth-century marble statue *Abduction of a Sabine Woman* in wax. He made the statue slowly burn away, along with a statue portraying the artist, as if they were candles in a church. It is one way of bringing flux into conversation with marble, using the warmth of the fire to deform the suggested image of marble and make it permanently vanish. The work tries to twist the ambition for permanence that is deeply ingrained in the code of marble and criticize its masculinist history by making the figure of the male artist disappear. As such, it creates room for something and someone else at the expense of what and who appeared destined to remain. The flux introduced here, however, is relative: the work does not erase itself since it remains a concept invented by the artist that can be—and has been—repeated.[9] Also, photographs officially document its Biennale materialization. The work does not represent a tabula rasa; it is an artistic intervention in the ambition to make a statement. As the expression of flux, seeking to destroy the code of marble's desired timelessness, fire is a destructive force that, in Fisher's mind, appears to be necessary to find "a very clear way of expressing himself." It is not a careful act of "gentle imitation" (Prettejohn 14–15) but a grand gesture reproducing the desire for artistic grandeur that is also part of the code of marble. By adding the elemental violence of fire and turning the work into a concept, the installation does not depart from but varies upon and problematizes the paradigm of marble sculpture. Walker's fountain uses this grand gesture to send its message, replacing the well-known monumental queen with a monumental anonymous woman. Roger places his statuary on pedestals. All these artworks rewrite and retain, including the potentially damaging and socially exclusive components of the classical marble code. What they have in common is that they can be seen as mindscapes, mental or psychological scenes that stage a contemporary conversation with the cultural legacies of marble.

In this sense, these works of contemporary art are "postclassical" (The Postclassicisms Collective): they do not take classicism for granted and try to position themselves vis-à-vis this cultural repertory in a global world with violent histories that need to be dealt with. For sure, classicism has been successfully deployed to create art that explores various sorts of questions, feelings, thoughts, ambitions, and experiences by, at times, resourcefully, carefully, beautifully, or violently making variations on what is offered from a "collective tradition" (Settis 63; Vout).[10] This repertory not only consists of artistic formulas (such as the kouros figure, the nymph, or the Corinthian column) but also of materials like marble, which has become a weighty cultural marker in itself, encoding objects with aesthetic, cultural, social, and historical features and legacies. Contemporary artists struggle with how to relate to these

---

9   As Holmes puts it, "A conceptual sculpture basically doesn't age, because you can always redo it" (68). The installation was repeated for the opening of the Pinault Collection in the Musée Bourse de Commerce in Paris in 2021.
10 I am grateful to my colleague Anneke Smelik for giving me this book and various other moments of inspiration, pleasure, and guidance. I would also like to thank Ann Demeester, Eric Moormann and the editors of this volume for their useful advice and suggestions while writing this essay.

legacies, to marble's luminosity, luxury, permanence, and materiality. They continue the task of classicism to the extent that they not only deconstruct the artistic language of classicism but also try to "perfect" it by making postclassical marble do the social and cultural work beyond and against the grain of the traditional code, reaching out to a shinier future.

Works Cited

Anguissola, Anna. "Masterpieces and Their Copies: The Greek Canon and Roman Beholders." *Serial/Portable Classic: The Greek Canon and its Mutations*, edited by Salvatore Settis, and Anna Anguissola, Fondazione Prada, 2015, pp. 73–79.
Babich, Babette. "Nietzsche's Philology and the Science of Antiquity." *Nietzsche as a Scholar of Antiquity*, edited by Anthony K. Jenson and Helmut Heit, Bloomsbury, 2014, pp. 233–61.
Barad, Karen. *Meeting the Universe Halfway: Quantum Physics and the Entanglement of Matter and Meaning*. Duke UP, 2007.
Barry, Fabio. *Painting in Stone: Architecture and the Poetics of Marble from Antiquity to the Enlightenment*. Yale UP, 2020.
Bernard, Seth G. "Pentelic Marble in Architecture at Rome and the Republican Marble Trade." *Journal of Roman Archaeology*, vol. 23, 2010, pp. 35–54.
Brinkmann, Vinzenz, and Ulrike Koch-Brinkmann. *Bunte Götter: Die Farben der Antike*. Liebieghaus, 2020.
Brown, Bill. "Thing Theory." *Critical Inquiry*, vol. 28, no. 1, 2001, pp. 1–22.
Chantraine, Pierre. *Dictionnaire étymologique de la langue grecque : Histoire des mots*. Klincksieck, 2009.
Fant, J. Clayton. "The Roman Emperors in the Marble Business: Capitalists, Middle-Men or Philanthropists?" *Classical Marble: Geochemistry, Technology, Trade*, edited by Norman Herz and Marc Waelkens, Kluwer, 1988, pp. 147–58.
Fry, Tony, et al., editors. *Steel: A Design, Cultural and Ecological History*. Bloomsbury, 2015.
Ghosh, Amitav. *The Nutmeg's Curse: Parables for a Planet in Crisis*. U of Chicago P, 2021.
Goldhill, Simon. "Marmoreal." *Liquid Antiquity*, edited by Brooke Holmes and Karen Marta, Deste, 2017, pp. 250–53.
———. *The Temple of Jerusalem*. Harvard UP, 2005.
Grand-Clément, Adeline. "Poikilia." *A Companion to Ancient Aesthetics*, edited by Pierre Destrée and Penelope Murray, Wiley, 2015, pp. 406–21.
Harloe, Katherine. *Winckelmann and the Invention of Antiquity: History and Aesthetics in the Age of Altertumswissenschaft*. Oxford UP, 2013.
Hochscheid, Helle. *Networks of Stone: Sculpture and Society in Archaic and Classical Athens*. Peter Lang, 2015.

Holmes, Brooke. "Interview: Urs Fischer." *Liquid Antiquity*, edited by Brooke Holmes and Karen Marta, Deste, 2017, pp. 62–69.
Horace. *Satires, Epistles, Ars Poetica*. Edited by Jeffrey Henderson, Harvard UP, 1929.
Kim, Clare, editor. *Kara Walker: Fons Americanus*. Tate, 2019.
Liefvoort, Suzanne van de. *Appearance Matters: Natural Luxury in Roman Domestic Decoration*. 2016. Radboud U, PhD dissertation.
Manfrini, Ivonne. "Entre refus et nécessité de la couleur : La sculpture grecque antique." *L' Antiquité en couleurs : Catégories, pratiques, représentations*, edited by Marcello Carastro, Millon, 2009, pp. 21–41.
Marchand, Suzanne L. *Porcelain: A History from the Heart of Europe*. Princeton UP, 2020.
Marthari, Marisa, et al., editors. *Early Cycladic Sculpture in Context*. Oxbow Books, 2017.
Mignolo, Walter D. *The Darker Side of Western Modernity: Global Futures, Decolonial Options*. Duke UP, 2011.
Moormann, Eric. *The Impact of Winckelmann on Europe*. Babesch, 2018.
Ostergaard, Jan Stubbe, and Anne Marie Nielsen, editors. *Transformations: Classical Sculpture in Color*. Ny Carlsberg Glyptotek, 2014.
Plate, Liedeke, and Anneke Smelik, editors. *Performing Memory in Art and Popular Culture*. Routledge, 2015.
Pliny. *Natural History IX-X*. Edited by Jeffrey Henderson, Harvard UP, 1952–1962.
The Postclassicisms Collective. *Postclassicisms*. Chicago UP, 2020.
Prettejohn, Elizabeth. *Modern Painters, Old Masters: The Art of Imitation from the Pre-Raphealites to the First World War*. Yale UP, 2017.
Riederer, J. "The Decay and Conservation of Marbles on Archaeological Monuments." *Classical Marble: Geochemistry, Technology, Trade*, edited by Norman Herz and Marc Waelkens, Kluwer, 1988, pp. 465–74.
Rohleder, Johannes. "Marble and Limestone." *Calcium Carbonate: From the Cretaceous Period into the 21st Century*, edited by F. Wolfgang Tegethoff, Birkhäuser, 2001, pp. 69–135.
Sassi, M. Michela. "Perceiving Colors." *A Companion to Ancient Aesthetics*, edited by Pierre Destrée and Penelope Murray, Wiley, 2015, pp. 406–21.
Settis, Salvatore. "Supremely Original: Classical Art as Serial, Iterative, Portable." *Serial/Portable Classic: The Greek Canon and its Mutations*, edited by Salvatore Settis and Anna Anguissola, Fondazione Prada, 2015, pp. 51–72.
Sluiter, Ineke. "Anchoring Innovation: A Classical Research Agenda." *European Review*, vol. 25, no. 1, 2016, pp. 20–38.
Smith, Zadie. "Kara Walker: What Do We Want History to Do to Us?" *Kara Walker: Fons Americanus*, edited by Clara Kim, Tate, 2019, pp. 32–53.
Spier, Jeffrey, et al., editors. *Beyond the Nile: Egypt and the Classical World*. Getty, 2018.
Stewart, Susan. *The Ruins Lesson: Meaning and Material in Western Culture*. Chicago UP, 2020.

Suetonius. "The Deified Augustus." *Lives of the Caesars I*, edited by K.R. Bradley, Harvard UP, 1998, pp. 150–309.

Vout, Caroline. *Classical Art: A Life History from Antiquity to the Present*. Princeton UP, 2018.

Waelkens, Marc, et al. "Quarries and the Marble Trade in Antiquity." *Classical Marble: Geochemistry, Technology, Trade*, edited by Norman Herz and Marc Waelkens, Kluwer, 1988, pp. 11–28.

Winckelmann, Johann Joachim. *Gedanken über die Nachahmung der griechischen Werke in Malerei und Bildhauerkunst*. Walthersche Buchhandlung, 1756.

Part III: Extractivism and Toxic Colonialism

5. Asbestos: The Fallout of Shipbreaking in the Global South

László Munteán

Asbestos is a naturally occurring mineral known for its insulating and fireproofing qualities afforded by its fibrous texture. Throughout its heyday in the twentieth century, it was used to create several composite materials, including asbestos cement, asbestos plaster, and fireproofing foams used in construction. Ropes, firefighter suits, gloves, theater curtains, ovens, and even cigarette filters also contained asbestos. Paradoxically, the qualities that made asbestos a trademark of safety also endangered the lives of those who worked with it. Inhalation of its microscopic fibrils lodged within each of its fibers can cause lung cancer, mesothelioma, and asbestosis—three of the most common asbestos-induced diseases—the symptoms of which may not appear until two or three decades after exposure. While many countries have banned the mining, use, and import of asbestos, detecting and removing it from buildings remains a major concern.

Lesser known is that asbestos was used extensively in shipbuilding as an insulating material for pipes, ducts, boilers, and machinery, as well as for guns and ammunition on warships. Shipyard workers have long been suffering the lethal consequences of their exposure to asbestos. Although the International Convention for the Safety of Life at Sea prohibits the installation of asbestos-containing materials on ships built after July 1, 2002,[1] this regulation does not pertain to vessels built before that date. Once older vessels reach the end of their service period, typically after three or four decades, they are sent to dismantling yards. Most of these yards are in the Global South, where hazardous materials can be recycled at a significantly lower cost than in the Global North. This essay probes the theoretical and ethical implications that thinking of (and with) asbestos as a material of culture entails in relation to shipbreaking.

---

1   https://www.imo.org/en/OurWork/Safety/Pages/Asbestos.aspx.

Ships That Matter

Recent scholarship has used the figure of the ship as a conceptual tool to reflect on European modernity in relation to colonial expansion and the Atlantic slave trade (Gilroy 4–40), the refugee crisis (Mannik), and global capitalism and containerized trade (Khalili; Martin). These approaches construe the ship as an object that facilitates the movement of people, goods, and commodities, providing the means of trade and negotiating and projecting national or imperial power. There is, however, an alternative way of looking at ships; rather than perceiving them as finished objects, it focuses on the materials from which the ships are made. Such a shift of perspective from form to materials is analogous to a transformation from an object into a thing, as per Bill Brown's distinction (4). When perceived as a thing, the boundaries that define the ship as an object are rendered porous, making the ship "leak," to apply Tim Ingold's favored term in an uncannily fitting context (7). From such a materials-based perspective, the ship breaks down into an assemblage of materials laden with their own histories, which requires that we attend to "the before and after of the object," which Brown describes as the temporality of "thingness" (4).

Karen Barad's notion of material-discursive practices helps further conceptualize the implications of a materials-based perspective on ships. In material-discursive practices, Barad maintains, "[t]he relationship between the material and the discursive is one of mutual entailment. Neither is articulated/articulable in the absence of the other; matter and meaning are mutually articulated" (Barad, "Posthumanist Performativity" 822). Following asbestos in material-discursive terms thus requires that we account for the differential and co-constitutive dynamics of its materialization as an effect of discourse and, vice versa, its discursive production as a material. For instance, when its ubiquity and low price are considered preconditions for the large-scale construction of passenger, cargo, and navy ships throughout the twentieth century, one should also consider colonialism as the geopolitical discursive condition that supplied asbestos for Royal Navy ships in both world wars. Most of the asbestos built into these warships was mined in the former British colonies of South Africa, Botswana, Zimbabwe, and Malawi (Hedley-Whyte and Milamed 191–92). While ships tend to be portrayed as the means that enabled colonial expansion and exploitation in the first place, this example illustrates their entanglement with these processes at the level of materials and the discourses that enabled their flow. This perspective also brings to the fore the materiality of human bodies that were in touch with asbestos in mining and the construction and dismantling of ships. Major shipyards in the Global North that are opening up about their illegal use of asbestos after its ban from shipbuilding are currently facing lawsuits by affected workers and their families (Munz; Strand). However, lawsuits concerning working conditions are not an option for workers in the shipbreaking yards in the Global South. Even if they are protected by law on paper, these laws are rarely enforced and often evaded by local authorities and owners of shipbreaking yards (Karim 125–26).

The Slow Violence of Toxic Colonialism

To navigate the assemblage of bodies, materials, economic interests, and political dependencies, it is necessary to consider the events that led to the concentration of the world's largest shipbreaking yards in three countries of the Global South: Pakistan, India, and Bangladesh. Here, almost ninety percent of the world's merchant ships are scrapped every year (Sawyer 555). One of the events that triggered this practice was the environmental catastrophe caused by the oil tanker *Exxon Valdez*, which ran aground near Alaska on March 24, 1989 (544). The oil spill that this caused resulted in the decision to replace all single-hulled oil tankers with double-hulled ones. As a result, many single-hulled vessels became redundant, forcing their owners to find cheap ways of disposing of them.

As stipulated by the Basel Convention of 1989,[2] each country is responsible for internalizing the disposal costs of its hazardous waste in its own territory. To circumvent this regulation and avoid the expense of having their ships dismantled in the Global North, shipowners often register their vessels in countries other than their own. More than half of the world's merchant fleet is registered under such "flags of convenience" provided by, among others, Panama, Honduras, Liberia, Malta, and the Marshall Islands, where low taxes and loopholes in the law allow shipowners to evade labor and environmental regulations (DeSombre 71). Once their service period ends, these ships are sold to cash buyers, who then resell them to the dismantling yards, usually under new names. Using cash buyers as intermediaries is one of the most common ways shipowners evade the responsibility for exporting toxic waste (NGO Shipbreaking Platform). The largest of these yards are located at Alang in India, Chittagong in Bangladesh, and Gadani in Pakistan. The gentle slopes of the shorelines in all three locations are ideal for running obsolete vessels to the beach at high tide and, once the water recedes, having them scrapped from bow to stern by tens of thousands of migrant workers using nothing more than blowtorches and their bare hands.

Since the *Exxon Valdez* oil spill, thousands of such vessels have been dismantled on these beaches. The redundancy of freighters in the wake of the financial crisis of 2008 and 2009, as well as the redundancy of cruise ships due to the COVID-19 pandemic, have added an extra boost to the shipbreaking industry in these countries. The cynical logic that sustains this cycle is that it creates a win-win scenario for the

---

2   http://www.basel.int/

shipping companies that want to make a profit by disposing of their ships that contain hazardous waste at a low cost. In addition, the shipbreaking yards in the Global South provide not only an unquenchable supply of high-quality steel to be melted down and reused but also a livelihood for at least one million people in India alone (Sawyer 547). The industry also supplies businesses along the coast that recycle and sell everything the ships contain. Such an interrelation of economic pressures inflicted on developing nations sustained by an imperial exercise of power disguised as mutually beneficial business relations is what Laura A. Pratt describes as "toxic waste colonialism," an inverse colonial dynamic predicated on the disposal of waste from the Global North in the peripheries of globalization.

Risking their lives every day for an equivalent of ninety euros per month, workers in this pervasive colonial dynamic are exposed to asbestos in combination with various hazardous materials. These include mercury, PCB (polychlorinated biphenyl), lead, arsenic, and oil residue, all of which take a heavy toll on human health and the environment. Most of these workers lack knowledge of the long-term consequences of their exposure to these materials, but even if they are aware of the risks, the work is often the best option they have to provide for their families. Latching onto the opportunities yielded by economic, legal, and political cracks and loopholes that often find their roots in earlier forms of colonial rule in the Global South, toxic waste colonialism operates by what Rob Nixon calls "slow violence:" a form of protracted and sustained damage inflicted through the "leaking" of such materials into human bodies and their environment.

Toward an Ethics of Intra-Action

Over the past two decades, the plight of workers in the shipbreaking yards of developing countries has been a subject of photography projects, most notably by Sebastião Salgado, Sean Smith, and Edward Burtynsky, as well as several documentaries such as *Shipbreakers* (2004) and *Toxic Tankers for Bangladesh* (2014). Work by such activist groups as the NGO Shipbreaking Platform, a coalition of environmental, human, and labor rights organizations, has been instrumental in raising awareness of the problem. While the ethical import of such efforts is crucial, the images circulating on the Internet tend to capture life in the yards in aestheticizing and exoticizing terms, inviting viewers to be shocked by the working conditions and simultaneously awestruck by the colossal size and skeletal forms of half-dismantled vessels. This draws on, as Mike Crang argues about Burtynsky's work, the aesthetic conventions of representing ruins and shipwrecks as sublime spectacles (24–26).

It is precisely the legacy of this western gaze to which Ann Stoler's notion of ruination provides an ethical alternative. Shifting the emphasis from "ruin" as a noun to "ruination" as a verb, she provides a conceptual tool to think of the ruins of colonial empires not as vestiges of a distant past but as "durabilities" that persist in the present under different disguises. "To think with ruins of empire as ruination is to emphasize less the artifacts of empire as dead matter or remnants of a defunct regime than to attend to their reappropriations, strategic neglect, and active positioning within the politics of the present" (350). Perceiving the global network of economic relations that vindicate the ways in which the shipbreaking industry is run in the Global South underlines the persistence of imperial formations and the exercise of slow violence under the disguise of business interests.

Reading Stoler through the lens of Barad's agential realism invites an ethical stance that asks us to contemplate ruination even if we are as far away from these locations as I am in the moment of writing. While corporations, shipowners, and governments should be held liable, Barad's understanding of agency as distributed among and emerging from the intra-action of different components of a phenomenon compels me to reconsider responsibility in this context. Thinking in the terms of quantum physics, Barad contends that "[q]uantum entanglements are not the intertwining of two (or more) states/entities/events, but the calling into question of the very nature of two-ness, and ultimately of one-ness as well. . . . Quantum entanglements require/inspire a new sense of a-count-ability, a new arithmetic, a new calculus of response-ability" (251). Where an approach predicated on the interaction of different actants attaches responsibility to one or another actant, in Barad's new calculus, responsibility "is an iterative (re)opening up to, an enabling of responsiveness" (265).

In this sense, even if we do not interact with asbestos (as a result of the safety measures and the bans on asbestos implemented in the Global North) and are not directly responsible for its disposal in the Global South, we nonetheless intra-act with asbestos as part of an assemblage that encompasses bodies, materials, and discourses in their entangled and differential becoming. One ramification of this understanding is that the ways in which we acquire the commodities that we use on a daily basis are entangled in economic and political networks sustained by ocean-going cargo vessels bound to be dismantled in the shipbreaking yards of the Global South. Rather than being "harbored" by its individual components, agency flows through these practices and constitutes the conditions of their possibility. Inasmuch as we are beneficiaries of these material flows as customers, consumers, or simply as bystanders, we are implicated (even if not complicit), to use Michael Rothberg's term. Confronting our implication in these processes, Rothberg insists, is an urgent political task and the condition of what he calls "long-distance solidarity" (10–12). If such solidarity is possible, we must acquire material literacy not only to know what materials things are made from but also to become response-able for their disposal and afterlife.

Acknowledgment

I want to thank Anneke Smelik and Liedeke Plate for their continued support of my work and growth as a scholar.

Works Cited

Barad, Karen. "Posthumanist Performativity: Toward an Understanding of How Matter Comes to Matter." *Signs*, vol. 28, no. 3, 2003, pp. 801–31.
———. "Quantum Entanglements and Hauntological Relations of Inheritance: Dis/continuities, SpaceTime Enfoldings, and Justice-to-Come." *Derrida Today*, vol. 3, no. 2, 2010, pp. 240–68.
Brown, Bill. "Thing Theory." *Critical Inquiry*, vol. 28, no. 1, 2001, pp. 1–22.
Crang, Mike. "The Death of Great Ships: Photography, Politics, and Waste in the Global Imaginary." *Environment and Planning*, vol. 42, no. 5, pp. 1084–1102.
DeSombre, Elizabeth, R. *Flagging Standards: Globalization and Environmental, Safety, and Labor Regulations at Sea*. MIT Press, 2006.
Gilroy, Paul. *The Black Atlantic: Modernity and Double Consciousness*. Harvard UP, 1993.
Hedley-Whyte, John and Debra R. Milamed. "Asbestos and Ship Building: Fatal Consequences." *Medical History*, vol. 77, no. 3, 2008, pp. 191–200.
Ingold, Tim. "Bringing Things to Life: Creative Entanglements in a World of Materials." *Realities / Morgan Centre, U. of Manchester*, 2010. NCRM working paper. https://eprints.ncrm.ac.uk/id/eprint/1306.
Karim, Saiful. *Shipbreaking in Developing Countries: A Requiem for Environmental Justice from the Perspective of Bangladesh*. Routledge, 2018.
Khalili, Laleh. *Sinews of War and Trade: Shipping and Capitalism in the Arabian Peninsula*. Verso, 2020.
Mannik, Lynda, editor. *Migration by Boat: Discourses of Trauma, Exclusion and Survival*. Berghahn, 2016.
Martin, Craig. *Shipping Container*. Bloomsbury, 2016.
Munz, Aaron. "Shipyard Workers and Asbestos." *Asbestos.com*, 20 Dec. 2022, https://www.asbestos.com/occupations/shipyard-workers/.
Nixon, Rob. *Slow Violence and the Environmentalism of the Poor*. Harvard UP, 2011.
NGO Shipbreaking Platform. "Cash Buyers." https://shipbreakingplatform.org/our-work/the-problem/cash-buyers/. Accessed 22 Jan. 2023.
Pratt, Laura A. "Decreasing Dirty Dumping? A Reevaluation of Toxic Waste Colonialism and the Global Management of Transboundary Hazardous Waste." *William and Mary Environmental Law and Policy Review*, vol. 35, no. 2, 2011, pp. 580–623.
Rose, Arthur. *Asbestos: The Last Modernist Object*. Edinburgh UP, 2022.

Rothberg, Michael. *The Implicated Subject: Beyond Victims and Perpetrators*. Stanford UP, 2019.
Sawyer, John F. "Shipbreaking and the North-South Debate: Economic Development or Environmental and Labor Catastrophe." *Penn State International Law Review*, vol. 20, no. 3, 2002, pp. 535–62.
Stoler, Ann Laura. *Duress: Imperial Durabilities in Our Times*. Duke UP, 2016.
Strand, Tara. "Mesothelioma and Asbestos Risk for Shipyard Workers." *Mesothelioma.com*, https://www.mesothelioma.com/asbestos-exposure/occupations/shipyard-workers/. Accessed 22 Jan. 2023.

6. Copper's Suppressed History Unearthed in Otobong Nkanga's Sensual and Embodied Art Practice

Mette Gieskes

"Copper . . . has been at our side since civilization began and has helped us thrive at every step of human history. It was used in almost everything . . .," Clarkdale's Arizona Copper Art Museum boldly asserts in its mission statement (Arizona Copper Art Museum). While the museum exudes pride about its dedication to artistic and artisanal applications of a metal that has been valued, financially and aesthetically, as one of the key material contributors to the realization of humanity's most impressive achievements, recently, more critical voices regarding the ways copper has been adapted to human ends have emerged within and beyond museum walls. Parallel to the flourishing in the humanities of new materialism, posthumanism, and decolonial studies, a number of artists has employed copper in ways that have highlighted the more disturbing—suppressed—side of people's engagements with the metal, some proposing alternative ways of coexistence with natural materials in the process. Chinese-American artist Mel Chin has, for instance, foregrounded the toxicity of metals like copper in gardens with accumulative plants that draw heavy metals like copper from contaminated soil. The metals are extracted from the plants and sold, bringing in money that Chin subsequently uses to cover the expense of regenerating toxic landfills. In his photos of metallic orbs in abandoned excavation sites of former South African mines, photographer Dillon Marsh reveals copper extraction's adverse environmental and humanitarian effects. Anishinaabe sculptor Michael Belmore employs materials like copper to examine the damaging effects on the landscape of human activity for capital gain. Last on this list is Belgium-based Nigerian artist Otobong Nkanga, whose work will be the focal point of this chapter. Nkanga has unpacked the ecological damage and human suffering caused by the extraction of materials like copper for the sustenance of our excessive lifestyle. The following pages investigate how several of Nkanga's installation, sculptural, and performance works bring to light the uneven distribution of resources like copper in the circulation of raw materials in the globalized world. Examining how Nkanga's works critically explore the mutilated landscape of a former Nigerian copper mine, the chapter also demonstrates that Nkanga's works poetically, or "poethically," in Denise Ferreira da Silva's words (245), articulate copper's sensory and aesthetic qualities, in some performances even following minerals' own forces and flows with her bodily movements, entangling human and nonhuman agents in reciprocal ways that strongly resonate with Timothy Ingold's notions of "improvisation" and "emerging meshwork" (435; 437).

A metallic material with a cubic crystalline structure, copper (Cu) owes its reddish-brown color to its reflection of red and orange light. When situated in moist air, it however acquires a protective greenish surface film called patina. Copper is a malleable, relatively soft, yet durable and ductile material, which is easily worked, can be polished to a shiny finish, and is an excellent conductor of heat and electricity. As the affordances of copper are many (Gibson), it has been applied in industry, agriculture, transportation, architecture, at home, and in museums. Most copper is used for electrical equipment, wiring, roofing, plumbing, industrial machinery, medical equipment, and energy conduction. It has also been utilized for weapons, cookware, tools, architectural moldings, roofs, paint pigments, engravings, and statues, in some cases combined with other metals into alloys like bronze and brass (Adamson et al.).

Though many people are aware of the fact that our daily lives, as well as our cultural and artistic practices, depend on materials like copper, which form society's foundation in the Marxian materialist sense, this interdependence has recently become the topic of scrutiny in publications and artworks that inquire into ways in which human and nonhuman actants have "emerged together" (Biemann 43). Increasingly, critical investigations have challenged the tendency of people in capitalist, (post-)industrial, and (post-)colonial societies to exploit "raw materials" and the landscapes from which they are extracted, practices that are based on an implicit view of the primacy of people amongst all beings, both organic and inorganic. Such anthropocentric views have led primarily Europeans and North Americans to a sense of entitlement involving claims of ownership and control over nature, part and parcel of a perspective that considers domination, colonization, and subjugation of people in other parts of the world legitimate as well. Similar to, but not building on, new materialists like Jane Bennett and Rosi Braidotti, contemporary artists such as Nkanga explore such unbalances through material and visual means, using materials like copper to imagine and embody other, more entangled, sustainable, and "response-able" ways of connecting human and non-human agents (Haraway 2). They tend to advance imaginative forms of cohabitation that do not exhaust ecosystems and people but are instead built on an awareness of the "reciprocal fragility" of Earth and human bodies (Wood 77).

Fig. 1: Otobong Nkanga, In Pursuit of Bling, 2014. Installation exhibition To Dig a Hole that Collapses Again, MCA Chicago, 2018. Photograph: Nathan Keay, MCA Chicago.

In 2014, Otobong Nkanga (born in Kano, 1974) gave copper and the mineral mica center stage in *In Pursuit of Bling*, an installation first exhibited at the Eight Berlin Biennale for Contemporary Art and recently acquired jointly by the Stedelijk Museum Amsterdam and Museum Arnhem (fig. 1). The work consists of two tapestries hung back-to-back, surrounded by thirty metal tables that are assembled according to the structure of a mineral atom. Some tables hold specimens of copper, malachite (a copper carbonate), and mica, the silicate mineral that grants shine to makeup, the cosmetic product providing luster to human bodies while contributing to the destruction of what Nkanga tends to conceive of as the body of our planet (Campbell-Betancourt 58). Some tables present archival photos or built-in monitors, showing images of mineral extraction and various uses of copper and mica (Ginwala 93). One tapestry represents a faceted mica stone and locations where the mineral can be found, while the other, *Transformation*, pictures humans' self-serving involvement in the extraction of copper ore. *Transformation* shows two schematic, truncated figures who seem to be standing on mineral-rich mountains and whose upper bodies have been replaced by structures containing molecular bonds and platforms that resemble the surfaces of both landscapes and mineral stones.

86   Part III: Extractivism and Toxic Colonialism

Fig. 2: Otobong Nkanga, Reflections of the Raw Green Crown, 2014 [video still]. Single channel HD video projection, color, sound, 2:52 min.

One of the videos shown in the current installment of *In Pursuit of Bring*, entitled *Reflections of the Raw Green Crown* (fig. 2), features the artist conversing with the copper spires of the late nineteenth-century Gethsemanekirche and the WWII-ruined Kaiser Wilhelm Memorial Church (Kaiser-Wilhelm-Gedächtniskirche), both situated in Berlin, her conical, malachite headdress similar in shape to the edifices' copper spire roofs (Kholeif 74). In the video, the artist's copper crown empathizes with the copper of the churches' spires, addressing it as follows: "you have traveled a long way through land and sea to be here to crown the tops of your captors' roofs. ... Who would have guessed the process you have been through. Uprooted, melted, polished, reshaped, and integrated to crown the finest in town." The voiceover also surmises that its deracinated and labored, silent material conversational partner "might remember Tsumeb," "the land of malachite," "[n]ow empty for all is gone," referring to the place of origin of the church's copper (Nkanga, *Reflections of the Raw Green Crown*).

The Namibian mining town Tsumeb was founded by the German colonial empire in 1905 to facilitate the extraction and subsequent transportation of resources like copper ore that prospectors found in high concentrations in a nearby mineral-rich deposit in 1875. Due to the oxidized copper's visual effect on the landscape's surface, this deposit was dubbed Green Hill. Before the German colonialists started blast-mining with dynamite, exploiting the land and the local population, the local San people had carved out small pieces of copper ore in less intrusive ways and engaged in small-scale trade with the Ovambo people. When Nkanga visited the former mine, which had been closed in 1996, she encountered an open pit rather than a hill, in addition to abandoned mining buildings, a patch of ore smelting refuse (Nkanga, *Remains of the Green Hill*), and the now disused railway that had been constructed to transport ore from Green Hill to the harbor in Swakopmund. The natural resource copper had been melted, transported, and given a destination in shining European monuments, displaced from and with no visible connection to its now depleted and contaminated place of origin (Kholeif 76).

Nkanga conceives of the raw copper stones and the photos of Green Hill on the tables of *In Pursuit of Bling*, as well as of the copper steeples of the Gethsemanekirche and the Kaiser Wilhelm Memorial Church in the video, as silent material witnesses that remember the past in the present (Nkanga, *Reflections of the Raw Green Crown*). The materials—once situated in Northern Namibian land, now topping European monuments and on view in European museum spaces—bear traces of colonialism, capitalism, and (post)industrialism, embodying memories of unfair labor, displacement, and ecological destruction. The minerals have come to index avarice and human and environmental injustice through their subjection to invasive extraction modes, circulation in the globalized world, and eventual use in grand, opulent monuments and multiple other applications. Though the copper on the spire of the damaged Gedächtniskirche was not part of the late nineteenth-century church design but applied between 1957 and 1962 as part of the efforts to preserve the church's remains as a ruin commemorating the allied bombings, chances are high that the copper that was added later also originates from Namibia: Germany has continued to import large amounts of copper from the country, up until today.[1]

In Pursuit of Bling confronts European museum visitors—consumers of the end products of raw materials and frequent passersby of copper-roofed buildings that speak of a heroic past—with the reality of the remote, voided mines. This confrontation is cogently established through a direct, palpable encounter with the mineral that is one of the essential material sources of out-of-balance relations between (formerly) colonized and colonizer, poor and affluent, and nonhuman entities and controlling humans. The work shows that in a globalized world, places that are far apart, like Tsumeb on the one hand and European cities such as Berlin, Amsterdam, and Arnhem on the other, are inextricably connected, disallowing an exoticizing, imperial gaze that locates the problems elsewhere.[2] One way in which this connectedness is enacted is through the inclusion of stones that have been in both places. In Nkanga's work, the material has obtained the power to speak, even literally in the videos. It invites viewers to consider how to coexist on Earth, now and in the future. *In Pursuit of Bling* forces us to consider the gaping wound left elsewhere, a void bestowing us with abundance: the presence of copper in western Europe is a direct result of the absence of the ore in the now cavernous Tsumeb landscape, implicating our excessive lives.

Another work of Nkanga's, *Solid Maneuvres* (2015) (fig. 3), is intended as an antimonument to the damaged landscape and negative space at Green Hill, an inverse variation on the artist's characterization of monumental buildings as pedestals of the copper that tops them. *Solid Maneuvres* is a series of sculptures composed of stratified layers of pressed, metal sheets resembling topographical maps on metal poles, two mountainous, one containing a depression. The surface of the sculptures and the floor below are sprinkled with crushed traces of materials with subterranean origins, like salts, mica-containing makeup powder, and copper particles—residues of an injured hill that are now imaginatively restituted to the land. In a 2015 performance by the same title, Nkanga activated the sculptures by enacting a kind of ritual in their midst, rubbing the pulverized elements between her fingers and scattering the dust onto various parts of her body, touching the material in an intimate,

---

1 I am thankful to Nkanga's studio manager Wim van Dongen for referring me to two sites providing recent data on international trade, including copper imports and exports: https://tradingeconomics.com/germany/imports/namibia/copper and https://oec.world/en/profile/bilateral-country/deu/partner/nam.

2 Jessica Horton and Janet Catherine Berlo similarly observe that the (indigenous) artists whose material-oriented work their article analyzes "locate their practices in an extensive and shared contemporary landscape that includes the space of exhibition, thus short-circuiting a romantic gaze that might locate indigenous art or bodies in nature somewhere else" (20).

sensual fashion. Through this performance, Nkanga ceremonially re-enacted the engagement with, or maneuvering of, materials and land of laboring bodies. Yet where the miners at Green Hill had operated under inhumane, alienating, and ecologically unsound conditions, incited to manipulate and exploit rather than responsively interact with the extracted ores, her own contact with the material was respectful and affective, receptive to what the artist calls the materials' own "performativity" (Nkanga, "Solid Maneuvers"). The suggestion is that in a postcolonial and post-anthropocentric world, our engagement with matter could be more in line with ritualized interactions with ancestral soil and lands of indigenous cultures.

Fig. 3: Otobong Nkanga, Solid Maneuvers, 2015/20 [video still]. Performance at exhibition There's No Such Thing as Solid Ground, Gropius Bau, Berlin, 2020. Performed by Nkanga, July 1, 2020, 40 min.

In the performance *Solid Maneuvres*, Nkanga's interaction with copper surpasses the discursive, though it makes viewers critically aware of the dialectical relationship between our daily, material lives and the socio-economic structures that support them. Nkanga's relation to the material in the performance is emphatically tactile. The artist has disclosed that, before she starts working with a material, she tends first to feel it with her body, sometimes even singing to it: "My heart has to palpitate, my skin has to have goose pimples/ I have to struggle with it, fight with it" (Arundhati Thomas). When visiting Green Hill earlier in 2015, she had also sung to the land, apologizing for all that had happened since the arrival of "foreign invaders" (Arundhati Thomas) in a spontaneous, sensuous, and healing performance of which footage can be found in the video *Remains of the Green Hill* (fig. 4). During this performance, Nkanga stood barefoot on a rock overlooking the Green Hill crater, practicing a kind of yoga while balancing stones from the mine pit on her head. Such caring and sensory encounters between body, landscape, and minerals exude respect for natural materials. Nkanga's intimate communion with minerals is an implicit counterforce to the violent and imposing ways of political and economic systems that have perpetuated social, global, and environmental injustice. In her performances, Nkanga does not act as an agent unilaterally, forcing a final form on inert matter, but in her "gestural dance with a modulation of the material" follows the minerals' own agential and sensory properties and flows, enacting an Ingoldian embodied ecology of materials (434).

Fig. 4: Otobong Nkanga, Remains of the Green Hill, 2015 [video still] – Performance Tsumeb, Namibia. Single channel HD video projection, color, stereo sound, 5:48 min.

Through her discursively critical yet also affective and sensuous interactions with—rather than actions upon—copper, Nkanga imagines alternatives to the ways of the Anthropocene, which, as Heather Davis and Etienne Turpin have argued, might be characterized as a primarily "sensorial phenomenon: the experience of living in an increasingly diminished and toxic world" (3). As such, she willingly takes on the burden that, according to Amitav Ghosh, all storytellers, including artists, should embrace: recovering in imaginary ways the agency and voice of non-humans (204).

Works Cited

Adamson, Glenn, et al., *Copper*, special issue of *Material Intelligence*, no. 4, 2002, www.materialintelligencemag.org/copper-4/.
Arizona Copper Art Museum. "Our Mission and History." *Copperartmuseum.com*, www.copperartmuseum.com/our-mission-and-history.
Arundhati Thomas, Skye. "Otobong Nkanga Excavates Material Histories." *Frieze*, no. 215, November 2020, https://www.frieze.com/article/otobong-nkanga-excavates-material-histories.
Bennett, Jane. "The Force of Things: Steps Toward an Ecology of Matter." *Political Theory*, vol. 32, no. 3, June 2004, pp. 347–72.
Biemann, Ursula. "On the Metachemistry of Oil and Water." *World of Matter*, edited by Inke Arns, Sternberg Press, 2015, pp. 30–43.
Campbell Betancourt, Diana. "Bodies, Breath, and Bling in Concert with the World." *Otobong Nkanga: Uncertain Where the Next Wind Blows*, edited by Tone Hansen and Karen Monica Reini, Henie Onstad Kunstsenter and Verlag der Buchhandlung Walther und Franz König, 2021, pp. 48–59.
Davis, Heather, and Etienne Turpin, editors. *Art in the Anthropocene: Encounters Among Aesthetics, Politics, Environments and Epistemologies*. Open Humanities Press, 2015.
Dongen, Wim van. Email to Mette Gieskes. 17 January 2023.
Ferreira da Silva, Denise. "Blacklight." *Otobong Nkanga: Lustre and Lucre*, edited by Clare Molloy et al., Portikus and Sternberg Press, in collaboration with Kadist and M HKA, 2015, pp. 245–53.
Ghosh, Amitav. *The Nutmeg's Curse: Parables for a Planet in Crisis*. The U of Chicago P, 2021.
Gibson, James Jerome. "The Theory of Affordances." *Perceiving, Acting and Knowing: Towards an Ecological Psychology*, edited by Robert Shaw and John Bransford, John Lawrence Erlbaum Associates, 1977, pp. 67–82.
Ginwala, Natasha. "The Refusal of Shine." *Otobong Nkanga: Lustre and Lucre*, edited by Clare Molloy et al., Portikus and Sternberg Press, in collaboration with Kadist and MHKA, 2015, pp. 89–95.
Haraway, Donna. *Staying with the Trouble: Making Kin in the Chthulucene*. Duke UP, 2016.

Horton, Jessica L., and Janet Catherine Berlo. "Beyond the Mirror: Indigenous Ecologies and 'New Materialisms' in Contemporary Art." *Third Text*, vol 27, no. 1, 2013, pp. 17–28.

Ingold, Tim. "Toward an Ecology of Materials." *Annual Review of Anthropology*, vol. 41, October 2012, pp. 427–42.

Kholeif, Omar. "To Dig a Hole." *To Dig a Hole That Collapses Again*. Museum of Contemporary Art Chicago and DelMonico Books•Prestel, 2018, pp. 74–84.

Nkanga, Otobong. Video *Reflections of the Raw Green Crown*, 2014. otobong-nkanga.com, www.otobong-nkanga.com/videos.

———. Video *Remains of the Green Hill*, 2015. otobong-nkanga.com, www.otobong-nkanga.com/videos.

———. Performance *Solid Maneuvers*, 2015. otobong-nkanga.com, www.otobong-nkanga.com/performances?lightbox=dataItem-kd4tohvp.

———. "Solid Maneuvers." Video. *Vimeo.com*, vimeo.com/436836601.

Wood, Catherine. "The Lady Who Swallowed a Rock." *Otobong Nkanga: Uncertain Where the Next Wind Blows*, edited by Tone Hansen and Karen Monica Reini, Henie Onstad Kunstsenter and Verlag der Buchhandlung Walther und Franz König, 2021, pp. 74–81.

7. The Coloniality of Materiality: Brazilwood, or Unlearning with Anton de Kom in the Mauritshuis

Oscar Ekkelboom

Anton de Kom wrote *We Slaves of Suriname* (1934) when he was banished to the Netherlands for being one of the foremost advocates of Surinamese independence from Dutch colonial rule. Although exiled from his motherland, he nevertheless tells his story from Sranan—the soil to which "the slave ships carried their African prizes, their living merchandise, our parents and grandparents" (De Kom, *We Slaves* 48). Prior to their arrival to Mother Sranan, before the era of slavery, De Kom explains that this land slumbered and "nothing changed in the dense forests of her unknown interior" (45). Indeed, it is only since coloniality that these forests and the enslaved people are subjugated, mutilated, and exploited for the enjoyment of modernity. As De Kom clearly articulates, the pleasures of modern culture are implicated in the suffering of others and the destruction of the Earth:

> You, white reader, may have learned in school that the Mauritshuis in The Hague is paneled with the most precious brazilwood. As you pause to admire this paneling, we ask you to consider that it was our mothers, who with this heavy burden on their head day after day (because Sunday was one institution that the Christian civilizers neglected to introduce in Suriname), trudged over hilly terrains, through pools and swamps, constantly threatened by the whip your ancestors wielded. (De Kom, *Wij slaven* 36; my trans.)

By exposing what I term the coloniality of materiality, De Kom awakens a white museum audience, immersed in the beauty of European aesthetics and craftsmanship, to the brutality of slavery and the contemporary experience of coloniality.

As a material, the brazilwood of the Mauritshuis' paneling appears to be key to De Kom's experience of the museum. These wooden decorations alone offer a case study for a decolonial analysis of the colonial wound the author addresses. However, during a fire in 1704, long before *We Slaves of Suriname* was written, the interior of the Mauritshuis, including the carpentry to which De Kom refers, was wholly destroyed. Yet, this historical fact by no means serves to discredit De Kom. To the contrary, his reflections on the historic and contemporary experiences of coloniality—that is, of slavery and the suffering of the Earth—open up a critical view on the methodologies that focus on the materials of culture. Thinking with De Kom, this chapter diverts from the dominant art historical reading of the museum centered on European canons and aesthetics. Instead, by inquiring into the coloniality of materiality, I aim to reconstitute that which the European trajectory of thought hides and erases so that epistemologies that understand the Earth and the museum differently can re-emerge.

Drawing on the notion of decoloniality and the insights it offers into the coloniality of power, being, and gender, as introduced by Aníbal Quijano and further elaborated, among many others, by Walter Mignolo, María Lugones, and Rolando Vázquez, this chapter introduces the coloniality of materiality. This notion brings European epistemology, which views the world through materials, in relation to the colonial matrix of power. Specifically, this chapter explores how Europe's modern civilizational project colonizes the Earth by materializing it both conceptually and through its actual destruction. I will argue that within the colonial matrix of power, these movements work in reciprocity. By bringing the coloniality of materiality into the same scope as the coloniality of power or being, I explore how modern thinking about materials, materiality, and material culture, as surveyed by Tim Ingold in his article "Toward an Ecology of Materials," renders invisible the destruction of the Earth and Earth-beings inherent in the production of materials. This chapter, therefore, first seeks to address the colonial difference that separates modernity's enjoyment of materials from coloniality's suffering. Second, it explores how modernity's conceptualization of materials is itself a negation of the destruction of the Earth.

Delinking from the Coloniality of Materiality

Decolonial thinking and doing, as practiced by the thinkers introduced above, urges us to ask different questions than those presented by postcolonialism or new materialism (Mignolo and Walsh; Vázquez). According to Vázquez, within new materialism, as in other scholarly accounts of materials, "critique becomes reduced to a form of presentism" because it confines itself to the affirmation that "reality is co-extensive with radical immanence" (128). This means that its critical thought is only concerned with that which occurs in material reality. In contrast, decoloniality is engaged with what is lost and erased through exploitation, denigration, or appropriation. Consequently, the forms of criticism that exclusively engage with materials are insufficient from the perspective of decoloniality. As Vázquez suggests, "decoloniality calls for a turn in our disposition towards the real, from enunciation to listening, from extraction to cultivation, from appropriation to reception ... from what has been dismembered to re-membering" (119). In other words, decoloniality seeks to reconstitute that which is not immanent or historically present (anymore). It is from this starting point that I provide a conceptual platform from which to consider the experience of a material that is lost—an impossible experience in the modern rational mind.

Within the colonial matrix of power, the coloniality of materiality concerns the negation and erasure of non-material realities. Underpinning this rejection, I argue, is an understanding of the Earth as a composition of materials. Ingold shows how deeply thinking of materials is rooted in modern epistemology. His own work builds on this tradition, as he considers the Earth as a convergence of materials in flow and transformation (Ingold 437). In doing so, however, he is inattentive to the possibilities of understanding the world in any other way than through matter. Moreover, Ingold and the discourse upon which he elaborates advance their understanding of the world—as a gathering of materials—as a universal truth rather than a worldview specifically located in European rationality. For example, Ingold universalizes his understanding of the Earth by considering materials not only in time, but as "the stuff of time itself" (439). As such, the coloniality of materiality negates and erases the possibilities of worlding that do not disintegrate the Earth into a gathering of materials, as does the worldview reflected by Anton de Kom when he writes about Mother Sranan. Of course, other civilizations have considered the world through materials. However, none of them impinged, appropriated, and capitalized on the globe and its inhabitants as much as Europe did. When speaking of experiences and knowledges outside the limits of western thought, decoloniality does not transcend rationality in some divine, mystical, or fetishistic manner but instead thinks beyond the frameworks of western immanence. In this particular case, speaking from a western institution, we may not be able to rationally grasp the implications of the material in the way De Kom experiences it. This, however, is only because we know that the original paneling has been lost. Therefore, to follow De Kom, modern knowledge and patterns of experience must be unlearned in order to learn to experience materiality in its material absence.

In contrast to previous accounts of materials, the coloniality of materiality considers materials as a disintegration of the Earth and Earth-beings. In doing so, it reveals that the modern conceptualization of the Earth as a gathering of materials is a precondition that enabled Europe to appropriate the Earth and Earth-beings as resources with the potential for extraction. A mountain, for example, only becomes a resource when certain minerals are discovered that can be extracted from it and are capitalized. Similarly, the body was disintegrated into a set of materials when anatomists dissected it into organs and fluids. Subsequently, that same body was turned into a resource when scientists made it possible to transplant those organs and fluids from one body to another. Yet, at what expense does modernity materialize the Earth and Earth-beings? In either case, the "source" is irreparably damaged. Therefore, I would argue, in every material lies the inherent destruction of the Earth.

Vázquez's decolonial path helps us to recognize the mechanisms and processes of the colonial matrix of power that produced European knowledge and experience as universal. Vázquez's work is, among other things, concerned with the formation of modernity and aims to understand this dominant framework of experience by inquiring into the regulation of the senses (17–18). Following Vázquez, this chapter asks how the Mauritshuis shapes the visitor's experience through the wooden paneling in the twentieth and twenty-first centuries. In a wall text about the museum building, the curators describe the situation before the fire: "The Mauritshuis had an impressive interior with paneling made of tropical wood, murals depicting Brazilian landscapes and large quantities of objects that Johan Maurits had brought back with him from Brazil" (Mauritshuis, room 1). Visitors are encouraged to imagine how impressed they would have been if they had stepped into the original interior of the building. This is not so different from the experience of pupils taught in schools, as described by De Kom. The adjective "impressive" forces visitors to imagine the spectacle of the wooden paneling—an aesthetic appreciation that provides them with an overwhelming experience. However, whether this appreciation concerns the materiality of the paneling or its craftsmanship remains uncertain.

A European Story of Brazilwood

Early European settlers in Abya Yala—broadly understood as the Americas—sought eagerly to extract its natural materials. The search for gold is well known through the numerous unsuccessful expeditions to the mythical city or kingdom of El Dorado and from European cultural works describing the quest. Lesser known is the European interest in brazilwood, a generic term for various kinds of hardwood. Throughout the sixteenth century, wood was the main product that Europe imported from Abya Yala. This can be observed in archives when looking at inventories of shiploads brought into the ports of Europe. The Portuguese first used the wood for dying fabrics, and later the material became popular for carpentry. However, the material's significance for Europe becomes even more apparent in European visual culture. Brazilwood acquired a particularly prominent place in the art of the seventeenth-century Dutch Republic.

A few years after architect Jacob van Campen completed the Mauritshuis in 1644, he took charge of the construction of Amsterdam's city hall—presently the Royal Palace of Amsterdam. The front and rear elevations of the building are equipped with marble tympanums designed by Artus Quellinus. Depicted on the rear tympanum, entitled *The Four Continents Paying Homage to Amsterdam*, we can see the personification of Amsterdam accompanied by personifications of the city's rivers Amstel and 't IJ accepting gifts offered by Asia, Europe, Africa, and America. "America" is represented by two men recognizable by their feather headdresses. One is offering a pot of undistinguishable goods; the other is sitting against a tree, offering mats and two tree trunks while smoking a pipe.

Among all these goods, the tree trunk, as a gift from "America," appears to be a recurring motif in Dutch seventeenth-century illustrations. *De nieuwe en onbekende weereld, of beschryving van America en 't zuid-land (The New and Unknown World; or, Descriptions of America and the South-Land*, 1671) by Arnoldus Montanus, for example, opens with an engraving by Jacob van Meurs that depicts a gift including a tree trunk by the personification of "America" and her entourage to the Europeans upon their arrival in Abya Yala. The same gift of a tree trunk can be seen in *The Map of Amsterdam with Cityscape* (circa 1682–88) by Johannes Kip and *The Map of Amsterdam* (circa 1674–82), possibly by (or after) Romeyn de Hooghe. Yet another example of the same motif painted by an anonymous artist is the *Allegory of the "Treaty of Friendship and Commerce between the States General of the United Netherlands and the United States of America"* (1782–85). These examples demonstrate that wood was not just another natural material that was taken from Abya Yala to Europe. Through these images, brazilwood acquired a symbolic meaning. To the Europeans, this humbly offered wood symbolized "America's" rich natural materials and the possibility of its extraction for their profit. In other words, the wood represented Abya Yala as a natural resource.

Through this modern reading of brazilwood, we encounter a modern/colonial difference. For, when talking about materials, I mean substances that are produced—and not extracted, because that implies the material foundation of the Earth—from that which De Kom calls Mother Sranan. Materials—including so-called natural or raw materials—such as stone, wood, metal, or leather, only become so through the disintegration and destruction of the Earth and Earth-beings. They only become material, real, or immanent through the artifice of materialization and production. I argue that materials, whether conceptual or produced, are, in fact, always an artifice. Therefore, from now on, this chapter leaves the modern conception of wood as a material and instead understands it as an artifice produced by destroying a tree or a forest. Consequently, the wooden paneling of the Mauritshuis must be understood in relation to the destruction of Mother Sranan.

This understanding of materials as artifice brings us to coloniality and, specifically, to what Vázquez terms "double erasure" (41). While modernity identifies itself as the entire horizon for intelligibility, it negates the historical process of erasing other worlds inherent in its constitution. For the coloniality of materiality, this means concretely destroying the Earth by producing materials. This ruination is negated by the pretension that these substances are extracted as naturally preexisting. In other words, modernity's understanding of the Earth as a gathering of materials erases the destruction of the Earth through the pretension of their natural appearance or immanence without human interference. Subsequently, when attempting to delink oneself from the coloniality of materiality—the effort of undoing the double negation of the destruction of the Earth—we should start with acknowledging the artifice of understanding the world as a convergence of materials.

The Colonial Difference

Returning to Anton de Kom's experience of the wooden paneling in the Mauritshuis, he draws our attention to another movement in Vázquez's decolonial path: the colonial difference, which marks the separation of the lives experienced through modernity and the lives lived under the conditions of coloniality (Vázquez 17–18). The difference looks at the disjunction between the pleasures and affirmation of modernity on the one hand and the suffering and erasure of others on the other. In no uncertain terms, De Kom links the paneling of the Mauritshuis directly to slavery. As such, he reveals a relationship between black suffering and white enjoyment and how this colonial difference persists to this day. What does this mean with regard to the coloniality of materiality? It highlights that we should not consider the Mauritshuis as a gathering of materials. Instead, the building must be read as an implicated entity entangled in coloniality, the history of slavery, and the destruction of the Earth.

How can this brief decolonial exercise of thinking with Anton de Kom help us delink ourselves from the coloniality of materiality? De Kom prompts his readers to oppose the double erasure of modernity, first by considering the material of the Mauritshuis' interior and not the artifice of aesthetics and craftsmanship. Second, he reminds us that it was the enslaved women who bore "this heavy burden on their head day after day." These women were forced to destroy their Mother Sranan to produce so-called materials, after which Europe could accept without qualm the wood as a grateful gift. This problematizes the Eurocentric idea of the Earth as an accumulation of materials, showing it to downplay the materials' inherent destruction of the Earth and Earth-beings, and thus obfuscates the possibilities to view the world through any means other than the material.

Depending on our positionality and the histories and legacies we bring to the museum, we can each experience the Mauritshuis differently. I arrived at this insight through De Kom's biography of the brazilwood of this building, which paradoxically makes the history of slavery and the destruction of the Earth tangible, even though the material is absent if considered from the perspective of modern epistemology. Although De Kom's statement about the paneling's material was at the time he wrote *We Slaves of Suriname* no longer true, we cannot claim that the conditions of slavery and his experience or imagination are false, nor can we argue that the history of slavery and the destruction of Mother Sranan is obliterated by the fire that destroyed the original wooden paneling. De Kom undoes the double erasure of the coloniality of materiality by reviving the brazilwood in a literary way. As a consequence, the lived experience of slavery can resurge into the museum in the present.

That is where decoloniality begins: with recognizing the possibilities of worlding the world differently.

Works Cited

Ingold, Tim. "Toward an Ecology of Materials." *Annual Review of Anthropology*, vol. 41, 2012, pp. 427–42.
Kom, Anton de. *We Slaves of Suriname*. Translated by David McKay, Polity Press, 2022.
———. *Wij slaven van Suriname*. Contact, 1934.
Mauritshuis. "The Building." Wall text, room 1, August 2022.
Mignolo, Walter, and Catherine E. Walsh. *On Decoloniality: Concepts, Analytics, Praxis*. Duke UP, 2018.
Montanus, Arnoldus, and Jacob van Meurs. *De nieuwe en onbekende weereld: of Beschryving van America en 't Zuid-land: vervaetende d'oorsprong der Americaenen en Zuidlanders, gedenkwaerdige togten derwaerds* [*The New and Unknown World; or, Descriptions of America and the South-Land*]. Jacob Meurs, 1671.
Vázquez, Rolando. *Vistas of Modernity: Decolonial Aesthesis and the End of the Contemporary*. Mondriaan Fund, 2020.

Part IV: Energyscapes of the Future

8. Lithium for the Metaverse: Myths of Nuclear and Digital Fusion

Niels Niessen

> *I'm so happy 'cause today I found my friends,*
> *they're in my head.* (Nirvana, "Lithium")

How does lithium feel? I don't think I have ever touched lithium, at least not in its elemental form, but increasingly this lightest metal is to be found all around us, for instance in smartphone batteries. A part of our everyday reality, lithium simultaneously remains the stuff of science fiction: lithium, especially lithium-6, is a key fuel for nuclear fusion, which brings the sun to earth. If nuclear fusion is ever harnessed as an energy source, human expansion will accelerate even more dramatically into extraterrestrial space and cyberspace. I therefore imagine lithium to feel *weightless* and *frictionless*, as in bodies defying gravity, whether in real life (IRL) or in the Metaverse, the virtual/augmented/mixed reality (VR/AR/MR) world recently popularized by Mark Zuckerberg and his avatar. But lithium is not manna from heaven. Like the black fossil golds that continue to propel a growth-addicted globe, this white gold (or white oil) will increasingly manifest itself as *the* post-fossil conflict mineral (along with cobalt, manganese, nickel, and graphite, which are also essential materials for today's batteries). Like fossil, lithium hurts, as the quest for it is driven by the same old burn-out logic that dominates the planet now.

Lithium is also an anti-depressant. As Kurt Cobain sings in the Nirvana song named after the drug on the 1991 album *Nevermind*, he is "not gonna crack" because today he found his friends in his head. Cobain's reference to imaginary friends is a fitting way to describe life in the Metaverse. In the Metaverse, the user tunes into a universal brain, logging out of their body and material reality. For transhumanists to reach Nirvana would mean *total fusion*: the mind uploaded into the cloud. This essay pierces this fusion myth.

Batteries

Lithium (Li, atomic number 3) is a soft, silvery-white alkali metal. Under regular conditions lithium is the least dense of all solid elements, and like all alkali metals, it is highly reactive and flammable. The name "lithium" derives from *lithos*, which is Greek for stone, as lithium was discovered from a mineral. In 1817, Swedish chemist Johan August Arfwedson detected the element while analysing petalite ore. Lithium does not occur freely in nature but only as part of usually ionic compounds (an ion being an atom or molecule with an electrical charge). The world's largest lithium reserves are in Chile, Iran, Australia, China, and Argentina. In Europe, the largest reserves are in Portugal. Lithium is mostly found in ocean water: five thousand times more than on land yet at extremely low concentrations, making the isolation of lithium from salt water a very complex operation.[1]

Lithium is used in rechargeable batteries for electronics such as smartphones, laptops, and cars. Currently, these are lithium-ion batteries, a type of rechargeable battery in which lithium ions move through an electrolyte (a medium that contains ions) from the negative to the positive electrode during use, and back when charging. Invented in the 1970s, lithium-ion technology was first used commercially in 1991 by Sony. In 2006, Tesla revealed prototypes of its Roadster model, a year later Apple launched the iPhone—two breakthrough products fuelled by lithium-ion.[2] For now, lithium-ion remains the industry standard, but in the coming decades this technology is expected to be replaced by solid-state batteries. Solid-state batteries still work with lithium ions moving through the battery. In contrast with lithium-ion batteries, however, the electrolyte is not a flammable liquid but a solid material. This makes them safer and also increases their energy density potential.[3]

In the transition from a fossil-based global economy to one fuelled by renewable energy sources, lithium will thus clearly continue to play a key role—or remain a key *actor*, as new materialism would have it. Already in 2014, Tesla and Panasonic agreed to cooperate on the construction of a battery manufacturing plant, and in 2020, Tesla secured the rights to a site in Nevada to produce lithium from clay deposits. Two years later, Tesla CEO Elon Musk tweeted that his company may indeed get into lithium mining directly: "Price of lithium has gone to insane levels! ... There is no shortage of the element itself, as lithium is almost everywhere on Earth, but pace of extraction/refinement is slow."[4]

---

1   See also: Royal Society of Chemistry.
2   See also Liu.
3   See also Phiddian.
4   See Clifford.

Lithium-6

I will return to the current reality of lithium mining, but I first want to speculate about lithium's future. Every once in a while, news about nuclear fusion pops up, as for example in early 2022 when researchers at the Joint European Torus (JET) experiment in Oxfordshire set a new record for the amount of energy produced in a sustained fusion reaction (Sample). JET is part of ITER, the International Thermonuclear Experimental Reactor megaproject headquartered in France that is co-funded by the European Union, China, India, Japan, Russia, South Korea, and the United States. *"Iter"* is Latin for *path* or *the way*, in this case to the neverland of "a potential source of safe, non-carbon emitting and virtually limitless energy," as we read on the ITER website.

In the case of terrestrial fusion experiments such as those conducted by ITER, fusion is fuelled by two forms of hydrogen: deuterium (^{2}H or D), which has one proton and one neutron, and tritium (^{3}H or T), which has one proton and two neutrons. In this deuterium-tritium (DT) fusion one deuterium nucleus fuses with one tritium nucleus, producing one helium nucleus (He, atomic number 2, named after the sun), one free neutron, and 17.6 megaelectron volt (MeV) of energy. Deuterium is a stable hydrogen isotope and is easily won from "heavy water" (D_2O), which makes up about 0.03% of all oceanic water. Tritium, however, is unstable (i.e., radioactive) and does not occur in nature. In 2022, there was less than twenty kilograms of tritium on earth, while the fission reactors that produce tritium—most of which are in Canada—are near the end of their lifetime. As *Wired* reports, before it even starts working "nuclear fusion is already facing a fuel crisis" (Katwala).

This is where lithium enters the picture, or more precisely lithium-6 (^{6}Li, so 3 protons and 3 neutrons), which is one of the two stable lithium isotopes on earth, the other being lithium-7. In fusion reactors, the walls are covered with a breeding blanket made of lithium-6 that, when bombarded with high-energy neutrons, produces tritium. The problem is that lithium-6—which is a controlled material also used in thermonuclear bombs (or H-bombs)—is not as abundant as fusion enthusiasts make it seem, because with current technology there is no industrial source of lithium-6. In natural lithium, the 6-isotope only has an abundance of 7.5 percent (the remainder being lithium-7), whereas for sustainable fusion 90 percent is needed. It is therefore still highly uncertain whether the production of tritium out of lithium-6 in a laboratory setting will work well enough in a reactor. As Steven Krivit writes, "If the test fails, the quest for fusion is over."

Meanwhile, fusion detracts a lot of resources from *truly* clean solutions while its quest perpetuates a dominant global culture obsessed with economic growth. Whether or not nuclear fusion is ever harnessed, its sustainable claim will remain science fiction. In much science fiction, by the way, fusion is often just a given, facilitating travel to the outer edges of the galaxy and the colonization of asteroids.

Here it has to be noted that the fusion drivers propelling most sci-fi imagination are fuelled by helium rather than tritium because terrestrial DT reactors are too heavy to outfit a rocket.

Magic

Let's stay in a speculative mode and extrapolate our technofeudal present, in which companies like SpaceX, Meta, and Amazon invade all spaces terrestrial and extraterrestrial. If fusion ever materializes, human expansion is expected to move further into outer space and "inward" in the direction of the Metaverse in order to further colonize people's attention. In science fiction, the Metaverse is an iteration of the Internet represented as a single universal and immersive virtual world. The name was introduced in the 1992 dystopian novel *Snowcrash* by Neal Stephenson, which describes a cyberspace in which "magic is possible." In 2021, the Metaverse became a household name when Mark Zuckerberg announced that Facebook was now Meta Platforms. "We'll be able to feel present," Zuckerberg rambles in his video presentation of the Metaverse, "like we're right there with people no matter how far apart we actually are."

Zuckerberg's optimism resonates with Big Tech's overall transhumanist belief in the fusion of human life and technology—the belief in technology as second nature. This belief is not new. In the case of the Metaverse—which is primarily an audiovisual medium—we are reminded of late-nineteenth century accounts of the cinematic experience as total immersion. As film philosopher André Bazin argued in his 1946 essay "Le mythe du cinéma total et les origines du cinématographe" ("The Myth of Total Cinema") the *idea* of cinema as an immersive medium preceded its technological realization. "There are numberless writings," Bazin contends, "all of them more or less wildly enthusiastic, in which inventors conjure up nothing less than a total cinema that is to provide that complete illusion of life which is still a long way away" (20). Cinema's magic thus paved the way for cinema as a technology, and can't we say the same about the Metaverse? Also, the Metaverse, before it is real, is preceded by the belief in a *magical* overcoming of the barriers inherent in human interaction. There is not one metaverse by the way, because besides Meta Platforms also companies like Microsoft and Epic (from the game *Fortnight*) are developing virtual worlds. The transhumanist dream is for these worlds to add up to one single Metaverse, overcoming the limitations of the human body that will remain immobile as in the cinema.

Resistance

To stay with cinema, Jonathan Beller argues that also in the digital era, the capitalist society of the spectacle remains characterized by a cinematic mode of production in which we "confront the logistics of the image" not only at the "scene of the screen" but wherever we turn (1). Increasingly, this mode of production depends on lithium, at the cost of people and the planet. An online search yields a number of documentaries and reportages that expose the socioecological reality of lithium mining. For instance, *Die Lithium Revolution* (2012, dir. Andreas Pichler and Julio Weiss, DE et al,) shows the tension between Bolivia's wish for autonomy in the exploitation of its lithium resources and German mining companies seeking to do business. Two other films, *En el nombre del litio* (2021, dir. Christián Cartier and Martín Longo, AR) and *Lithium: New Gold Rush in the Andes* (2021, Matthias Ebert, DE), take us to Salinas Grandes in Argentina, where indigenous communities resist lithium mining, as the amount of water needed for the process will contaminate their habitat. "We filed complaints and have held demonstrations to try to slow the expansion," a local activist says, "the government has already issued permits for several projects, but no one is giving us any specifics" (fig. 1). Meanwhile, in the Portuguese north, a village is threatened to be swallowed by the largest lithium mining site in the EU. "Are these electric cars so good for the environment?" asks Aida Fernandes in *The Dirty Truth behind Green Cars* (2020, DE/FR), "they will have to destroy all these mountains."

Fig. 1: Screenshot from Lithium: New Gold Rush in the Andes, 2021.

There is a certain irony in watching these lithium documentaries on a smartphone or laptop screen, because as Padraig Murphy et al. write in "New Materialism, Object-Oriented Ontology and Fictive Imaginaries" (2021), the devices attached to these screens "might have within its network the geopolitics of lithium deposits on Bolivian salt lakes" (5). In new materialist fashion, the authors draw attention to the *thingness* of media objects and practices through which imaginaries circulate, including documentaries about environmental degradation. While I do share this materialist perspective on our media-saturated culture, I am not so sure about the *new* materialist practice of calling non-living objects like smartphones *agents*, at least not when agency is attributed indiscriminately to human and non-human forms alike. In difference with new materialists' radical de-anthropocentrism, I think that a minimum of posthumanist humanism remains needed: a belief in people's ability to make meaning (the founding belief of cultural studies), in their ability to tell stories and weave social textures, and in their creation of *common* and communal spaces (as opposed to profit-driven and automized environments like the Metaverse). In other words, we need to somewhat hold on to the possibility of a collective human subject, while at the same time queering, decolonizing, and posthumanizing this subject. To say with new materialism that objects are actants (Bruno Latour) or that matter is vibrant (Jane Bennett) may be ontologically poetic, it also diverts attention from agency as resistance. I therefore prefer a *cultural* materialist understanding of agency as people's individual and above all collective consciousness of, and emancipation from, power, with power understood as the interplay between material structures (e.g., lithium mining, data colonialism) and ideological discourse (the myth of total fusion).

Nirvana, or the Metaverse as Lithium

To some this minimal posthumanist belief in agency may sound naïve in light of algorithmic control and climate catastrophe. It is as if saying that, after all, there *is* an alternative in response to Mark Fisher's *Capitalist Realism: Is There No Alternative?* Fisher argues how capitalism occupies the horizons of the thinkable, magically incorporating all critiques against it. He refers to Kurt Cobain. "Cobain knew," Fisher writes, "that he was just another piece of spectacle, that nothing runs better on MTV than a protest against MTV; knew that his every move was a cliché scripted in advance, knew that even realizing it is a cliché" (9).

And yet, I would argue that Nirvana's music and poetry *do* express a belief in the world, if only because Nirvana gives voice to the dissonance inherent in postmodernist life, or what Fisher calls capitalist realism. Take "Lithium," which depicts psychotic breakdown, both at the level of content (the manic "I'm so excited, I can't wait to meet you there and I don't care") and form (the narrator losing their mind;

the bipolar song structure alternating between the subdued verses and the explosive choruses) (see also Huber). The lithium of the title dulls these emotions while the song sets up a parallel between the drug and religion: "'cause I've found God." Lithium thus is the opium of the people in a bipolarizing world that isolates and exhausts people. Twenty years after *Nevermind*, Nirvana continues to resonate. As capitalism morphs into a technofeudal system dominated by Big Tech, people are increasingly invited to act as mindless addicts of immersive media streams all feeding into the Metaverse: a digital Nirvana luring in the cloud. Let us keep some belief in collective human agency and resist this myth of total fusion that destroys both people and the planet (fig. 2).

Fig. 2: *Nirvana at climate protest in Munich, 2022. Photograph by Pola Jane O'Mara and Niels Niessen.*

Works Cited

Arte Documentary. *Portugal: The Dirty Truth behind Green Cars*. 2020. https://www.youtube.com/watch?v=QvrCzN3_WNM

Bazin, André. *What Is Cinema? Vol. 1*. Translated by Hugh Gray, U of California P, 2005.

Beller, Jonathan. *The Cinematic Mode of Production: Attention Economy and the Society of the Spectacle*. UP of New England, 2006.

Clifford, Catherine. "Elon Musk Says Tesla May Have to Get into the Lithium Business Because Costs Are So Insane." *CNBC*, 8 April 2022, https://www.cnbc.com/2022/04/08/elon-musk-telsa-may-have-get-into-mining-refining-lithium-directly.html.

Die Lithium Revolution. Directed by Andreas Pichler and Julio Weiss, Gebrueder Beetz, 2012.

DW Documentary. *Lithium—New Gold Rush in the Andes*, *YouTube*, 2021, https://www.youtube.com/watch?v=LZjiEggYglM.

En el nombre del litio [In the Name of Lithium]. Directed by Christián Cartier and Martín Longo, Calma Cine and Farn, 2021.

Fisher, Mark. *Capitalist Realism: Is There No Alternative?* Zero Books, 2009.

Gebrüder Beetz Filmproduktion and Polarstarfilms. *Die Lithium-Revolution*, 2012.

Heptinstall, Simon. "The 25th Anniversary of the Lithium-Ion Battery." *Kyria*, 2016, http://www.kyria.co.uk/blog-the-25th-anniversary-of-the-lithium-ion-battery/.

Huber, Chris. "The Meaning of Nirvana's 'Lithium'." *Extra Chill*, 10 December 2021, https://extrachill.com/2021/12/nirvana-lithium-meaning.html.

Katwala, Amit. "Nuclear Fusion Is Already Facing a Fuel Crisis." *Wired*, 20 May 2022, https://www.wired.co.uk/article/nuclear-fusion-is-already-facing-a-fuel-crisis.

Krivit, Steven B. "Lithium, Lithium, Everywhere, and None to Use for Fusion Reactors." *New Energy Times*, 27 January 2022, https://news.newenergytimes.net/2022/01/08/lithium-lithium-everywhere-and-none-to-use-for-fusion-reactors/.

Liu, Zhao. "The History of the Lithium-Ion Battery." *ThermoFisher Scientific*, 10 November 2019, https://www.thermofisher.com/blog/materials/the-history-of-the-lithium-ion-battery/.

Meta, "The Metaverse and How We'll Build It Together—Connect 2021." *YouTube*, 2021, https://www.youtube.com/watch?v=Uvufun6xer8.

Murphy, Padraig, Pat Brereton, and Fiachra O'Brolchain. "New Materialism, Object-Oriented Ontology and Fictive Imaginaries: New Directions in Energy Research." *Energy Research and Social Science*, no. 79, 2021, pp. 1–6.

Nirvana. "Lithium" (song). *Nevermind*. DGC Records, 1991.

Owl WiS. "How Lithium Ion Battery Works | Working Principle." *YouTube*, 8 November 2021, https://www.youtube.com/watch?v=YFdokb9Nwto.

Phiddian, Ellen. "Lithium-Ion Versus Solid State: Reassessing Battery Safety." *Cosmos*, 8 March 2022, https://cosmosmagazine.com/technology/energy/are-solid-state-batteries-safer-than-lithium-ion/.

Royal Society of Chemistry. "Lithium." https://www.rsc.org/periodic-table/element/3/lithium.

Sample, Ian. "Nuclear Fusion Heat Record a 'Huge Step' in Quest for New Energy Source." *The Guardian*, 9 February 2022, https://www.theguardian.com/environment/2022/feb/09/nuclear-fusion-heat-record-a-huge-step-in-quest-for-new-energy-source.

The Dirty Truth behind Green Cars. ARTE, 2020.

9. Harnessing the Sun in Tech-on-Climate Discourse

Rianne Riemens

The Materiality of the Sun

While we all have an idea, or an image, of what the Sun is, its materiality can be hard to comprehend. The Sun is a yellow dwarf star of 4.5 billion years old. It is not a solid entity but instead consists of different regions made up of hydrogen and helium that go through cycles of high and low activity. The distance between the Sun and Earth is 150 million kilometers, while the Sun itself has a diameter of 1.4 million kilometers. Despite the distance, the Earth's very life depends on the heat and light produced by the nuclear reactions in the Sun's core (at an astonishing 15 million degrees Celsius) (fig. 1). The Earth and all other objects in our solar system are secured in their place by the Sun's gravity. Our planet's existence is thus tethered to the Sun, which is currently estimated to be halfway through its lifetime. In another 5 billion years, the Sun will morph into a giant star, making life on earth impossible (NASA).

The Sun's vital material role in sustaining life on Earth makes it a constant protagonist in human cultures, and a subject in many religions and myths. Most historical religions, for example, include a Sun god: the Incas worshipped Inti, the Egyptians had Ra, and the Greeks their Helios. These Sun gods were seen as central deities that bring light and provide life. Scientific knowledge has given us—and keeps giving—more detailed knowledge about the Sun's importance: it provides humans with Vitamin D and enables plants to grow through photosynthesis, to give two examples. But the Sun can endanger the same life it makes possible, something which has become increasingly apparent in the ongoing climate crisis. As the Earth's atmosphere continues to trap the Sun's heat, temperatures rise, causing droughts and heatwaves.[1] But while the Sun is connected to the damaging effects of the climate crisis, it is also framed as part of the solution: the Sun's very light could provide an alternative climate-safe source of power in the form of solar energy.

---

1 Note that the fact that the Sun's heat gets trapped in the atmosphere does not mean that the Sun causes climate change. This "greenhouse effect" is caused by human activities that release gases such as CO_2 (NASA, "Causes").

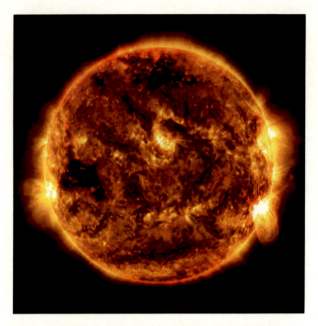

Fig. 1: The Sun emits a mid-level solar flare (a burst of radiation), captured by NASA's Solar Dynamics Observatory on October 1, 2015. Source: NASA/SDO].

While myths and religious narratives revolving around the Sun have existed for centuries, in the light of the climate crisis, new myths emerge about the Sun as energy source. In this chapter, I ask: what myths about the Sun's materiality are reproduced in contemporary discourse surrounding the climate crisis? More specifically, I will focus on "tech-on-climate discourse:" the production of promotional materials regarding the climate crisis by Big Tech companies. A focus on this field reveals how the Sun is mediated as a material of digital culture, functioning as a symbol of a green future that is made possible by Big Tech. I argue that the Sun is harnessed as a discursive marker of a greener future that disregards the complex reality of the Sun and solar energy.

Digital Culture and the Climate Crisis

The climate crisis urges countries and economies to decrease the use of fossil fuels and increase the use of renewable energy. While an energy transition sounds straightforward, it comes with a complex cultural transformation. A growing group of scholars in the field of energy humanities puts oil and energy at the center of their research in order to understand the ways in which energy is interwoven with our everyday lives (e.g., Szeman and Boyer; Wilson et al.). To better understand the relation between energy and everyday life, the tech sector that boosts a lot of today's energy use cannot be overlooked. Tech companies have become powerful economic actors because of the ownership of essential software and hardware, the collection of data from their billions of users, and the interconnection of services on which many corporate and individual users depend. But the sector also consists of an enormous global physical infrastructure of factories, offices, data centers, and energy sites that requires large amounts of materials, land, and human labor to function (Hu). Because their large environmental impact forms a reputational risk, tech companies such as Amazon, Alphabet, Apple, Meta, and Microsoft, also known as the "big five," are taking explicit positions as pioneers in the energy transition. While tech companies do invest in renewable energy and the recycling of finite materials, I argue that their green framing is more a matter of marketing strategy than of environmental concern.

Through their promotional materials the companies present a vision of the future centered on sustainability and innovation. In the images that platforms reproduce, meant to symbolize sustainability and innovation, the Sun and solar energy play a central role. Take for example the video "The Future of Energy" (2020) by Amazon's cloud service Amazon Web Services (AWS), in which a promise of smart sustainability is signified by the Sun. A voice-over claims that "our" energy use needs to be "more sustainable, more intelligent, and more efficient than ever before." Considering its focus on the future of energy, the video is shot at an unexpected location: an oil production plant. For Amazon, being sustainable is not about moving away from fossil fuels, but about using and processing these more efficiently. The video frames Amazon's core values of efficiency and intelligence as a promise of sustainability, by including images beaming in sunlight. The video contains shots filmed at dawn, in which the Sun reflects on a field of solar panels. In another shot, sun rays give the oil plant and the workers a warm, orange glow. The Sun plays a twofold role in the video: it functions as a source of natural light and as a form of energy. Both forms of representation of the Sun embody Amazon's positive future vision, in which solar panels can peacefully exist next to fossil fuels. Such a dream of an ideal future, which highlights the generating potential of energy, is an example of an "energy imaginary" that tech companies create in their tech-on-climate discourse (Williams, "This Shining Confluence").

While the use of solar imagery might seem innocent, as a means to produce corporate energy imaginaries they deserve critical scrutiny. The "Future of Energy" is not a science-fiction movie, it is a promotional video that Amazon uses to convince businesses of the values of their cloud service. The video and webpage on which it appears are full of corporate vernacular: AWS stands for sustainable and responsible innovation, transformation, and acceleration ("AWS Energy"). These promises are accompanied by a still from the "Future of Energy" video showing the sun rays glowing on Amazon laborers. The Sun is thus mobilized as a symbol of Amazon's climate discourse.

Amazon, however, is not the only company that looks to the Sun for salvation. In the "Better" video by Apple (2014), CEO Tim Cook's voice-over states that Apple wants to be a better company and make the planet a better place. The video has, in comparison with Amazon's video, a cleaner appeal in line with the identity of the brand and consists of attractive shots of immaculate factory interiors and green energy sites.[2] Although Apple's video is set at a different location, both videos beam in sunlight and present the Sun as a source of light and energy. Whereas smartness and efficiency are key terms in Amazon's green energy imaginary, Apple's commercial centers on the word "better," with Cook stating that "better is a force of nature." In the video, a parallel is drawn between technology (innovation) and the Sun, with both presented as forces of nature that drive humanity forward with their infinite generative potential.

The Energy Imaginary as Naive Fantasy

In the examples of Apple and Amazon, the Sun appears as a central and attractive visual element. By associating themselves with the Sun and the infrastructures of solar energy, tech companies frame themselves as enablers of a bright and sustainable future. The After Oil Collective uses the term "solarity" to refer to "a state, condition, or quality developed in relation to the sun, or to energy derived from the sun" (n.p.). In the book *Solarities: Seeking Energy Justice*, the collective writes that many have turned toward the Sun for its positive qualities, a turn that "is replete with desire and hope" (5). This hope goes beyond the promise of an energy transition. Imre Szeman and Dominic Boyer argue in *Energy Humanities: An Anthology* that the Sun is seen as a solution to the present as a whole; as a promise of stability. These qualities of solarity are harnessed in tech-on-climate discourse: as a source of hope in times of crisis. By drawing on the positive qualities of the Sun as a provider of infinite warmth and light, a new green future vision arises that is both hopeful and abundant.

However, I would argue that in the case of tech companies' energy imaginaries, the positive attitude toward solarity leads to a false framing. In general, tech companies aim to positively imagine their climate impact by foregrounding infrastructural artefacts such as green energy sites and data centers bathing in sunlight, while fossil fuels and e-waste remain obfuscated. Tech-on-climate discourse thus constantly

---

2   For a more extensive analysis of Apple's brand identity and the idea of technology as second nature, see Niessen.

plays with the balance between visibility and invisibility, in which the Sun plays an instrumental role: it is used to highlight that which companies want to foreground. As Szeman and Barney write, solar imaginaries blur "concept, fantasy, and infrastructure together in a manner that makes it difficult to disentangle solar fiction from solar reality" (1–2). The material reality of tech companies' infrastructure and the potential of solar energy become entangled with an idealized version of a tech- and solar-powered future. This future disregards the fact that the generation of solar energy through solar panels and batteries also depends on finite materials that need to be mined and cannot be infinitely expanded to feed Big Tech's hungry machine.

Tech companies thus frame themselves as philanthropic institutions that want to do good by, as Mél Hogan explains, "partnering with nature" (631). This idea of partnership fails to consider the impact of the underlying economic, infrastructural, and material forces that make continuous growth possible. Jesse Goldstein describes this framing as an element of green capitalism: a form of greenwashing that presents technological innovations with the goal of "planetary improvement." As Hogan writes: "in order to green their cycles of production, Big Tech is 'investing' in nature and in public infrastructure in ways that not only sustain but also unwittingly serve to encourage consumption" (636). What tech companies present as a partnership with nature is, in fact, a continuation of the extractivist logic of fossil-fueled petrocultures (Wilson et al.). A transition to renewable energy alters the infrastructural presence of tech companies, but does not break with the logic of continuous growth and consumption. The Sun is thus strategically "applied" as a shiny veneer to symbolize a fantasy of a cultural transition that does not actually take place.

The growth narrative is also harmful because it frames nature as an ecosystem that can be controlled and monetized. Portraying "nature" as an ecosystem that can thrive if it is technically managed offers tech companies a powerful position, but creates false hope about the future of the climate crisis.[3] In this limited vision, the Sun as material is being molded and mediated in a way that benefits tech companies. Following anthropologist Tim Ingold, I suggest that the materiality of the Sun is appropriated for specific, economic purposes; the Sun as raw material is converted "into the finished forms of artifacts" (Ingold 432). The Sun as artifact is a mediated object, distinct from the Sun as raw material, revealing a flawed and simplified framing of the relationship between Sun, solar energy, Big Tech and the climate crisis. This is the myth that tech companies produce: an optimistic narrative that consists of a mix of fact and fantasy.

---

3   For more on the Earth as programmable object see Gabrys.

Beyond the Myth of Energy without Mediation

While the Sun and its solar infrastructures play an obvious promotional role in tech-on-climate discourse, the impact of Sun myths should not be underestimated. The After Oil collective refers to the myths surrounding solar energy as a dream:

> The dream of solar is that we can access energy as energy: energy without mediation, energy without the need for fuel and so without leaving any trace of its use. This is the dream of infinite energy without needing to worry about its impact, either as extraction or as emission. (6–7)

This solar dream, or fantasy, presents a non- and never existing future, but one that nonetheless has real consequences. As Hogan writes, the myth of green tech companies partnering with nature is made up of "thin narratives that deploy textual and visual rhetorical strategies intended to obfuscate and overwrite resource exploitation" (647). The result is a staged version of the material effects of tech companies that shows a misrepresentation of solar energy as infinite and clean resource.

The misrepresentation of the Sun's materiality is, I argue, illustrative of how tech companies frame nature at large in economic and managerial terms. In this framing, Rhys Williams writes, "the natural world in its entirety may come to be seen as simply an inefficient and outmoded system of production" ("Turning Toward the Sun" 161). Such managerial perspectives, when applied to nature and the Sun, might be expressed in projects such as the geo-engineering of large scale Sun deflectors, as promoted by tech mogul Bill Gates.[4] These methods might accelerate the planet's crisis they intend to avert because of their potentially detrimental effects, but also as solutionist fantasy that never relinquishes the need for growth.[5] New myths about the ways in which the Sun's materiality can be controlled need to be countered by stories that acknowledge that an energy transition also entails a cultural transition in terms of values and practices regarding "the why and how of energy" (Wilson et al. 4). What we need is a form of "cultural sustainability," a cultural and theoretical production of new future visions that bring together the Sun, solar energy, technology, humans, and nonhumans in a nature-culture continuum (Meireis and Rippl; Smelik). And while these stories might also envision people and landscapes bathing in sunlight, they should not obfuscate the complex reality of solarity and the energy transition.

---

4   See Gates' recent book on climate change for an insight into his views on geo-engineering.
5   See for example the discussion on the possibilities and risks of such experiments in the Guardian (Carrington).

Works Cited

After Oil Collective, Ayesha Vemuri and Darin Barney, editors. *Solarities: Seeking Energy Justice*. U of Minnesota P, 2022.

Amazon Web Services. "The Future of Energy." *YouTube*, uploaded 6 Mar. 2020, https://www.youtube.com/watch?v=9k-LBQG5Q6E.

Apple. "Apple Better – HD commercial." *YouTube*, uploaded by The Commercial Cinema, 14 May 2014, https://www.youtube.com/watch?v=J7ArPgBRR94.

AWS. "AWS Energy." https://aws.amazon.com/energy/. *Amazon*. Accessed 4 Dec. 2022.

Carrington, Damian. "'Dimming the Sun': $100m Geoengineering Research Programme Proposed." *The Guardian*, 25 March 2021, https://www.theguardian.com/environment/2021/mar/25/top-us-scientists-back-100m-geoengineering-research-proposal.

Gabrys, Jennifer. *Program Earth: Environmental Sensing Technology and the Making of a Computational Planet*. U of Minnesota P, 2016.

Gates, Bill. *How to Avoid a Climate Disaster: The Solutions We Have and the Breakthroughs We Need*. Alfred A. Knopf, 2021.

Goldstein, Jesse. *Planetary Improvement: Cleantech Entrepreneurship and the Contradictions of Green Capitalism*. The MIT Press, 2018.

Hogan, Mél. "Big Data Ecologies." *Ephemera – Theory and Politics in Organization*, vol. 18, no. 3, 2018, pp. 631–57.

Hu, Tung-Hui. *A Prehistory of the Cloud*. The MIT Press, 2015.

Ingold, Tim. "Toward an Ecology of Materials." *Annual Review of Anthropology*, vol. 41, 2015, pp. 427–42.

Meireis, Torsten, and Gabriele Rippl. Introduction. *Cultural Sustainability: Perspectives from the Humanities and Social Sciences*, edited by Torsten Meireis and Gabriele Rippl, Routledge, 2019, pp. 3–11.

NASA. "The Causes of Climate Change." *NASA Global Climate Change: Vital Signs of the Planet*, https://climate.nasa.gov/causes/. Accessed 4 Dec. 2022.

———. "Our Sun." *NASA Science: Solar System Exploration*, https://solarsystem.nasa.gov/solar-system/Sun/in-depth/. Accessed 29 Sept. 2022.

Niessen, Niels. "Shot on iPhone: Apple's World Picture." *Advertising and Society Quarterly*, vol. 22, no. 2, 2022, http://doi.org/10.1353/asr.2021.0023.

Smelik, Anneke. "Fractal Folds: The Posthuman Fashion of Iris van Herpen." *Fashion Theory*, vol. 26, no. 1, 2022, pp. 5–26.

Szeman, Imre, and Dominic Boyer, editors. *Energy Humanities: An Anthology*. John Hopkins UP, 2017.

Szeman, Imre, and Darin Barney. "From Solar to Solarity." *The South Atlantic Quarterly*, vol. 120, no. 1, 2021, pp. 1–11.

Williams, Rhys. "'This Shining Confluence of Magic and Technology': Solarpunk, Energy Imaginaries, and the Infrastructures of Solarity." *Open Library of Humanities*, vol. 5, no. 1, 2019, pp. 1–35.

———. "Turning Toward the Sun: The Solarity and Singularity of New Food." *The South Atlantic Quarterly*, vol. 120, no. 1, 2021, pp. 151–62.

Wilson, Sheena, et al. *Petrocultures: Oil, Politics, Culture.* McGill-Queen's UP, 2019.

Part V: Materials of the Nation

10. Dutch Peat

Tom Sintobin

"Unland"

The Roman historian Tacitus is claimed to have said that "peat is land that is not to be ridden and water that is not to be navigated" (Tonnis 8). Neither liquid nor solid, "wet lands," as peat lands, fens, bogs, and moors are commonly called (Proulx), obstruct conventional means of transportation and thereby escape human control in this respect. This hybrid matter also resists categorization in several other ways. Peat lands, for instance, seem to resist the opposition between past and present since they consist of accumulating dead plant and sometimes animal matter that does not fully decay due to the acidic and anaerobic conditions of the bog. This is especially true for so-called high moor peat, which is characterized by peat moss (of the *Spagnum* family), a plant whose bottom part is dead while its upper part keeps growing. One could say that high moor peat is dead and alive at the same time. As Penné and Sepp (298) have argued, this undecidedness turns peat lands into a prime example of what Roland Barthes has called "the neutral": phenomena rebelling against "the yes/no (+/-) model," baffling "the paradigm" (6).

In the Netherlands of the nineteenth century, this undetermined place was called "onland" (Van der Woud 40), or "unland" in English. In line with "ancient Judeo-Christian belief," this dangerous place was treated as a divine gift for humans to use "as they wish" (Proulx 14). And use it they did: as a soil to cultivate buckwheat and to create new agricultural land, as substrate for horticulture, and as a reservoir of cheap fuel in the form of peat. It has even been argued (and contested) that the Dutch Golden Age would not have been possible without huge reserves of peat (de Zeeuw). Non-functional meanings have been ascribed to the bog as well: it was a place of mystery, and, from 1850 onwards as Paulissen et al. have shown (7), increasingly became seen as a biodiverse and beautiful place embodying old values (Sintobin and Corporaal 160), to which people are attached (Paulissen et al. 7), and that deserves protection (Schouten et al. 58).

Even nowadays, peat lands continue to provoke conflicting responses. A good example is the debate on De Deurnsche Peel, a nature reserve in Noord-Brabant. Nature and water agencies Staatsbosbeheer and the Waterschap Aa en Maas herald peat lands as the one thing that could stop global warming due to their capacity to store CO2 and advocate the full restoration of biodiverse peatlands in their original state with the help of the European funding program LIFE+. Locals, however, fear the return of desolate, mosquito-infested wetlands and prefer to preserve the new wooded ecosystems and cultural heritage that have resulted from centuries of peat cutting (De Graaf). This chapter, however, does not study peat as an object of representation but the ways in which artists are exploring its possibilities as an artistic material in its own right, a practice that is clearly gaining prominence in the twenty-first century. It will focus on the use of peat in three different contexts: in choreography, in art-in-nature projects, and in galleries.

Choreographing Peat

Föld, a modern dance choreography by Krisztina de Châtel, premiered on 24 June 1985 in the Amstelkerk in Amsterdam and has been staged regularly in the Netherlands (e.g., 1985, 1997, 2005, 2012) and abroad (e.g., Paris, 1985; Hungary early 1990s and 2005). The latest series of reprises started on 9 May 2022 at Internationaal Theater Amsterdam (and was followed up by performances in cities such as Alkmaar and Maastricht). "Föld" is the Hungarian word for "Earth," and during the performance the dancers gradually break through the circular wall of earth that limits their movements. Peat was chosen, according to De Châtel, because normal soil was too hard, humid, and coarse. Although peat poses its own challenges—it dries out and is expensive—it "feels soft and fine and yet sticks to everything: mouth, eyes, nose and sweaty body" (Embrechts).[1] Demonstrating the interaction between earth and bodies is the entire idea of this choreography. De Châtel talks about "struggling" ("strijd leveren") and stresses that costumes were discarded if the peat did not stick to them. Indeed, *Föld* has been compared to ancestral rites, in which primeval man fights (Schenke) and cultivates the earth (van Nieuwpoort). The idea of a universal fight of man with nature has not changed over the years, but present-day commentators seem to interpret it differently, for instance by stressing that the heap of peat represents our planet, which is not being cultivated but rather destroyed by man/the dancers (Colée). Other commentators argue that this fight should not necessarily be interpreted as a victory for man (Embrechts). This new interpretation was not an effect of changes in the choreography—De Châtel changed just one move and decided to use only male dancers—but of shifting contexts of reception. Judging from the large audiences and the standing ovations the performance drew in 2022, this theme is currently more appealing than ever according to De Châtel.

---

1   All references in this paragraph are to newspapers consulted through the online database Nexis Uni, which does not mention page numbers.

Art-in-Nature

De Châtel merely selected peat for its particular qualities, more specifically for its impact on human bodies. The original context of the material does not play a role; peat just happens to be the best material to enable her to tell a universal story. This is different for artists participating in outdoor projects, in which peat art is put into the environment its material stems from. In 2003, for instance, the exhibition *Peatpolis.nl* was held in Barger-Compascuum. This village has considerable symbolic value since it lies in the heart of what was once the largest high peat land in the Netherlands and Germany, the Bourtanger Moor. This large-scale artistic project under the curatorship of Adri de Fluiter is an example of "art-in-nature." "The surroundings and the work of art form such a unity that a unique situation arises that cannot be exchanged for anything else" (De Fluiter 95). Seventeen Dutch and international artists took up the challenge to help create an art city in this high moor reserve by making use of peat.

In their descriptions as preserved in the book *Peatpolis.nl*, most of the artists refer to the history of wetlands. There are references to different pasts: Celtic (Jan van Lisdonk), prehistoric (Anton Watzeels; Michael McGillis; Lorna Green), mythical (Miriam Monchen, Yvonne Struys), and also to that of peat workers (Miriam Monchen; François Davin; Arno Arts) or to peat lands as a spa (Wenche Kvalstad Eckhoff). Simultaneously, many artists stress the actuality and physicality of their relationship with peat. In line with folk beliefs, peat is treated as a living organism that has eyes looking back at the visitor (Carlotta Brunetti) and a skin (Mark Evert Kramer). Cherie Sampson writes about the "presence of my body in the interior of a peat hut" as "an encounter with a personification of nature that is devouring, life-giving and female" (39). Kvalstad Eckhoff's manifestation had people actually taking mud baths (22–23), and Johan Sietzema describes himself trudging through the peat bog (59).

Since this exhibition was plagued by bad weather, working on it became an extremely bodily experience indeed. Several artists testified to their hardships: Arno Arts's building site was flooded by the endless rain, so he had to drain it; Michael McGilles discovered that the logs he had to work with were much smaller than he had assumed and had irregular shapes, making it hard to stack them (Van Ruiten "Op internet"). Miriam Monchen still remembered twenty years later that the peat logs she was working with were warped because of the rain. For visitors, *Peatpolis.nl* was a bodily experience as well. Seeing it all required a five-kilometer walk through the mud. Even the former Queen Beatrix, after arriving by helicopter, had to wear boots to be able to visit the site (Van Ruiten, "Boer Bob"). All this shifted attention away from peat as part of an ecosystem to peat as an artistic material, with its own characteristics and demands that differ from other artistic materials such as language, marble, and bronze, which enable the erecting of monuments for eternity.

Even before the end of the exhibition, Monchen's artworks were knocked down by the wind (figs. 1 and 2).

Fig. 1. and Fig. 2: Miriam Monchen, *Veenwieven* [Women of Peat Lands], before and after the storm. Photograph: ©Miriam Monchen.

Almost a decade after *Peatpolis.nl* and unrelated to it, artist Henk de Lange started using peat after a stay in Ireland. An early work of his was *Natuurtempel (Temple of Nature)*, which was constructed in Appelscha in 2012 and became part of the Land Art project in Flevoland a year later. Standing three meters tall, this construction of peat blocks reinforced with iron stayed there for eight years. De Lange was fascinated by the transformation his artwork underwent. Its angle changed, as did its texture, depending on the weather, showing cracks in times of frost or heat. Parts of it started to crumble, and plants and moss grew on it. Galleries that want to exhibit art made of peat that has not yet dried out completely need to moisten it regularly, De Lange stresses.

This "liveliness" is precisely what attracts De Lange to this material. Even fully dry, peat is not easy to work with, he explains, because its consistency is unpredictable, with branches sticking out of it and hard or soft parts showing up unexpectedly. It is therefore of little use to plan the theme of the artwork in advance. On the contrary, it is necessary to leave room for spontaneity since the material itself indicates into what it can be transformed. De Lange's *Dodo*, for instance, was originally intended as part of a series of human figures, but he had to change his idea halfway through. Peat also poses physical demands. De Lange has a half-open workplace for his art and wears a face mask, for manipulating peat generates much dust. On the other hand, the fact that peat is light allows him to keep working with it despite his joint complaints. De Lange makes use of peat from the north of Germany or Estland, but very occasionally also Dutch peat, which he buys from Staatsbosbeheer or from a renovation project in Friesland that got rid of old peat blocks that had been insulating the roof.

Peat Art

Dioni ten Busschen has worked with peat since 2010 and, as stated on her website, makes "sculptures, objects, furniture and wall coverings" inspired by the "natural environment of the peat." She has a permanent exhibition in the Peatart Gallery in Amsterdam but also regularly exhibits in other cities in the Netherlands, as well as in Sweden and Germany, often in peat history museums. Religious motifs play an important role in her work, with works such as *Holy Stone, Self-Sacrifice, Lamb of God, Fertility Mascot, Table with Funeral Gifts*, and *Praying Hands* (ten Busschen). There are also body parts (*Noor Mees, Hand* [fig. 3]) and objects (*Dish Large, Small Primal Pot*). The potential meanings of these works are closely related to the peat material. Although these artworks do not directly refer to peat lands, it seems logical to interpret them in that context because of what they are made of.

Fig. 3: Dioni ten Busschen, Hand, peat, 10x12x10 cm, 2011. From The Forgotten People of Soosaare. ©Dioni ten Busschen.

Hand, then, is automatically seen as a mummified hand, all the more so because of the very intricate and parchment-like surface structure of the material. *Self-Sacrifice* shows a person who took her own life by jumping into the swamp, while *Dish* turns into a representation of an archaeological find in the bog. This also results in very complex meanings, as is the case with *Lamb of God*—a Christian sacrificial symbol that coalesces with a heathen sacrificial place. In other words, peat as a material seems to play a much bigger role in the process of signification than clay, for instance, would do. Ten Busschen herself mentioned that she does not have a background in working with clay and that she found that clay "pushes you too much in the direction of what it is not." Peat has agency, according to the artist; in my talk with her, she said that the material "told me how it wanted to be treated" and that peat "did not like" being outside. Ten Busschen stresses that peat is a challenging material to work with. It demands patience and the respect and love that a thousand-year-old material that stems from a living organism deserves. This slowness of processing forces one, she claims, to reflect on what it means to use materials altogether, regardless of the objects they happen to constitute. In other words, working with peat draws her attention to any materials as "the stuff that things are made of," as Ingold formulates it ("Materials" 1).

Ten Busschen works with peat from Estland that has been harvested in a sustainable way, that is, without destroying the living top layers. Another one of her projects, *A Second Peat-Art Life for Plastic Waste*, in which she covers compositions of waste plastic with peat to turn them into useful objects, also stresses sustainability. In a sense, peat is used to neutralize one of the most prominent kinds of waste in our present-day society: just like peat locks up CO_2, it prevents plastics from falling apart into microplastics. Ten Busschen creates the twenty-first-century equivalent of natural peat: it becomes an archaeological site, stopping time and preserving entire units of the past.

Hein van Delft started using peat in 2015 after encountering it in De Deelen near Heerenveen, a bog where peat was cut until 2021. As a garden and landscape architect, Van Delft has always been fascinated by natural materials. Walking, especially in the northern part of the Netherlands, allows him to find things to experiment with by way of trial and error. "Letting materials slip through my fingers" is crucial for Van Delft, and "in the case of peat this is connected to an entire history, to see the relics of plants or wood that has been a tree centuries ago, to feel it and to think of how I could express something with it." He calls peat a very dirty material to use: it pigments anything that comes into contact with it. Initially, he would experiment with it in his bathroom before he acquired a studio.

A central concept in Van Delft's poetics is connection. His art aims at showing the essential connectedness of things (landscape, nature, history, and mankind) and thus confirms Ingold's claim that a landscape is to be perceived as "an enduring record of—and testimony to—the lives and works of past generations who have dwelt within it, and in so doing, have left there something of themselves" (*The Perception* 189). That is why Van Delft combines peat with fragments of the kind of clothes peat workers used to wear and with the sheep wool typical of the region. For his work *Neerslag (Rain)*, which forms part of the 2022 exhibition for *Stroomopwaarts (Upstream)* in Het Tripgemaal in Gersloot, he used high peat from Estland. Van Delft admits that he would have preferred to use Dutch peat to stress the authenticity and the locatedness of his work, but that was impossible to find. Combining the three materials reveals how similar they ultimately are: the fibers of the clothing, the fluffiness of the high peat, and the strands of wool perfectly intermingle.

Van Delft explicitly refuses to work in the sentimental, idyllic, and romantic way that is so common when people or museums talk about the past. There are no landscapes left without humans, he claims, so he refrains from the nostalgic longing for a prehuman nature. This explains the specific shape of works such as *Neerslag*, but also of *De Deelen (The Parts)*: it is reminiscent of the kind of lacquer profiles landscape architects use, testifying again to Van Delft's non-sentimental, systematic approach to landscapes. Not coincidentally, Van Delft's first exhibition was at gallery 9 in Amsterdam, which, according to its website, tends to show "abstract art, often geometrical but sometimes also organic and material."

The Liveness of Peat

Despite obvious differences, some patterns become manifest in these artworks. The artists often point out that their encounters with peat are not monodirectional. Peat pigments everything that comes into contact with it: houses (Van Delft), but also bodies and their skins (De Châtel) and lungs (De Lange). Working with peat is not purely cognitive but a bodily experience that activates all the senses (De Châtel, De Lange, Van Delft). Peat has its own demands and even agency: one has to respect it (Ten Busschen) and carefully listen to the way it wants to be treated (Ten Busschen, De Lange). It strongly responds to changes in temperature and humidity (De Châtel, De Lange, Monchen) and thus introduces unpredictability and room for spontaneity. It bears and shows the traces of its organic origins (De Lange, Van Delft, Ten Busschen) and, in doing so, draws attention to its histories, both those from the past and the new histories that are born out of the meeting between artist and material. Interestingly, the association between peat and the problem of carbon emissions, often brought up in recent debates, does not (yet) play a significant role in this artistic discourse.

While peat lands (and their uses) have nowadays almost entirely disappeared in the Netherlands, they are still very much present as signs: in the extraordinary number of place names referring to "veen," in Dutch expressions such as "turf naar de venen sturen" ("to send peat to the peat lands"—like water to the sea), in dead metaphors that use "turf" for voluminous books or small persons, as a topic in literature and newspapers, in the branding campaigns of regions, and so on. Very few people have ever smelled the pervasive odor of burning peat that, until deep in the nineteenth century, hung over many Dutch cities. And yet, many people regularly come into contact with the real thing, possibly without realizing it, for instance when they take a bag of potting soil from the shelves of a gardening center or water their houseplants. From this perspective, peat is obviously an object with a clear function that has been disconnected from its origins. This may sound strange, since working with peat and new plants in a garden necessarily involves touching, shaping, smelling, and looking at the material, with all its irregularly shaped and sized particles—and yet it is only now through the peat artworks that I realize that, as I plant my seedlings, I am working with relics of plants that could be many centuries old. And as I let time that had stood still for centuries slip through my fingers, and peat dust color my hands, I contemplate how I am actively contributing to the destruction of my own planet by literally throwing fossil fuels to the wind. In my neighbor's garden, the radio plays: "But even sitting in the garden one can still get stung" (Faithless).

Acknowledgment

I would like to thank Dioni ten Busschen, Krisztina de Châtel, Henk de Lange, Miriam Monchen, and Hein van Delft for the inspiring conversations about their peat works.

Works Cited

Barthes, Roland. *The Neutral*. Translated by Rosalind Kraus and Denis Hollier Columbia UP, 2005.
Busschen, Dioni Ten, editor. www.dioni.nl.
Colée, Ronald. "'Föld' opnieuw te zien tijdens de Nederlandse Dansdagen in Maastricht" ["'Föld' to Be Seen again at the Dutch Dancing Days in Maastricht"]. *Dagblad De Limburger*, 28 Sept. 2022.
Delft, Hein van. Email 25 Nov. 2022.
Embrechts, Annette. "Föld is 37 jaar na de première nog altijd een ware uitputtingsslag voor dansers" ["37 Years After its Premiere Föld Still Exhausts the Dancers"]. *De Volkskrant*, 9 May 2022.
Faithless. "The Garden." *Sunday 8PM*, Cheeky Records, 1998. Transcript of lyrics.
Fluiter, Adri de. "Peat Art." *Peatpolis.nl*, edited by Janny Baker and Michiel Gerding, International Peat Society, 2003.

Gallery nine. www.gallerynine.nl/gallery/Gallery_9_NL.html

Gerding, Michiel. "Peat Art and Peat Culture." *Peatpolis.nl*, edited by Janny Baker and Michiel Gerding, International Peat Society, 2003, pp. 10–16.

Graaf, Peter de. "Hoogveenherstel of natuurverwoesting? Help, de Peel verzuipt" ["Restoring High Peat or Destroying Nature? Help, the Peel is Drowning"]. *De Volkskrant*, 9 Dec. 2021.

Ingold, Tim. "Materials against Materiality." *Archaeological Dialogues*, vol. 14, no. 1, 2007, pp. 1–16.

———. *The Perception of the Environment.* Routledge, 2000.

Nieuwpoort, Marcel-Armand van. "Verrassende choreografie De Châtel hoogtepunt van Holland Festival" ["Suprising Choreography De Châtel Highlight of Holland Festival"]. *Het Financiële Dagblad*, 8 July 1985.

Paulissen, Maurice, et al. "Place Meanings of Dutch Raised Bog Landscapes: An Interdisciplinary Long-Term Perspective (5000 BCE-Present)." *Landscape Research*, 2022, https://doi.org/10.1080/01426397.2022.2118246.

Penné, Lesley, and Arvi Sepp. "De verbeelding van moeras en veen: Figuraties van de drassige bodem als topos van de gemeenschap in de hedendaagse Duitstalig-Belgische literatuur" ["The Representation of Bog and Peat: Figurations of Wet Lands as Trope for the Community in Present-Day German-Belgian Literature"]. *De Moderne Tijd*, vol. 5, no. 3–4, 2021, pp. 292–310.

Proulx, Annie. *Fen, Bog and Swamp: A Short History of Peatland Destruction and its Role in the Climate Crisis.* 4th Estate, 2022.

Ruiten, Joep van. "Boer Bob redt Peatpolis, laat Beatrix maar komen" ["Farmer Bob Saves Peatpolis, Beatrix is Welcome"]. *Dagblad van het Noorden*, 4 June 2003.

———. "Op internet ziet turf er héél anders uit" ["On the Internet Peat Looks very Different"]. *Dagblad van het Noorden*, 20 May 2003.

Schenke, Menno. "Ballet Föld fascinerend" ["Ballet Föld Fascinating"]. *Algemeen Dagblad*, 26 June 1985.

Schouten, Matthijs, M. van Ool, and A. Kempenaar. *Veen, turf en Vincent van Gogh* [*Peat Lands, Peat and Vincent van Gogh*]. Staatsbosbeheer, 2003.

Sintobin, Tom, and Marguérite Corporaal. "Turf is nu eenmaal een vruchtbaar terrein voor de fantasie. De literaire verbeelding van veen en veenderij in Nederlandse literatuur, 1909–1940" ["After All Peat is a Fertile Territory for Fantasy. The Literary Representation of Peat and Peat Cutting in Dutch Literature"]. *De Moderne Tijd*, vol. 5, no. 3–4, 2021, pp. 268–91.

Tonnis, Wim. "Piet, Pete and Peat." *Peatpolis.nl*, edited by Janny Baker and Michiel Gerding, International Peat Society, 2003.

Woud, Auke Van der. *Het landschap, de mensen: Nederland 1850–1940* [*The Landscape, the People: The Netherlands 1850–1940*]. Prometheus, 2021.

Zeeuw, J.W. de. "Peat and the Dutch Golden Age: The Historical Meaning of Energy-Attainability." *AAG Bijdragen*, vol. 21. Landbouwhogeschool Wageningen, 1978, pp. 3–32.

11. Milk: Material Entwinements and the Making and Unmaking of Healthy Bodies

Tess J. Post

In January 2020, a video campaign funded by the Dutch government and the European Union entitled *Nederland draait op zuivel* ("the Netherlands runs on dairy") was launched to promote national dairy consumption. A cheese sandwich is tossed on a plate, a glass of milk eagerly deposited next to it, with a voice-over proclaiming, "this is the way we have lunch in the Netherlands." According to the campaign, if it were not for the strength that cows' milk provided, the Dutch would not have been able to build their renowned sea dikes, and the landscape would have looked radically different. The land would not be inhabited by cows but by sea-cows because the country would be flooded with water.

What is this campaign telling us? In a near ludicrous manner, it reiterates a rhetoric with a long history, revering milk as a vital material, its strength reciprocally flowing between bodies and matter. Milk, in this instance, is mobilized affectively by being tied to the resilience and prosperity of the Dutch nation. A campaign such as this only exists because it has a rich reservoir of cultural meaning upon which to draw. In *Mythologies* (1957), Roland Barthes called milk a "totem-drink" in the Netherlands, attributing its venerated position to the extensive mythology that surrounds it (79). In these mythologized tales of milk, there is a congruence between the land's wealth, the cow's health, the people's strength, and the Dutch nation's prosperity. Milk campaigning potentializes national belonging, articulating an affective appeal that continues to dictate milk's popularity in the Netherlands today.

Milk, however, is a "leaky" material, and as with all resilient totems, there is also latency and excess. The white liquid ostensibly transforms the human body, providing strength and ableness, but milk also affects the animal body. Animal agriculture breeds animals to physical extremes, the impaired body is made productive and economically valuable, causing this industry to be the chief source of disability among animals (Taylor, "Animal Crips" 104). I aim to explore how milk as a material is used to make certain others and how milk itself is made.

Following Tim Ingold's prompt that to "understand materials is to be able to tell their histories" (434), I will trace the advent of the popularity of cows' milk and outline several examples from Dutch dairy advertising from the early and mid-twentieth century. I examine the role played by these advertisements in configuring milk consumption as part of an affective economy shaping the materialization of certain bodies (Ahmed 121). As the healthy individual and national body became a prime focus of milk advertising, cows were subjected to extensive breeding programs intended to engineer the ideal *"melkkoe"* ("dairy cow"), to make an otherwise naturally varying substance into a predictable and hygienic resource. Arguably, when considering these realities as interwoven occurrences, we do not merely grasp milk as the naturalized and familiar object it is made out to be, but also encounter it as a "thing" that demands our attention and emerges in relation to other materials (Brown 4).

Cultivating the National Body with Milk

Milk of animal origin is subject to rapid spoilage if not handled, cooled, or preserved correctly. In the late nineteenth century, the Dutch milk industry started to flourish due to new dairy technologies, hygienic improvements, and selective breeding programs for cows (Reinders and Vernooij 19). Milk production and distribution became more efficient and hygienic as farmers transitioned to new industrial means. The "dirtiness" of milk was thus palliated through the development of scientific tools and knowledge that captured and modified the unpredictable material nature of milk, which further helped to consolidate milk as a Dutch commercial household staple. By the 1930s, dairy farmers were increasingly competitive, and more milk than ever was being produced. To stimulate the consumption of milk, the Dutch government nationalized large parts of the dairy industry and funded the establishment of the *Crisis-Zuivelbureau*, an organization tasked with creating propaganda for Dutch milk. Milk was not only marketed as a complete source of nutrition, but it was also promoted as being relatively cheap, very healthy, and, most importantly, of quintessential Dutch origin. After World War II, the *Crisis-Zuivelbureau* was renamed *Nederlands Zuivelbureau*, and the nationwide advertising continued. Sayings that are still often used today, such as *"melk is goed voor elk"* ("milk is good for everyone"), were popularized by these two national dairy associations.

Crisis-Zuivelbureau and *Nederlands Zuivelbureau* propaganda was extensive and not only limited to printed advertisements. It also included large-scale physical manifestations, such as dairy weeks and milk exhibitions, drawing hundreds of thousands of visitors (fig. 1). Notable examples include *"De Melkweg,"* and *"De zuiveltentoonstelling"*. The Nijmegen dairy week of 1936 accompanied the festivities of the International Four Day Marches—the largest multiple-day marching event in the world. The city's main road was transformed into a *"melkweg"* ("milky way or street"), and its grassy lawns were lined with life-size wooden cows and large billboards reading *"melk hoort bij sport"* ("milk belongs to sports") and *"niets beter voor uithoudingsvermogen dan melk"* ("nothing better for stamina than milk"). A local newspaper reported how these "symbolic [cow] figures show us the meaning and value of milk for our bodies" ("*symbolische figuren die ons de betekenis en de waarde van melk voor ons lichaam doen zien*") and that more milk consumption will increase our national prosperity ("Zuivelpropaganda tijdens de Vierdaagsche," "De Zuivelweek"). These dairy weeks included cooking demonstrations, milk bars, film exhibitions, and dairy parades. The milk-themed metamorphosis of Nijmegen is but one example of the dozens of dairy weeks that were organized from the 1930s to the 1950s. They are a testament to the comprehensive propaganda of the dairy associations that created them. By connecting milk to such grand and festive events, milk drinking became an affective endeavor—a form of ingestible belonging.

Fig. 1: "*De Zuiveldagen Te Heerenveen,*" Leeuwarder Nieuwsblad, 7 March 1936. *This photograph of a dairy parade in Frisia in 1936 provides an example of what such parades looked like. The texts on the vehicle read "health" and "agriculture," with a woman dressed in traditional milkmaid clothing sitting on a vehicle adorned with milk bottles.*

Milk consumption was promoted to increase individual and collective work productivity, health, and happiness. Dairy campaigns attributed superhuman strength to consuming milk while rendering sickly those who did not consume enough. The cartoons of the 1950s campaign *Met melk meer mans* (*More Power with Milk*) attest to this rhetoric, featuring short narratives of people suddenly capable of enormous physical feats after drinking milk (figs. 2–5). A sick man visiting a doctor is happy and full of health after drinking three glasses of milk as prescribed; a bedridden older man dances happily with a nurse; a man smilingly carries not only a piano but also its deliverer up the stairs; and a joyful mother lifts her two children so high up that they can feed a giraffe at the zoo, all after drinking a glass of milk. It is important to note that these campaigns were brandless, made to promote milk as a general material. Many advertisements did not even disclose their commercial nature, but presented themselves as informative articles backed by science rather than money.

Figs. 2–5: Met melk meer mans (More Power with Milk). Advertisements, Nederlands Zuivelbureau (Netherlands Dairy Agency), 1956.

Milk was marketed as an indispensable material for the cultivation of healthy bodies and a prosperous Dutch nation. Campaigns such as *Melk, onze nationale drank* (*Milk, Our National Drink*) in 1935 and *Nêerlands Zuivel, voedt u goed!* (*Dutch Dairy, Feed Yourself Well*) in 1936 demonstrate the commercial alignment of individual bodies with a national body politic. Illustrated advertisements from the second campaign were accompanied by the phrase "*zuivel kweekt gezonde kinderen en een krachtig volk*" ("dairy breeds healthy children and a strong population"). The Dutch verb "*kweken*," meaning to breed, grow, or cultivate, evokes a usage reminiscent of animal breeding and physical anthropology. This type of terminology evinces a material connection: dairy foodstuffs cultivate healthy bodies able to collectively create a strong nation. A tangible implementation of this narrative was the introduction of "*schoolmelk*" ("school milk") in the mid-1930s. To foster physical and mental well-being, the Dutch government subsidized the country-wide provision of milk in primary schools. School milk became so popular that by the 1950s, almost every primary school in the Netherlands participated in the program (Reinders and Vernooij 119).

Aside from the mandatory milk consumption in schools, dairy promotions were often directed at children. For instance, the *Melkbrigade* ("milk brigade," also known as *M-Brigade*) was a pseudo-militaristic campaign of the 1950s and 1960s resembling a youth movement, with over 400,000 Dutch children as members during its heyday ("Ere-Brigadier"). When children drank at least three glasses of milk daily, they acquired cotton patches with an "M" to proudly display their membership. The *Melkbrigade* organized milk quizzes, fieldtrips, parades, and theatrical shows in concert halls with famous Dutch people who endorsed milk. In these instances, an emotive sense of being is formulated through specific consumption patterns. In the case of the *Melkbrigade*, milk was made desirable, connected to entertaining experiences for children and adults, and constructed as an integral part of "Dutchness."

In this way, the article or commodity being promoted accumulates affective value. Sara Ahmed explores how certain emotions stick to objects, considering how affect is a form of capital and how the circulation of objects and their emotive associations shapes the material world. Accordingly, feelings appear in objects or, indeed, *as* objects (Ahmed 121). Ahmed argues that affective economies help to align individual bodies with communities and can thus shape "the body of the nation" (121). As such, the affective circulation of milk enables the articulation of an imagined community. Importantly, which emotions "stick" to particular objects is also "bound up with the 'absent presence' of historicity"—that is, affective economies normalize certain objects by obscuring particular aspects, such as their histories of production, exchange, or circulation; in other words, their material entwinements (Ahmed 120).

Making the Milkable Body

By taking milk as a relational fluid that shapes Dutch bodies and matter, the campaigns discussed above bring into play affective economies and create a realm of imagined national belonging. However, what happens if we truly consider milk as the relational fluid it is, and not just in the way it has been served up to us by these campaigns? When we consider milk not as a static object but as a particular subject-object relation, we may better grasp its "thingness" (Brown 4). Bill Brown writes how things are "what is excessive in objects" as the force by which objects become "values, fetishes, idols and totems" (5). Whereas an object is banal and naturalized to us, it becomes a thing when we encounter its unfamiliarity. Tim Ingold notes how "things can exist and persist only because they *leak*" (483). Thingness thus leaks into the demarcation of a material as an object and, in so doing, amounts to latency and excess (Brown 5). In the vast symbolism of the object, we find hints of its thingness—its unfamiliarity—because of the inherent relationality of material.

Let us return to milk and attend to its latency and excess. While the national dairy associations were marketing milk as a way to increase bodily health and national productivity, the cows producing that milk endured severe physical transformations. From the 1950s onwards, the Dutch dairy industry has been amply subsidized by the European Economic Community and the European Union, a funding that continues to this day ("EU-subsidies" 5). By the mid-twentieth century, the milk production of Dutch cows was the highest in the world (Theunissen and Jansen 280). Decades of intensive breeding, veterinary interventions, and agricultural engineering had paid off in *"veeverbetering"* ("cattle improvement"). Whereas the average Dutch cow produced 2500 liters of milk annually in 1910, this had increased to 4000 liters by the 1950s and is now over 8000 liters per annum ("Nederlandse landbouwproductie 1950–2015"; "Meer melkvee").

The cows' milk we know today is the product of an appetite for pure and perfectible cattle and the result of a long and complex genealogy of breeding practices. The preoccupation with clean and purebred (*"raszuiver"*) cattle frequently mirrored and informed broader societal discussions and practices concerning human racial and hygienic purity (Theunissen and Jansen 282). A harrowing example is the recruitment of cattle breeders by National Socialist officials for social policy-making (Bauman 258). Richard Walther Darré, a leading *Blut und Boden* ("blood and soil") ideologist, compared the breeding of cattle to the breeding of humans and took inspiration from his years of working in livestock genetics (Zelinger 372).[1] An article in the Dutch anti-Semitic paper *De Misthoorn* from 1940 similarly reports how a farmer

---

1   Darré was a race theorist who wrote *Neuadel aus Blut und Boden* (1930), in which he developed the Blut und Boden ideology about the mutual relationship between a people and the land they occupy and cultivate, and formulated a systemic eugenics program to actualize this

proudly keeps a milk registry for his purebred cattle (*"De zuivere bron..."*). Dutch soil is described as flowing into the purebred cows whose health, in turn, infuses their pure milk and ultimately feeds the strength of the "Germanic spirit" and *"volkskracht"* ("nation's power") of the (White) Dutch people. This passage parallels the contemporary *Nederland draait op zuivel* campaign, except that it overtly reiterates a racial rhetoric that usually remains latent. Here, we see spelled out something intrinsic in many of the milk campaigns previously discussed—that milk signified Whiteness and that it not only served to affectively consolidate national identity, but also racial identity.

Milk is negotiated discursively through ideas of purity and hygiene, calculability and economic profit, and such ideas materialized in the breeding of cows and the production of milk. The dairy industry creates hyperproductive beings in one very specific environment with one particular goal—producing the most milk. In her seminal work *Beasts of Burden* (2017), writer, activist, and artist Sunaura Taylor addresses how the animal agricultural industry generates disability. Writing at the convergence of disability studies, animal ethics, and ecofeminism, Taylor elucidates the material interwovenness of various dis/abled bodies. Namely, the milk industry normalizes and commercializes forms of impairment, making the disabled animal body productive and desirable while simultaneously obscuring that disablement. By specifically selecting the genes of cows who produce the most milk, their udders become almost too heavy for their bodies (Taylor, *Beasts of Burden* 32). Aside from their congenital corporeal status as the result of rigorous breeding practices, many cows suffer from psychological distress and additional ailments. A healthy cow in a factory farm is an oxymoron (Somers and Soldatic 38). The material environment of the factory farm is in itself disabling, with small enclosures that inhibit movement and slippery, feces-laden floors that cripple cows. Whereas cows can live up to twenty years, cows in the dairy industry are "milked to death" in a matter of a few years, easily replaced by one of the many female calves they give birth to.

Taylor also addresses the effect on humans performing manual labor on farms and in slaughterhouses, who are disproportionally exposed to distressing conditions. The milk industry relies on low-paid migrant labor, where the proximity to impaired and dead animals places them at greater risk of zoonotic diseases and dangerous pathogens and where the high-paced machinery and pressure to be ever more productive leads to bodily injuries (Timmermans and Clevers). Pollution and antibiotic resistance generated through factory farming put the health of many more people at risk (Marchese and Hovorka 3). Milk is heralded as the key to productivity, health, and able-bodiedness, but it also brings illness, disability, and death to those implicated in its production. Arguably, the "thingness" of milk is present both

---

ideology. Blut und Boden became a key slogan in Nazi ideology, legitimizing the implementation of unspeakable violence.

in its excess—the surplus of expendable (animal and human) bodies it creates, and in its latency—the underlying senses of White supremacy that easily transpire.

Conclusion

In this essay, I have sought to understand what is made with the material of milk and what the material itself is made of. Milk as a material is configured vis-à-vis specific bodies, enabling certain (able, White, human) bodies to be affectively aligned with Dutch national identity, while other bodies are made disposable. The cultivation of the perfect dairy cow has changed their physicality to a point where their bodies support a kind of material determinism, confined in their flesh to fulfill the role that was instilled in their very anatomy through decades of selective breeding. Exploring these aspects in tandem shows how a bodily substance is both made and expected to make others. Within the vast state-sponsored promotion of milk as a vital material for the health of the nation and its corporeal constituents, we can sense that milk's visceral connection to other—human and nonhuman—bodies is never far away. The health and productivity ascribed to milk ingestion by humans stand in stark contrast to the reality of a cow's existence. In the matrix of making and unmaking desirable corporealities and various degrees of able-bodiedness, some material realities remain largely unseen.

Works Cited

Ahmed, Sara. "Affective Economies." *Social Text*, vol. 22, no. 2, 2004, pp. 117–39.
Barthes, Roland. *Mythologies*. Translated by Richard Howard and Annette Lavers. Hill and Wang, 2012.
Bauman, Zygmunt. *Modernity and the Holocaust*. Polity Press, 1989.
Brown, Bill. "Thing Theory." *Critical Inquiry*, vol. 28, no. 1, 2001, pp. 1–22.
"'De Melkweg' trok meer dan 125.000 bezoekers." *Het Binnenhof*, 9 July 1953.
"De Zuiveltentoonstelling in Berlijn: Hoe het gras in drinkbare melk verandert." *Haagsche Courant*, 25 August 1937.
"De Zuivelweek." *De Gelderlander*, 24 July 1936, p. 9.
"De zuivere bron...." *De Misthoorn*, 26 October 1940.
"Ere-Brigadier Klaas Bloot beloont moedige M-brigadier." *Het Vaderland*, 9 April 1960, p. 10.
"EU-subsidies voor Nederlandse vlees- en zuivelbedrijven: Onderzoek naar de miljoenensubsidies voor de productie en promotie van dierlijke producten." Report. *Dier en Recht: Advocaat van de Dieren*, Amsterdam, 2021.

Ingold, Tim. "Toward an Ecology of Materials." *Annual Review of Anthropology*, vol. 41, 2012, pp. 427–42.
Marchese, Alyssa, and Alice Hovorka. "Zoonoses Transfer, Factory Farms and Unsustainable Human-Animal Relations." *Sustainability*, vol. 14, 2022.
"Meer melkvee, forse toename melkproductie." *Centraal Bureau voor de Statistiek*, 28 October 2015.
"Met melk meer mans." *Het Vaderland*, 17 November 1956.
"Met melk meer mans." *Provinciale Drentsche en Asser Courant*, 16 June 1956, p. 2.
"Met melk meer mans." *Trouw*, 20 October 1956, p. 5.
"Nederland Draait Op Zuivel." Campaign. *Nederlandse Zuivel Organisatie (NZO)*, January 2020.
"Nederlandse landbouwproductie 1950–2015." *Centraal Bureau voor de Statistiek*, 31 January 2017.
Reinders, Pim, and Aad Vernooij. *Alles van Melk: Geschiedenis van de Nederlandse Zuivelindustrie*. WBooks, 2013.
Somers, Kelly, and Karen Soldatic. "Productive Bodies: How Neoliberalism Makes and Unmakes Disability in Human and Non-human Animals." *Disability and Animality: Crip Perspectives in Critical Animal Studies*, edited by Stephanie Jenkins et al., Routledge, 2020, pp. 35–56.
Taylor, Sunaura. "Animal Crips." *Journal for Critical Animal Studies*, vol. 12, no. 2, 2014, pp. 95–117.
———. *Beasts of Burden: Animal and Disability Liberation*. The New Press, 2017.
Theunissen, Bert and Inge Jansen. "Hoe de Nederlandse melkveerassen ontstonden en wat dat betekent voor hun behoud als levend erfgoed." *Tijdschrift voor Geschiedenis*, vol. 133, no. 2, 2020, pp. 279–302.
Timmermans, Chiel, and Richard Clevers. "Misstanden vleessector onder druk verzwegen." *Het Parool*, 11 July 2020.
Zelinger, Amir. "Race and Animal-breeding: A Hybridized Historiography." *History and Theory*, vol. 58, no. 3, 2019, pp. 360–84.
"Zuivelpropaganda tijdens de Vierdaagsche." *De Tijd: Godsdienstig-Staatkundig Dagblad*, 22 July 1936.

12. Wool

Michiel Scheffer

During the spring of 2022, there was much commotion in the Netherlands about the vast quantity of Dutch wool that was being thrown away. Anger about the wasting of wool led to a march in the former wool city of Tilburg. It was also a topic at the Dutch Design Week in Eindhoven later that year.

In this chapter, I argue that the wasting of wool was mistakenly attributed to the emergence of fast fashion and/or to the shift of manufacturing to China; and that the debate, both in the media and amongst academics, demonstrated a disregard for the materiality of wool. Indeed, the main reason why wool is discarded in many European countries is because breeders chose quality of meat over quality of wool. Wool is defined by its fiber length, its fineness, and its strength. These three variables determine the value (and hence the price) of the fibers. Wool is a long fiber, between five and nine centimeters. The longer fiber gives less pilling and greater longevity. Wool has a fineness between fifteen and forty microns (μm) and higher quality wool fabrics (measured in gr/m) require fibers below twenty microns. Fibers above thirty microns are only usable as filling material or in the production of carpets. Additionally, whereas in the 1960s, the majority of suits were made using fabrics of 500gr/m with fibers over twenty-five microns, the current standard for suit fabric is approximately 240gr/m and fibers below twenty microns (Scheffer, *Trading Places* 113). The dominant Dutch sheep breed, Texels, produces the coarser wool qualities, whereas finer qualities require Merino sheep (the meat of which is considered less tasty) as mainly held in Australia.

Coarse wool itches, as some people may remember from the post-World War II years, especially garments made from used blankets. However, coarse wool was not always discarded. In 1970, it represented forty percent of world wool production and was used in blankets, felts, coarser knitwear, coats, and carpets (Burlet). More recently, however, the demand for coarser qualities has dropped. For example, hardly anyone carries a blanket in their car anymore now that cars are well heated and break down less frequently, thus no longer leaving people literally out in the cold. Similarly, in their centrally heated homes, people today sleep under duvets instead of blankets; and better heating and insulation have made the wearing of thick, heavy knitwear largely superfluous. Coats are more often made from synthetic fibers, for a more casual or sporty look. Wool carpets are a luxury, and most often replaced by cheaper, stronger, and fireproof polyamide carpets, or by hard floors.

Above all, the debate on wasted wool revealed the conflict between the visual representation of fashion and the materiality of textiles. The simple reason why wool is discarded is because it is technically no longer suitable for textile use. Wool from sheep kept for meat or milk production is too coarse to be used in the manufacture of clothing. Some coarse wools can be used in the production of tweed fabrics, however, the demand for such fabrics, especially for jackets, is rather limited, as it has a very specific aesthetic and function. Tweed may be the fabric of choice for the landed gentry, especially in a hunting context, but it is much less suited to everyday use in centrally heated offices. However, the perception of value associated with tweed is only partly a consequence of representation (the landed gentry at the weekend); it is also the result of material factors, such as the properties of wool and its material processing.

Understanding the Material Characteristics of Wool

The limitations of using all kinds of wool can only be understood from grasping the material characteristics of wool. Wool comes in different fineness and length. It is sheared mainly from sheep and goats, and for some very fine qualities, from rabbits and llamas. Some animals are specifically bred for wool. Goats are kept for cashmere and mohair, llamas for alpaca and vicuña. These animals produce very long and fine hairs to be used in luxury menswear. The Merino sheep in Australia produces wool that can be used in most quality apparel. All of the animals named above are farmed for their wool, with shearing done yearly during their lives. Meat is in effect merely a by-product. In contrast, in Europe, sheep are mainly kept for their meat, their milk and wool constituting by-products. Wool from these animals is used as filling material for mattresses, duvets, and cushions, however, as production exceeds demand, most of the wool produced is now thrown away.

Wool processing is labor and resource intensive (Burlet) and shearing needs to be done by experts. Furthermore, the wool has to be graded by quality as different parts of the animal's body produce different qualities of wool. These tops are then cleaned of fats and dirt (grass, mud, and feces) by combing, washing, and carbonizing them. Depending on the fiber type, the wool then needs to be combed (to select the longer fibers) and/or carded (to disentangle and mix the fibers into a web or so-called sliver). The resulting fiber is then ready to be roved, spun, twinned, woven, or knitted, and to be dyed and finished to make a softer fabric. Wool is spun in so-called long frames (compared to short frames for cotton). The weaving process must be done at lower speeds than for cotton or synthetic fibers, which further increases the price of wool products, in addition to which the finishing of wool fabrics is also more complex than for cotton. Wool textiles, because of their complexity and the interlinkages of the different production sequences, were preferably made in vertically integrated mills or in districts of firms covering the whole supply chain.

The seasonal character of wool, the complexity of manufacturing, and its high cost make wool unsuitable for fast fashion. As a result, wool is mainly used for men's suits, high-end knitwear, and luxury carpets. Today, wool represents only one percent of the world's fiber use, compared to twenty percent before WWI. So, it has become a rather a niche product with its own dynamics, less exposed to mass market trends than other fibers, such as cotton. Wool is expensive: some five to ten times more expensive than cotton or polyester (Harmsen), which together now represent eighty-five percent of the fibers used in textile production. Fast fashion relies much better on cotton, polyester, or viscose fabrics, which can be printed or embroidered.

Wool production conforms to a specific pattern of globalization. Although China is now a major player in all stages of wool production, Italy is still the leading producer of high-end woolen and worsted products. Europe still leads the world in the manufacture of tailored clothing: Biella concentrates the top end of fine worsteds, combed wool yarns, and fabrics whereas Prato is a leader in the processing of regenerated wool: discarded garments (often made from Biella fabrics) that are recycled for yarns for knitwear or for coarser fabrics for coats or tweed-type fabrics. No other large wool districts have survived in the EU, although single isolated firms exist, and there is a revival of small-scale wool craft initiatives in many EU countries.

The reduction in the micronage and weight per meter of fabrics has been made possible by the breeding of sheep toward finer fleeces, better selection and grading of woolen tops, and better combing and spinning methods. Wool has thus become a luxury product and no longer a necessary means of surviving poorly heated houses and outdoor cold. In the 1990s, wool came to be considered mainly from an aesthetic visual perspective, with increased interest in the meaning of fabric patterns (also called "weaves") such as pied-de-poule, Prince de Galles, herringbones, and caviar. Often blended with silk or, more cheaply, with polyamide, wool represented an immaterial lightness of being—further enabled, for example, by Giorgio Armani's skill to drape and structure jackets with minimal lining and interlining. The visual effect is thus double: the weave or pattern that enhances a three-dimensional look, and the drape, either close to the body or enabling a wave effect (Scheffer, "Fashion Design").

With the emergent focus on sustainability, the material itself is making a comeback, demanding a better understanding of the intricacies of sheep and shearing, and of the various merits of carding and combing. While the wool industry has almost disappeared from cities that previously formed the backbone of the industrial revolution—cities such as Aachen, Roubaix, Bradford, and Tilburg (Scheffer, *Fatal Clusters*)—there are dreams of, and policies for, strategic autonomy (as presented in the EU textile strategy in 2022) in Europe that are symbolized by the Merino sheep of the Camargue, the tweed weavers of the Hebrides, and numerous local artisanal initiatives from the outskirts of Amsterdam to the Lüneburger Heide, and from Grasse to Catalunya. All of the above, however, must first overcome the fact that we have lost a thorough understanding of the materiality of wool and of the physical and chemical processes needed to obtain an acceptable product. Terms such as sheering, scouring, carding, combing, warp, weft, gauges, singeing, and selvages have all but disappeared and are better known in a figurative rather than literal sense. In order to rebuild value chains, their literal meanings and material effects need to be grasped.

Understanding Materials to Understand Culture

As Anneke Smelik argues in an article on polyester, we have to understand the materiality of our products to understand cultural change. Fashion derives its significance and its impact from the transformation of the human imagination into images and texts. In an era of supposed abundance and ephemerality, almost everything seemed possible. Indeed, after the liberalization of the textile trade in 2005, a vast choice of materials, the abundance of cheap labor in Asia, and pockets of skills in Europe provided a palette of materials that could form the palimpsest for any fashion discourse. In that context, fashion became an endless re-combination of well-known features (Sapir). However, due to the disruption of global supply chains and increasing production costs in Asia, it is now imperative we make a sustainable turn. While manufacturing in Europe declined between 1960 and 2015, the material limitations of products become ever more urgent to understand.

What may this understanding entail? First, it needs to start with a basic understanding of organic chemistry, as all textiles derive from polymers, which are built from carbon atoms combined with hydrogen, oxygen, and nitrogen. The properties of textiles derive from the chemical structure of these polymers. Second, we need to understand that these polymers need to be extracted or constructed from biomass (instead of petroleum). However, we also need to understand the production processes that may add or remove properties that are material (e.g., softness) or that have immaterial significance (e.g., colors with symbolic meaning, such as tartans). Third, we therefore need to understand the industrialization and economics of polymer and fiber production. The combination of properties and processes increases costs and defines the value or the perception of value to the consumer.

Value in products is partly material and partly immaterial. The material value comes from the costs of inputs (raw material, processing, and energy) and of labor processes. The immaterial value derives from design, branding, and marketing. They are both elastic: sensitive to cost competition (thus driven downwards) and to differentiation (thus driven upwards). Scale reduces costs, but also reduces exclusivity, and hence, value. Exclusivity (as well as scarcity), conversely, increases costs but also increases value. Luxury derives from both variables: the use of costly materials (so-called *matériaux nobles*) and processes (e.g., made-to-measure), and thus a degree of exclusivity, but also an intensive mobilization of brand value, for instance through logos. In a strategy of global presence, scale can be achieved by a global presence combined with exclusivity, as each store has only a few items of each style. Therefore, in luxury products, price elasticity due to immaterial factors is larger than for basic products in which material properties take precedence. The topic of price elasticity in relation to material and/or immaterial properties is under-researched. Consultants have often used an educated guess of a fifteen percent price premium for each extra material feature (Scheffer, *Trading Places*). Fiber manufacturers use the same benchmark. What value an immaterial feature or the combination of adding material and immaterial features actually adds to the product for consumers has not been measured or studied.

In the case of wool, the raw material and the labor-intensive nature of processing drive up costs. For instance, the small scale of Harris Tweed® production, but also the mobilization of geographically unique features (i.e., Scotland's rolling hills), create an exclusivity that might justify a high price. While wool is far more expensive than polyamide or polyester, it also has an exclusivity in both scale and a narrative that can justify a higher price—all the more so if used in tartan designs, thus strengthening a Scottish narrative, or if tailored in a made-to-measure process. In terms of use value, wool production in Europe delivers qualities that are too coarse to justify high prices. Therefore, the price and poor intrinsic value need to be compensated with an appealing narrative. In the case of Harris Tweed®, the narrative that creates coherence between sheep grazing in the highlands and a craft-wise production in the Hebrides, leading to a product representing the looks of the British landed gentry, serves to justify a price gap with synthetic fibers, but also with high-quality industrial wool.

Use value and the value attached to material properties also possess a cultural dimension. In European culture, wool's softness and, consequently, drapability, are highly appreciated, while in Japan crispiness and stiffness are preferred. These preferences lead to higher valuation for hemp and flax in Japan compared to Europe, where high prices in wool are usually associated with softness and fineness. Cotton and polyester, having far lower costs, but also lower prices, are largely appreciated for their comfort properties and easy maintenance (Shishoo), although they also have shorter lifespans and shed micro-fibers. They have mass appeal because of the combination of materials costs and well-accepted properties, such as comfort and easy care.

The appreciation of material and immaterial values is particularly relevant in relation to the transition the world has to make toward a fossil-free economy. By 2050, all textiles will have to be biobased. Wool could be a part of that story, but also linen and hemp have to extend their niche appeal. Cellulosic, wood-based fibers will grow in market share, while cotton production will remain stable (Harmsen). In contrast, polyesters and polyamides will have to be replaced by biopolymers. These biopolymers are likely to offer less performance than polyester. In any case, these materials may be more expensive than the current fibers. Is the urgency of sustainability going to be enough to convince consumers to pay a higher price? How much do materiality and materials (better properties) count? Or should brand appeal or design enhance the materials' immaterial value? This opens a field of research in which researchers in cultural studies, polymer chemistry, and textile technology should work together with economists and marketing researchers. The work of Anneke Smelik, for instance on Dutch fashion and sustainability, opened that avenue, but there is a long march ahead. Better put on a good woolly for the walk!

Works Cited

Burlet, Jean-Etienne. *La laine et l'industrie lainière*. Presses Universitaires de France, 1972.

Harmsen, Paulien, et al. "Textiles for Circular Fashion: The Logic behind Recycling Options." *Sustainability*, vol. 13, no. 17, 2021, p. 9714. https://doi.org/10.3390/su13179714.

Sapir, Edgar. *Anthropologie*. Tome 1, *Culture et personnalité*. Seuil, 1967.

Scheffer, Michiel. *Trading Places: Fashion, Retailers, and the Changing Geography of Clothing Production*. 1992. Utrecht U, PhD dissertation.

———. "Fashion Design and Technologies in a Global Context." *The Fabric of Cultures: Fashion, Identity, and Globalization*, edited by Eugenia Paulicelli and Hazel Clark, Routledge, 2008, pp. 128–43.

———. "Fatal Clusters: Tilburg, The Evolutionary Pattern of the Tilburg Wool Industry." *Comeback Cities: Transformation Strategies for Former Industrial Cities*, edited by Nienke van Boom and Hans Mommaas, Rotterdam NAI Publishers, 2009, pp. 202–17.

Shishoo, Roshan. "Importance of Mechanical and Physical Properties of Fabrics in the Clothing Manufacturing Process." *International Journal of Clothing Science and Technology*, vol. 7, no. 2/3, 1995, pp. 35–42.

Smelik, Anneke. "Polyester: A Cultural History." *Fashion Practice*, forthcoming.

Part VI: Affordances of Edible Matter

13. Yes, There Are No Bananas

Timotheus Vermeulen

A man strolls across the boardwalk. He is wearing an ill-fitting black suit and a thin tie. Bowler atop his head. Cane in one hand. In the other: a banana. He stops, peels the banana. Takes a bite. A second later, another mouthful, then carelessly drops the peel on the pavement. The man checks the sole of his left shoe and sets off to continue on his way. But as he takes his first step his right foot slips on the dropped peel, and in a single continuous motion he falls on his back.

This is a description of a scene from Charlie Chaplin's 1915 short *By the Sea*, but it might just as well have recounted a sequence from another Chaplin film, *The Circus*, or indeed, with some minor adjustments, instances from Samuel Beckett's play *Krapp's Last Tape*, a *Donald Duck* cartoon, the video game *Mario Kart*, any one of a hundred *American Funniest Home Videos*, the Adam Sandler comedy *Billy Madison*, the puppet show *Sesame Street*, or an early twentieth-century Billy Watson cabaret act. The "banana peel gag" is such a cultural commonplace that the moment we see a dropped banana peel on our screen, on stage, or on the pages of a comic book, we assume someone will slip on it—the vaudeville relative of Anton Chekhov's gun. Indeed, even at the time that Chaplin performed the gag it was already such a cliché that his contemporary Buster Keaton in *The High Sign* made a point of dropping a banana peel precisely so as not to slip on it.

In this essay I consider the role—and thus the ontology—of the banana in the banana peel gag and cultural narratives like it. For the banana is not just an inspiration to slapstick comedy. Few fruits seem to speak to our imagination as much as the banana. We invoke the banana to talk about ecological devastation ("Panama disease") and sexual potency ("is that a banana in your pocket or are you just happy to see me?"); corporate capitalism ("banana barons") and civil disobedience (the Guatemalan coup of the 1950s, prompted by disagreement over crops); praise ("top banana") but also disdain ("banana republic"); peace, prosperity, and joy (Victorian postcards) as well as bad luck (the fisherman's tale about bananas on a fishing boat) and depression (the ironic use of the song "yes, we have no bananas" during the 1930s Outdoor Relief protests in Belfast); wars (the "banana wars"), violence (the pretense that the banana is a gun), racism (the racial slur "banana" for Asian-Americans; audiences at football games in Europe throwing bananas at black players), exoticism (impressionist paintings using the banana as symbol of a pre-civilized existence), sexist representation (Josephine Baker's banana dress, Chiquita's caricature of Carmen Miranda as exotic, sexy Latina) and exploitation (the so-called Banana Bar in Amsterdam in the 1990s, a well-known sex club where women performed sexual acts with bananas) (for detailed accounts of many of the above, see Jenkins; Koeppel; Lovell; Piatti-Farnell; Wiley). The recently closed Washington Banana Museum in Auburn, WA, which I imagine the reader is as surprised to learn as I was existed at all, held over 6000 cultural representations of the banana (Lovell). The banana, writes cultural historian Lorna Piatti-Farnell, is an "omnipresent icon" (103). What I am interested in is the relation between this diverse cultural genealogy and the edible yellow, elongated, and curved berry from which it derives. How are these incomparable stories all afforded by the qualities, properties, and history of a single berry; and how in turn is that berry's unity of identity maintained across such diverse accounts? I consider these questions by looking at two versions of the same joke a hundred years apart: Chaplin's above skit, and Maurizio Cattelan's art installation *Comedian* from 2019.

In posing these questions, I'm inquiring after the relationship between "objects" and "things"—as well as, more generally, metaphor and materiality. Following, of course, the philosopher none of us ever really knows how to deal with, Martin Heidegger, and more recently theorists like Bill Brown and Tim Ingold, I take object as a material presence understood exclusively in relation to a subject, which is to say as use, or value, something "ready-at-hand": an actualization of one or some of its material affordances. The banana we buy at the grocer's is an object: we buy it to eat it, actualizing its affordances of sweetness, softness, edibility, nutrition, etc. In contrast, a thing is a material presence before, between and/or after it has a function, before one or some of its affordances are actualized as this or that at the expense of all the other possible uses. As Brown writes, a thing is what we encounter when an object stops "working for us: when the drill breaks, the car stalls, when the windows get filthy" (4). It is a relationality of the thing's material affordances to usages that is as of yet indeterminate, not delimited by this or that context of signification. A thing, thus, is not an essence as much as a contingency: a process and multiplicity; all that its material affords it to be. Objects are to things what crystals are to air in JD Ballard's novel *Crystal World*: they fixate what is in flux, reduce a multiplicity to a singularity, close in and off what was an opening onto. Brown writes that a thing is a suspended object (suspending the relation to a subject). But in this sense, an object is thus also a suspended thing (it forestalls becoming).

In our experience, the thing comes after the object: it is the object's limit, where the relationship between object and subject breaks down. Ontologically, however, it precedes it, too. The banana's objecthood is afforded by the banana's thingness, even if it is irreducible to it. Since the object is a relation between a thing and a subject, it crystallizes the thing and its affordances only insofar as it can be seen from the subject's interests, angle, distance, embodied qualities, cultural context, etc. It is both more than the thing (since in its relation with the subject it extends beyond the thing), and less (since it is not all of the thing, not all of its material affordances).

In the banana peel gag the banana is less than a thing in that it relies on some but not all of the berry's qualities: the banana skin's divisibility (the skin can peel off and partition into separate shards), its durability (the skin takes time to disintegrate), and its slipperiness (the peel's insides turn gradually smoother and moister as they rot). Yet it is also more than a thing, since the reason these qualities historically have been recognized in the banana (and the orange) as opposed to, say, the apple, or blackberry, is related to the berry's complex relation to the societies in which the gag was developed. As the food journalist Dan Koeppel has shown, the banana peel's divisibility, durability, and slipperiness were turned into a comedic trope in response to the berry's mass import to and subsequent ubiquity in nineteenth-century America. Cultivated on an industrial scale, this non-native fruit was so popular that its skins soon littered the streets. Reports of people slipping on them and injuring themselves appeared in newspapers across the country. Rumor has it that people even died (Koeppel). The banana became a symbol thus not just of the successes but also the perceived excesses of modernity: a speeding up of time and a contraction of space, an emphasis on movement and exchange, mass production and crowded centralized consumer hubs—cities. "On almost every corner," one city newspaper supposedly lamented in 1870, "there is a fruit stand, around which the pavements are littered with these dangerous parings, and not a day passes that someone does not receive a fall from stepping on them" (qtd. in Stans). Many cities passed laws to forbid people from disposing of peels on the street, New York systematized its garbage disposal and initiated the country's first recycling project as a result of the problem (Koeppel). The banana peel gag historically objectifies the banana not just because the banana skin is divisible, but because this multiplication is perceived as a hazard; because its divisibility, that is, confirms a distinct cultural discourse: xenophobia. The fear of the proliferating exotic berry becomes a fear of the other. The banana in the banana peel gag is thus both more than the thing, since its nature, co-determined as it is by cultural discourses, is irreducible to the berry's material affordances, and less, since it actualizes but three of those affordances.

There is no point in Chaplin's rendition of the banana peel gag where the banana is not an object, is not at once more and less than a thing. The banana is so culturally overdetermined that it is always already an object or rather a series of objects; its thingness is forever forestalled even if it is in each objective iteration intimated. Whilst Chaplin eats the banana, it is an object of consumption, for him as much as for the viewers, actualizing the thing's affordances of edibility. The moment he drops the banana skin on the pavement, which is to say the moment the banana is discarded as an object of consumption, is however not a suspension of the banana's relation to the subject, but a form of recycling. As soon as the peel is dropped, it becomes a "peel" one might slip over: another object, initiating another relationship to a subject, deferring but drawing on other qualities of the thing: its divisibility, slipperiness, etc. The abovementioned history matters here, as do genre expectations, since this gag is more likely to take place in a slapstick comedy than in a Western—and in fact I would say that even as the banana is an object of consumption, it is also always already an object of comedy. But Chaplin's performance plays a part, too. The comedian does not just let the skin slip from his fingers. He shifts the object from one hand to the other (explicating its handholdable size, friendliness of touch, and lightness) whilst repositioning his body toward the camera, and throws it up in the air (signaling at once that the banana affords to be thrown, and that, as the pun goes, "time flies like an arrow; fruit flies like a banana"). The set-up alerts us to and anticipates the banana's new role in this narrative, the changed context. The banana peel gag's banana suspends not the object but the thing, continually slipping from one object cycle to the next like a moebius loop, actualizing ever new affordances.

A hundred years on, Maurizio Cattelan's sculptural installation *Comedian* (2019) inverts Chaplin's joke. The artist taped a banana to a white wall at Miami Basel with silver duct tape. It came with a manual for the buyer which stipulated the banana should be replaced every ten days: bananas rot, after all, in the process changing color, form, and consistency, among other things. Here, as the work's title suggests, the object figures in a comedic context. It pits the thing's qualities, conventions, and history against the aesthetic and socio-economic context of this art fair: rot versus collecting, low culture versus high culture, wide availability versus exclusivity, bottom price versus high market value. Moreover, though the banana's material evidently affords taping it to a wall for a maximum of ten days, one cannot but wonder whether the tape affords loosening and refastening repeatedly. The banana is explicitly the object over which the whole of this exclusive and self-important scene for the very rich might slip—and which it might be argued to have achieved, since the installation sold for 150.000 USD. Yet before two days had passed, another artist tore the banana off the wall and ate it. The banana, in other words, in a single move had slipped, or, more accurately, had been grabbed, from one context to another—it had become another object, actualizing another material affordance.

What my concise discussion of the banana's recursive objectification in the banana peel gags of Chaplin and Cattelan shows is that the banana may well never be a thing. Even where it "stops working," "stalls," or "breaks," this is not so much an ontological disintegration (a change of planes, if you will) as a reconfiguration (a change on the same plane): we are not confronted with the banana as contingency or multiplicity, for all that its qualities might afford it to be in as of yet to be determined relationships, but as the actualization of one or some of its material affordances in a specific interaction. Of course, further study is required to test this hypothesis, of other cases and cultural tropes objectifying and de-objectifying alternative material affordances. But if the well-known song "Yes, there are no bananas" is anything to go by, we might have a hard time finding anywhere a banana is not always already a "banana." Indeed, as a new banana disease spreads across the continents, ruining crop after crop, there might soon be no bananas left at all.

Works Cited

Brown, Bill. "Thing Theory." *Critical Inquiry*, vol. 28, no. 1, 2001, pp. 1–22.
Heidegger, Martin. "The Thing." *Poetry, Language, Thought*, translated by A. Hofstadter, Harper and Row, 2001, pp. 161–84.
Ingold, Tim. "Materials against Materiality." *Archaeological Dialogues*, vol. 14, no. 1, 2007, pp. 1–16.
Jenkins, Victoria Scott. *Bananas: An American History*. Smithsonian Institution Press, 2000.
Koeppel, Dan. *Banana: The Fate of the Fruit That Changed the World*. Penguin, 2008.
Lovell, Ann Mitchell, curator. *The Washington Banana Museum: An Online Museum*, http://www.bananamuseum.com.
Piatti-Farnell, Lorna. *Banana: A Global History*. Reaktion, 2016.
Stans, Lea. "The History of Those Darn Banana Peels." *Silent-ology*, 1 April 2015, https://silentology.wordpress.com/2015/04/01/the-history-of-those-darn-banana-peels/
Wiley, James. *The Banana: Empires, Trade Wars and Globalization*. U of Nebraska P, 2008.

14. Coca(ine)

Brigitte Adriaensen

According to Canadian anthropologist Wade Davis, "Coca is no more cocaine than potatoes are vodka" (18).[1] He seems to imply that we should disconnect cocaine as an object from its material origin, the coca plant. The reason why he makes such a strong statement is his aversion to the stimulant cocaine and the violent conflict it has given rise to, together with a profound wish to protect the coca plant and the indigenous cultures attached to it.

Cocaine was discovered by Albert Niemann, a German graduate student, in 1860. Among critics, the reduction of cocaine to a capitalist commodity is common, as is the veneration of the coca leaf as a raw, natural material—one that carries with it a distinctive spiritual power. Coca and cocaine are thus seen as two entirely different things with separate histories (Britto 14). From such a perspective, the "war on drugs" rhetoric unjustly demonizes both the alkaloid and the plant. Or, to put it differently: the forced eradication of the coca leaf is the consequence of a flawed strategy. Not only should the coca leaf not be reduced to its chemical derivate, cocaine (other uses are increasingly being explored), but also the eradication of the illegal drug traffic should be oriented toward decreasing consumption (in the Global North) instead of destroying production (in Latin America) (Davis 30).

Much can be said about this discussion, but first, it is useful to observe that the dichotomy between coca and cocaine breaks down if we take a closer look. The perception of the coca leaf as a "raw material" is problematic. As Adam Drazin states, it is necessary to attack "the myth of rawness," as it seems to be based on the "mistaken notion that materials are more 'natural' than objects" (24). This implies an "ideology of nature," according to which indigenous cultures are portrayed as a pristine territory with immaculate rituals.

In fact, the coca plant has always been part of cultural negotiation and gave way to different cultural processes and dynamics from as early as 2000 BC (Davis 24). The coca leaf was already a symbol of power and authority during the Inca empire. Later, yet long before cocaine became a global commodity, the Spanish converted the coca

---

1   All translations of Davis and other quotations from authors published in the special issue of OPCA are by the author.

leaf into merchandise. Today, indigenous communities in Bolivia, Peru, and Colombia are selling other products made from the coca leaf (coca tea, coca biscuits, etc.). While this is institutionally encouraged in Bolivia and Peru, where the coca leaf is protected as cultural heritage constitutionally and in law, the situation in Colombia is far more complex. The Nasa indigenous people from the Calderas *resguardo*[2] in Tierradentro launched the product Té Coca Nasa in 1999, which they wanted to bring onto the market, stimulating rural development in the region. However, in 2007 the Colombian Institute for the Control of Medicines and Food decided that the production and trade of products made from the coca leaf needed to be restricted to indigenous territories, which blocked the community's ambitions to develop a sustainable and profitable business model that could help them out of poverty. David Curtidor Argüello, one of the co-founders of the enterprise Coca Nasa, denounces the paternalism and the "microracisms" inherent in Colombian law (47). In his view, the court's decision to allow the use and commodification of the leaf only within indigenous territories does not recognize the community's intellectual and cultural ownership of the leaf. Limiting coca's use to the indigenous territories reduces the plant to a pristine, spiritual power, reinvigorating the colonial and racial power dynamics in which it is still entangled.

While the coca leaf is often stereotyped as the "raw material," cocaine is typically seen as essentially immaterial. In his book *Narcocapitalism*, the Belgian legal scholar Laurent de Sutter foregrounds an intrinsic relation between cocaine and capitalism, stating that "cocaine only exists in an economic system appropriate to its volatility, its illegality, its addictiveness and its immateriality" (43). Such a perspective renders cocaine essentially immaterial—a view countered by several historians who introduced commodity studies within drug studies. Using Wallerstein's world-systems theory as a source of inspiration, they began empirically analyzing how different substances, including peyote (Dawson), marihuana (Campos), and cocaine (Topik et al.), became crucially involved within the global commodity chains that were used to build the world economy from colonialism onward. In his groundbreaking monograph *Andean Cocaine: The Making of a Global Drug* (2008), historian Paul Gootenberg examines how coca developed into cocaine as a "glocal" commodity from a regional, national, and transnational perspective from 1850 to the present day. Taking his firm belief that "not all drug history originates in Washington" (Gootenberg and Campos 4) as his starting point, Gootenberg pays special attention to the development of crude cocaine in Peru as an intermediate substance from which the alkaloid can be extracted, and which largely facilitated the trade. His take on cocaine is also influenced by Appadurai's "social lives of things" and Kopytoff's "cultural biography" of commodities, as he analyses channels of both economic and noneconomic flows in

---

2   "*Resguardo*" is equivalent to the English "reservation" but has precise connotations in both colonial and republican terms, which is why it is used here instead of its English equivalent.

which, among others, politics, legal systems, and medicine play an important role. The agency of things, or affects circulated by those materials, are not part of his research: "In drug studies, commodity or material perspectives are sorely needed for cooling down the burning and distorting passions that often surround mind-altering, contested, forbidden goods" (Gootenberg, *Andean Cocaine* 8). He, therefore, proposes to treat "drugs as 'mere' commodities in the way they are built up and accepted like other exchangeable things and in the ways they acquire, carry, and convey meanings" (8).

A different approach to the materiality of cocaine can be found in the work of the Australian anthropologist Michael Taussig. In *My Cocaine Museum* (2004), he proposes to consider cocaine as a substance that "shapes the country" (11) and a fetish: "gold and cocaine are *fetishes*, which is to say substances that seem to be a good deal more than mineral or vegetable matter. They come across more like people than things, spiritual entities that are neither, and this is what gives them their strange beauty" (18). Taussig travels to the Southwest Pacific region in Colombia to see how cocaine—and coca—together with gold have impacted communities for many centuries and how they are part of what Tim Ingold calls the "meshwork of things" ("Toward an Ecology" 437).

Taussig is fascinated by the specific materiality of things. He proposes an ecology of things, foregrounding the affective relation between things and humans. In the following quote, he talks about the digging of gold, which takes center stage in *My Cocaine Museum*:

> it could also mean that the language of stories is the language of things, with a twist. And this twist is that the language of things is privy to the people who live day by day with those things, have been cruelly forced by circumstances of world history to work those things, and nevertheless eventually grow to regard these things with empathy, loyalty, and some fondness, even while hating them. (66)

Although Taussig mentions neither new materialism nor Bill Brown's work explicitly in his book, there seems to be a clear connection. In his 2001 article "Thing Theory," Brown not only refers to earlier work by Taussig but also holds a similar view on things and materiality: "The story of objects asserting themselves as things, then, is the story of a changed relation to the human subject and thus the story of how the thing really names less an object than a particular subject-object relation" (4).

Thinking about cocaine and coca as subject-objects, or as semi-subjects, is particularly interesting if we consider the stimulant's mind-expanding nature. Indeed, psychoactive plants such as the coca leaf, but also cocaine, not only invite us to think in terms of an ecology of things but also in terms of an ecology of mind. Ingold rephrases Andy Clark's theory of the "extended mind" as follows: "the theory postulates that the mind, far from being coextensive with the brain, routinely spills out into the environment" ("Toward an Ecology" 438). He adds that thanks to this "leakage of the mind," "the world becomes a kind of 'distributed mind'" (438). In fact, Ingold also insists on the leakage of *things* (438), but in the case of psychoactive plants, the question is whether *things and minds* can be neatly separated. Even if we do not all consume coca(ine), the same can be said of sugar, coffee, or tea, which are all psychoactive substances and stimulants. How could we actually think of our world without the agency of these substances on our energy levels and performance? To what extent did these substances determine world history, and should we not think *"from"* these materials instead of *"about"* them, as Ingold suggests (437)? Following Hermann Herlinghaus in this respect, "[n]arcotics were indispensable commodities and psychoactive *agents*, destined both to second the practices of colonization and subjugation, on the one hand, and become fuels of industrial civilization, on the other" (9; emphasis added). In other words, acknowledging the role of coca(ine) in the global chains of commodities should not lead us to ignore their own agency from a material perspective.

While I have enumerated several arguments why it seems contradictory to separate coca from cocaine, Davis' desire to separate the two materials is also understandable. In recent decades, not only cocaine but also the coca plant has become increasingly demonized in Colombia. For many years, the United States has financed the large-scale destruction of coca plantations through the use of the widely used herbicide glyphosate (known by its brand name Roundup). In 2006, for example, 172,000 hectares were fumigated with helicopters (Ramírez 38). Although glyphosate was declared a health risk by the World Health Organization in 2015, terrestrial fumigation continued ("Colombia Suspends"). When the rightwing president Iván Duque came to power in 2018, the use of the herbicide again increased significantly ("Colombia Coca"). Two weeks before handing over the government to the newly elected leftwing president Gustavo Petro, who had declared that he would stop fumigation during his term in office,[3] the former president bought 263,000 liters of the same herbicide from the American enterprise Del Monte Agrosciences SAS (Romero Peñuela). If Davis invites us to dissociate coca from cocaine, he does so because, in his eyes, the crusade against the coca plant is unfair and causes unnecessary damage. Moreover, this crusade limits coca to its alkaloid, while many other possible uses also exist.

---

3   In his first discourse to the General Assembly of the United Nations, on September 20, 2022, Gustavo Petro drew a clear parallel between the "failed war on drugs" and the destruction of the Amazonian Forest. His call to stop the war on drugs is also a call to save the plant ("Colombian President").

Davis' article was included in a recent special issue of the OPCA (Observatorio del Patrimonio Cultural y Arqueológico)[4] from 2020, entitled "Coca as Cultural Heritage: Perspectives and Tensions in Colombia." In this issue, the editors ask if the coca leaf should be designated as national cultural heritage in Colombia. They point out that it was hard to find authors willing (and daring enough) to participate in such a controversial issue. In their words, many would have been able to contribute in a significant way, but only a few were ready to do so because the topic, "as is the case with 'cholera' or 'pandemic', is marked by death" (4). Coca is taboo. So, why is this the case?

First and foremost, cocaine can be considered to have fueled the ongoing violence in Colombia since the 1960s. While the internal armed conflict was certainly not only about cocaine, the cocaine business was used by the various parties concerned as a means to fund their activities.

Second, the taboo surrounding coca as cultural heritage might also be linked to the Greek notion of "miasma." In *My Cocaine Museum*, Taussig introduces the concept to explain the force that breaks loose when a rule of importance within the community is broken. When this happens, "all hell breaks loose as a sacred barrier has been violated and pollution issues forth" (126). Could it be that the disruptive potential of the plant is so strong that a taboo emerges, which then makes it hard to deal with the topic?[5]

There is also a third reason. While cocaine is a product derived from the coca plant, the two have been consistently dissociated in cultural discourse, especially in Colombia. According to Colombian historian Lina Britto, the reason why Colombia became so strong in drug trafficking from the 1970s onward (rather than Bolivia or Peru), is because, in Colombia, illegal trafficking was taken up by middle-class *mestizo* communities from Medellín and Bogotá. According to Britto, it is therefore unsurprising that the illegal cocaine trade had its epicenter in Colombia: "Deprived of a historical legacy and a cultural heritage that gave symbolism to coca, those pioneers of the drug traffic did not see any problem in launching themselves to the conquest of the international market of the alkaloid once it started emerging in the 70s" (14).

In other words, in Colombia the cocaine business was dissociated from the coca leaf at the same time that indigenous communities were, for decades, made invisible and marginalized by the Colombian governments. The situation was different in other Andean countries, where the coca leaf has been related to indigenous cultures since colonial times. However, this does not mean that there was no racism

---

4 OPCA is an independent research institute that is associated with the Universidad de los Andes in Bogotá.
5 In the broader research project *Poison, Medicine or Magic Potion* (Adriaensen), in which this article is embedded, we aim to delve more deeply into indigenous views of the plant's spiritual power and agency.

involved: elites in Peru and Bolivia did not want to spoil their high-class reputation by trafficking a product associated with an inferior race and class. The point is that in Colombia, the middle-class *mestizos* managed to dissociate the business from the ancestral indigenous uses of the plant. For the same reason, the drug business is typically associated with the *mestizo* urban drug culture (in television series, music, or films), while the coca plant itself—with its own history and alternative uses—is often kept out of sight. In this sense, talking about the future of Colombia means building a more inclusive society and acknowledging that not only the peasant *mestizo* communities (who are the main cultivators of the plant), but also the indigenous communities have to be heard. Coming back to Britto, "the destiny of the plant is the destiny of democracy in Colombia" (15) if we understand democracy, in the editors' sense, as "a political agreement regarding the plurality and the protection of the incredible diversity of worlds of meaning and knowledges that conform the social fabric and the historical framework of the nation" (4).

So, how can the label of "cultural heritage" contribute to saving the plant, and thus Colombian democracy? The editors of OPCA's special issue propose to nuance the rather static notion of "cultural heritage" by pointing out that the coca leaf should not be considered a substantive, but rather an adjective. Their argument is that "regardless of the activism of its producers and managers, it is an attribute that is negotiated, a transaction motivated and directed to capitalize symbols rather than an essence proper of the savage state of places, objects, and practices" (Jaramillo and Salge Ferro 4). In fact, they argue that the question is not whether coca is heritage or not. Indeed, the condition for talking about heritage is not "something that preexists and thus can be discovered under the infinite layers of time, but rather something that is constructed in the social concert" (4). In this way, the editors argue that Colombia needs to recognize coca as cultural heritage. At the same time, they acknowledge that the coca leaf has no essence, and is thus not an object that can be objectified by humankind. They seem to approach Ingold's view on the properties of materials, when he states that these cannot be "identified as fixed, essential attributes of things, but are rather processual and relational. They are neither objectively determined nor subjectively imagined but practically experienced" ("Materials" 14).

However, there is a clear difference between Ingold's statement and the editors' issue. Although they do not specify what kind of heritage they speak about in either the title or the introduction, one of the contributions, written by lawyer Paula Aguirre Ospina and anthropologist David Ramírez Ramón, includes a clear defense of the coca leaf as *intangible* (in Spanish: "immaterial") cultural heritage, the aim of which is to "recognize, identify, and divulgate the cultural intangible manifestations that represent, under international standards, the cultural diversity of the human beings" (51). The authors of the article specify that according to Colombian law, the coca leaf itself cannot become *intangible cultural heritage*, as this concept is legally restrained to cultural uses and practices related to an object within a living community (55). However, from the perspective of the material turn within cultural studies, reducing the plant or leaf to an intangible status seems rather problematic. The plant's agency, as a psychoactive substance, is again relegated to the domain of "nature" and separated from the cultural sphere in which it is embedded.

For now, we can conclude that the coca leaf and cocaine are both things and materials that are closely intertwined. They serve as important materials of spiritual, indigenous cultures, but have also been decisive in local and global cultures of drug consumption, and in this respect, they seem to have led to different cultural expressions. However, as materials themselves, they have also been invested with cultural meanings and prejudices, which have necessarily affected legislation, trade, and power dynamics. While coca and cocaine have been studied mainly as commodities, future research should delve more into their status as semi-subjects and especially their agency within the expanded-mind theory. How can we perceive the impact, not only of coca and cocaine *as matter* but also as *psychoactive substances?* Indeed, we must go beyond studying their role within chains of commodities and networks or their status as "intangible cultural heritage" within Andean communities. If we want to understand and bring together the "two faces" and the "double history" of coca (Britto 9), we need to turn to the material properties of the plant as a substance and its psychoactive force within the *meshwork of things*.

Acknowledgment

This article is part of my research project *Poison, Medicine or Magic Potion*, funded by the Dutch Research Council. I am profoundly grateful to Anneke Smelik for her continuous support and intellectual input in the application process of this project.

Works Cited

Adriaensen, Brigitte. *Poison, Medicine or Magic Potion: Shifting Perceptions of Drugs in and from Latin America (1820–2020)*. Radboud University, 2022–2027. https://www.ru.nl/en/research/research-projects/poison-medicine-or-magic-potion.

Aguirre Ospina, Paula, and Ramírez Ramón, David. "Los usos ancestrales de la hoja de coca como patrimonio intangible de Colombia: un reconocimiento pendiente." *OPCA*, no. 17, 2020, pp. 40–50.

Appadurai, Arjun. 1986. "Commodities and the Politics of Value." Introduction. *The Social Life of Things: Commodities in Cultural Perspective*, edited by Arjun Appadurai, Cambridge UP, 1986, pp. 3–63.

Britto, Lina. "Historia doble de la coca." *OPCA*, no. 17, 2020, pp. 8–17.

Brown, Bill. "Thing Theory." *Critical Inquiry*, vol. 28, no. 1, 2001, pp. 1–22.

Campos, Isaac. *Home Grown: Marijuana and the Origins of Mexico's War on Drugs*. U of North Carolina P, 2012.

"Colombia Coca Crop: Trump Tells Duque to Resume Spraying." *BBC*, 3 Mar. 2020. https://www.bbc.com/news/world-latin-america-51722456.

"Colombian President Gustavo Petro Calls for an End to the War on Drugs in Historic UN Address." *Peoples Dispatch*, 20 Sept. 2022. https://peoplesdispatch.org/2022/09/20/colombian-president-gustavo-petro-calls-for-an-end-to-the-war-on-drugs-in-historic-un-address/.

"Colombia Suspends Spraying Illegal Coca Fields with Herbicide over Cancer Link." *The Guardian*, 15 May 2015. https://www.theguardian.com/world/2015/may/15/colombia-herbicide-glyphosate-coca-fields-cancer.

Curtidor Argüello, David. "La Coca, patrimonio de los pueblos: El usurpador eres tú." *OPCA*, no. 17, 2020, pp. 42–49.

Davis, Wade. "Sobre la coca y la cocaína." *OPCA*, no. 17, 2020, pp. 10–33.

Dawson, Alexander S. *The Peyote Effect: From the Inquisition to the War on Drugs*. U of California P, 2018.

Drazin, Adam. "To Live in a Materials World." Introduction. *The Social Life of Materials: Studies in Materials and Society*, edited by Adam Drazin and Susanne Küchler, Bloomsbury Academic, 2015, pp. 3–28.

Gootenberg, Paul. *Andean Cocaine: The Making of a Global Drug*. U of North Carolina P, 2008.

Gootenberg, Paul, and Isaac Campos. "Toward a New Drug History of Latin America: A Research Frontier at the Center of Debates." *Hispanic American Historical Review*, vol. 95, no. 1, 2015, pp. 1–35.

Herlinghaus, Hermann. *Narcoepics: A Global Aesthetics of Sobriety*. Bloomsbury, 2013.

Ingold, Tim. "Materials against Materiality." *Archaeological Dialogues*, vol. 14, no. 1, 2007, pp. 1–16.

———. "Toward an Ecology of Materials." *Annual Review of Anthropology*, vol. 41, 2012, pp. 427–42.

Jaramillo, Luis, and Manuel Salge Ferro. "La coca como patrimonio cultural: Perspectivas y tensiones en Colombia." *OPCA*, no. 17, 2020, pp. 4–7.

Kopytoff, Igor. "The Cultural Biography of Things: Commoditization as Process." *The Social Life of Things: Commodities in Cultural Perspective*, edited by Arjun Appadurai, Cambridge UP, 1986, pp. 64–92.

OPCA. *La coca como patrimonio cultural: Perspectivas y tensiones en Colombia*. 2020, no. 17.

Ramírez, María Clemencia. "Interculturalidad y replanteamiento del uso de la hoja de coca." *OPCA*, no. 17, 2020, pp. 34–41.

Romero Peñuela, Natalia. "Los 263.000 litros de glifosato que el gobierno Duque le dejará al de Petro." *El Espectador*, 31 July 2022. https://www.elespectador.com/c

olombia-20/conflicto/los-263000-litros-de-glifosato-que-el-gobierno-ivan-du
que-le-dejara-al-de-gustavo-petro/#.
Sutter, Laurent de. *Narcocapitalism*. Polity Press, 2018.
Taussig, Michael. *My Cocaine Museum*. U of Chicago P, 2004.
Topik, Steven, et al., editors. *From Silver to Cocaine: Latin American Commodity Chains and the Building of the World Economy, 1500–2000*. Duke UP, 2006.

# Part VII: Material Practices in Digital Culture

15. The Ephemeral Materiality of Sound

Vincent Meelberg

Can sound be considered material, even though it is often characterized as ephemeral and intangible? If we take Adam Drazin and Susanne Küchler's definition of material as a starting point, it may seem as if sound is not a material. According to Drazin, materials are specific categories of matter (xxxvii), with matter considered to be all the stuff around us, consisting of atoms and molecules. Sound can be considered the vibration of molecules, usually air molecules, but sound does not consist of these molecules themselves. Instead, sound is the act of vibration rather than a material that consists of atoms and molecules. In other words, sound is energy that makes materials like air vibrate.

Sound, however, does appear to have materiality. Christopher Cox defines sonic materiality as sound's "texture and temporal flow, its palpable effect on, and affection by the materials through and against which it is transmitted" (149). This definition is compatible with Tim Ingold's definition of materiality as the quality of something that manifests itself in the physical world ("Toward an Ecology" 439). Sound can make things happen and enable things to vibrate. As a result, even though sound as such is not material, it does have materiality. Sound itself seems intangible, but it can affect and make other objects and things vibrate, including human listeners. Sound is vibration, which is a temporal phenomenon, and the manner in which these vibrations manifest themselves as resonances constitutes the materiality of sound.

This almost paradoxical nature of sound and its materiality pose particular challenges for those who work with sound. Traditionally, composers have not worked with, or sculpted, sound directly. Instead, they used, and many still use, musical notation to create their musical works. As a result, they do not engage with actual sounds directly but work with visual representations of sounds. Only since the development of recording techniques have musical creators been offered the opportunity to work with and on sound more directly by manipulating recordings of sound.

Digitization has offered musical creators further possibilities to interact with sound in a far more direct way. When working with software programs that allow for sound manipulation, musical creators may experience the sensation of almost literally touching sound. The gestures with which these manipulations are executed result in a particular affective relationship between musical creators and the sounds they work with.

Moreover, digital technologies have radically changed the material nature of sound. Sound can be considered an intangible thing, where "thing" is conceived "not of an externally bounded entity, set over and against the world, but of a knot whose constituent threads, far from being contained within it, trail beyond, only to become caught with other threads in other knots" (Ingold, "Bringing Things" 4). As a thing, sound leaks, is an excess, and transcends categorization. Digitization, however, has turned sound into a tangible object that can be categorized, manipulated, and understood relatively unproblematically. Sound has become a "completed form" (Ingold, "Toward an Ecology" 439) that can be controlled. As a result, digitization has changed and expanded the affordances of sound for musical creators.

An example of a digital device that has changed the affordances of sound is the Tasty Chips GR-1 granular synthesizer. GR-1 is a sample-based digital device that allows users to load audio samples, feed live audio through it, and manipulate it by dividing it into smaller parts or grains. This process is called granulation and allows for changing the audio in ways that "still represent the original sample to a completely mangled and scattered manipulation of the original. Imagine what it would sound like if you heard thousands of little sound particles (grains) swarming around to reconstruct any sample you present to it [sic]. Depending on what source sample you want to use, results can be lovely, soft, and soothing but also chaotic, aggressive, and unpredictable and everything in between" ("GR-1 Granular synthesizer"). Granular synthesis, which is a digital technology, enables the manipulation of sound in many predictable and less predictable ways.

The YouTube review and tutorial of the GR-1 synthesizer done by Loopop in 2020 offer a good introduction to what this device is capable of and how to operate it. The video begins by providing an overview of the interface of the synthesizer. This interface enables a physical, embodied interaction by the user between the sounds that are created and the users' bodies, with embodied interaction understood as the creation, manipulation, and sharing of meaning through physical relations with artifacts (Dourish 125). An interface is a boundary between two areas or systems (Chatzichristodoulou and Zerihan 1). In the case of GR-1, the interface consists of a screen, twenty-five buttons, fourteen knobs, and eight sliders that together act as a boundary between the algorithms the synthesizer's firmware consists of and its user. This interface enables physical interaction through particular movements called gestures, which are physical actions through which human subjects structure their environment (Leman and Godøy 4) between the sounds and the users' bodies. At the same time, however, all interfaces put constraints on the kinds of choices their users can make.

When looking at the layout of the interface of GR-1, it immediately becomes apparent that the screen is a critical element. This screen enables the visual representation of the sounds processed in GR-1 and provides the user with visual feedback. Users can see their actions on the sounds, which helps them make musical choices. Between 1:40 and 2:30 in the Loopop video, for instance, the reviewer selects fragments of sound by moving the large horizontal slider located under the screen and, at the same time, looking at the screen, which displays both the waveform and the fragment that is currently selected by moving the slider. Listening seems to play a negligible role in this selection process. As GR-1 allows for the manipulation of sound through a visual representation of sound, the focus seems to be on what can be seen rather than what can be heard. In other words, what users of GR-1 actually manipulate via the device's interface are visual representations of sound in time. Nevertheless, GR-1 enables the manipulation of sound in ways that were impossible before, which is done via embodied interactions with the interface.

In the Loopop video, an example of creating new sounds with GR-1 can be found between 12:29 and 13:29, where the sound of a glass being tapped is transformed into a grainy drone sound. With the aid of GR-1, a short, high-pitched sound has been turned into a sustained, washy soundscape. As a result, the materiality of the sound has changed as well. After all, how a short, high-pitched sound vibrates radically differs from how a grainy, sustained drone sound resonates. The materiality of these sounds, considered as resonances that can be felt, has different affective qualities, with affection understood as the inducement of autonomous bodily reactions when confronted with another entity (Massumi xvi). Sound has these affective qualities not because it represents or signifies something other than itself but because of what it does, how it operates, and what changes it effectuates (Cox 157).

These affective qualities of sound, in turn, are responsible for the performative potentiality of sound, that is, the capacity of sound to instigate a change in the users responsible for creating that very same sound. Therefore, when operating GR-1, two kinds of movement are at play: the conscious movements of users to create sounds by interacting with the interface of GR-1 through gestures and involuntary movements induced through affection by the sounds that are created. Since sound has these affective qualities because of its materiality, its performative potentiality is also a result of its materiality.

The fact that granular synthesis, the type of synthesis that the GR-1 is based on, enables the manipulation of sound in previously impossible ways also results in new affective relations between these sounds and their creators. New sounds entail new vibrations and thus new sonic materialities offering new affective potentialities. Digital technologies thus expanded the possibilities to create new sounds and evoke new sonic affections.

However, expanded possibilities do not automatically imply expanded control. Often, the results of interacting with sound through digital devices such as GR-1 are, to an extent, unpredictable, despite the control the interfaces of these devices seem to suggest. Even when digitized, sound retains its thingly character, a character that

Bill Brown describes as a "story of a changed relation to the human subject and thus the story of how the thing really names less an object than a particular subject-object relation" (4). Sound remains able to both problematize and make explicit the relation between listeners and sound through its potential to leak, subvert, surprise, and transcend categorization.

Works Cited

Brown, Bill. "Thing Theory." *Critical Inquiry*, vol. 28, no. 1, 2001, pp. 1–22.
Chatzichristodoulou, Maria, and Rachel Zerihan. Introduction. *Interfaces of Performance*, edited by Maria Chatzichristodoulou et al., Ashgate, 2009, pp. 1–5.
Cox, Christopher. "Beyond Representation and Signification: Toward a Sonic Materialism." *Journal of Visual Culture*, vol. 10, no. 2, 2011, pp. 145–61.
Dourish, Paul. *Where the Action Is: The Foundations of Embodied Interaction*. MIT Press, 2001.
Drazin, Adam. "Materials Transformations." Preface. *The Social Life of Materials: Studies in Materials and Society*, edited by Adam Drazin and Susanne Küchler, Bloomsbury, 2015, pp. xvi–xxviii.
"GR-1 Granular Synthesizer." *Tasty Chips Electronics*. www.tastychips.nl/product/gr-1-granular-synthesizer/.
Ingold, Tim. "Bringing Things to Life: Creative Entanglements in a World of Materials." *Realities / Morgan Centre, U. of Manchester*, 2010. NCRM working paper. http s://eprints.ncrm.ac.uk/id/eprint/1306.
———. "Toward an Ecology of Materials." *Annual Review of Anthropology*, vol. 41, 2012, pp. 427–42.
Leman, Marc, and Rolf Inge Godøy. "Why Study Musical Gestures?" *Musical Gestures: Sound, Movement, and Meaning*, edited by Marc Leman and Rolf Inge Godøy, Routledge, 2010, pp. 3–11.
Massumi, Brian. "Note on the Translation and Acknowledgements." *A Thousand Plateaus: Capitalism and Schizophrenia*, by Gilles Deleuze and Félix Guattari. Translated by Brian Massumi, Continuum, 1987, pp. xvi–xix.
"Review: Tasty Chips GR-1 // Granular Synthesis Explained // Full Workflow Tutorial." *YouTube*, uploaded by Loopop, 12 Mar. 2020, www.youtube.com/watch?v= 1RWOoEj3mwU&t=1551s.

16. Tracing the Voice's Digital Materiality

Nuno Atalaia

This chapter analyses how recent developments in speech processing technologies—digitizing and storing vocal utterances as data—frame the voice as a material. To do so, however, goes against the more traditional western understanding of the voice as a cultural category of questionable materiality. Already in Aristotle, the voice was seen as an intermediary between physical anatomy and metaphysical meaning-making. Through their signifying voice—*phone semantike*—humans were able to access the abstract realm of language, distinguishing themselves from other animals and their production of meaningless sounds—*aggramatoi psophoi* (Butler). For Aristotle, the voice both belongs to and escapes from the material.

This is not to say that the voice's materiality has been a mute subject in cultural analysis. Quite the contrary: we need only think of Roland Barthes' fascination with the voice's non-semiotic sonic properties, what he called "the grain of the voice" (Barthes). Paul Zumthor, a contemporary of Barthes, went so far as proposing a dedicated study of what he called the *order of the vocal*, as the activities and elements of the voice which escape the linguistic (Zumthor). But such efforts still replicate the Aristotelian divide by partitioning the material realm of sounds—*psophoi*—from that of language.

Following Tim Ingold, it is as though the voice is always denied its own "hard physicality," an existence outside "the socially and historically situated agency of human beings." More so, by being set apart from the world's "material character" and its processes, the voice remains, at least partly, in a metaphysical realm. I aim to supplement current debates on vocal materiality by centering my analysis on the digital technologies capturing and processing the vocal into data. Vocal digitization, I claim, is something very new and very different from what humans make of and with their voices.

The current expansion of vocal digitization is made possible by the large infrastructures under the possession of a few large monopoly-driven corporations, such as Google and Amazon. A key element of this expansion, and this text's object of analysis, is the ongoing adoption of digital voice assistants (DVAs). DVAs, such as Alexa and Siri, are systems through which humans can vocally interact with different objects while at the same time giving these systems access to the same humans' voices.

What drives my analysis is more than a speculative interest in these talking machines. Rather, it is motivated by the ongoing encroachment of large tech companies on the daily lives of an ever-greater number of humans. This encroachment is often facilitated by the unquestioning adoption of technologies such as DVAs, without considering the consequences their digital infrastructures might entail. To trace the voice's digital materiality is also to question how this material stands to be commodified and by whom.

DVAs and the Voice as a Material Affordance

Let us consider Amazon's recently released 2022 Superbowl halftime ad, starring the actress Scarlett Johansson, her husband Colin Jost, and the company's flagship DVA, Alexa ("Watch Alexa's 2022 Commercial for the Big Game"). The short film begins with Jost calling out to their assistant to set up their home for watching the Superbowl game. In a few seconds, the fireplace ignites, the living room's lights shift, blinds are drawn, and we hear the DVA's female-coded voice announce: "rosé is chilling". Impressed by the display, Johansson speculates on Alexa's "mind-reading" abilities; the ad takes a dark turn with a series of quick vignettes where the assistant humorously calls out the couple's secret opinions of each other, even denouncing their falsities to dinner guests. The ad returns to the original setting, in which the couple agrees it is best their DVA cannot read minds.

The ad organizes itself into two clear registers: firstly, factual, showcasing the different voice-activated automations Alexa makes possible; then, fictional, humorously portraying a soft dystopia of awkward moments. The border between fact and fiction, however, is constantly crossed. For example, in the speculative vignettes, Alexa responds to the unvoiced opinions of its users via actually existing automations such as activating a kitchen appliance or playing a song. The casting of Scarlett Johansson also harkens back to her performance as the fictional Samantha in Jonze's *Her* (2013). Finally, there is a play with the audience's expectations of what is possible through Alexa: when *Her* was released, the ad's first half would have been as speculative as the second. This ad underlines how vocal digitization brings a volatile fluidity to the borders separating what is fantasy and what is fact when it comes to talking machines.

In this ad, there is a (half-hidden) variety of computational devices connected through dispersed digital infrastructure that frame the voice as a material affordance of our surroundings. The voice is integrated into the "transforming and transformative life of materials" (Drazin 21). As Adam Drazin notes, "materials as social phenomena happen not only when wood becomes a table . . . but when your table is wood" (4). With DVAs, and the digital infrastructures of tech corporations, your table and the many items it supports can also be voice. This vocal materiality, rather than the result of an interpretative effort such as Barthes', is a consequence of the application of specific technologies.[1] Therefore, its analysis requires a technical understanding of the digital systems that make it possible.

In the following sections, I focus on two aspects of vocal digitization: input—the capture of vocal sounds from human sources to a technological medium—and output—the production of vocal sounds from non-human sources. I will conclude with a few critical remarks on what it means for these technologies to be almost entirely under the control of a few tech corporations. DVAs and their development are part and parcel of these corporations' history: they make DVAs possible and dictate how the voice is made digital.

Input: From Recording to Speech Processing

The history of speech processing—the technologies allowing humans to use machines through their voices—predates that of DVAs considerably, though with limited success. By 2011, when DVAs first appeared, speech processing had mostly stagnated, with little to no funding available since the 1970s (Ekman). DVAs were made possible by two major shifts in speech processing: one at the level of its actual operations and the other at the level of its organization.

Firstly, the models used for speech processing moved from the actual transcription of recorded sentences to a method that probabilistically reconstructed words and sentences through data extracted from these recordings. Using statistical models, different language maps were created based on the probability of one vocal sound preceding another (Pieraccini). These systems did more than greatly increase the accuracy of speech processing: they also made this process dependent on the production of vocal data from a human's vocal utterances. Therefore data, more than an abstraction involved in these systems, is a product resulting from these systems (Gitelman and Jackson).

Secondly, the many operations behind speech processing systems—including those described above—were dispersed through the cloud computing infrastructures of the corporations that own and sell DVA-operated devices. This is why, in Amazon's ad, Alexa can bring Johansson and Jost's home to life at the sound of their voice. A smart speaker or a fridge equipped with a microphone can parse a vocal recording to digital data with little computing power needed. However, there are

---

1   Though Barthes' fascination with the grain of Fischer-Dieskau's voice might not have been possible were it not for the technologies recording and reproducing the singer's renditions of Schubert.

heavier operations necessary to transcribe this data into text, then interpret this text into a desired outcome, and finally coordinate this desired outcome among different devices. All of these processes take place in one of Amazon's neighborhood-sized data centers (Vlahos).

The voice, now digitized, enters a material flow: collected by machines, stored into digital infrastructures, and processed into actions made by the same or other machines. Furthermore, vocal data does not evaporate once an action takes place; it persists well beyond DVAs and their operations. Vocal data can be repurposed, sampled, and processed into systems that only tangentially relate to the daily experience of DVA users. One field of research in which vocal data is fast becoming a valuable material is healthcare. Vocal biometrics—a specific category of data made possible through speech processing—can already be applied to diagnostic models able to predict and track diseases ranging from depression to coronary heart disease (Sigona). Vocal biometrics can also be used to deduce emotional states, independent of a human's intention or the linguistic content of their spoken utterances. Amazon already owns the patent for an emotion-tracking system which could soon be included in its DVA's design: ironic, considering Amazon's dystopian portrayal of a mind-reading Alexa (Jin and Wang).

The voice's digital materiality, therefore, not only exists beyond the historically situated agency of humans but has the potential to undermine this very agency. Rather than a metaphysical vehicle of meaning, vocal data, and the information to be extracted from it, become a material repository of a human's interiority, regardless of its linguistic content. But, as the next section illustrates, speech processing does not only allow machines to capture a human's voice: it also equips them with voices of their own.

Output: From Ventriloquism to Voice Synthetization

The digital development of machinic voices is an equally vital component of DVAs. By the time of Apple's release of Siri in 2011, the industry standard for making machines talk was known as concatenative speech synthesis. In this method, you would first ask a human to record themselves saying various sentences. These recordings would then be fragmented into their smaller components, from short words to isolated syllables. Through text-to-speech software programs, these components are reorganized to produce new utterances based on written sentences. Though the human speaker is detached from the non-human device by several technical layers, this method can still be said to fall under what Steven Connor categorizes as ventriloquism: the performances creating the illusion of transferal of a human's voice to a non-human object or disembodied entity.

Though countless devices could have the same voice, a singular human voice was still required. The actress Susan Bennet, for example, would enjoy moderate fame for voicing Siri's utterances. This method of speech synthesis was used to voice all four major platform DVAs: Apple's Siri, Microsoft's Cortana, Amazon's Alexa, and the earlier iterations of Google's voice-user-interface systems. Even when these companies offered different voices—in terms of gender coding or language, for example—each alternative was still modelled after another individual voice. However, as Google released its flagship "Google Assistant" in 2016, the company radicalized the production of machinic voices.

The same year, the large tech company also released a new way of creating human-sounding voices by applying Artificial Intelligence (AI) software to pre-existing vocal data (Oord et al.). The name of this system was Wavenet, and it could "generate raw speech signals" (1) from large samples of undifferentiated data without needing an intermediary voice or any textual input. These "raw" vocal sounds were detached from any semantic element; Google had created a system able to reproduce Barthes' famed "grain of the voice." Even more striking, the vast majority of this process took place without the need for any human supervision.

In 2017, Wavenet was combined with text-to-speech software to create Tacotron 2, allowing these AI-generated voices to be articulated into words and sentences (Wang et al.). This system made it possible to create a limitless number of voices and program them with different traits, from gender expression to regional accents. AI-powered speech synthesis software has since become the industry standard, leading all DVAs to abandon their previous human counterparts. Aristotle's framing of the voice as the result of complex anatomy is not put into question: what is put into question is whether this anatomy needs to be human.

These voices can no longer be called an instance of ventriloquism: they spring from vocal data's material flow, all made possible by myriad computational devices and the digital infrastructures owned by tech corporations. The voice announcing that the "rosé wine is chilling" in Alexa's ad is, therefore, radically different from the voice with which the DVA was first released in 2014. These voices are materials: they exist as artefacts, reorganized and redesigned from the commodified resource our voices become once digitized.

Dehumanizing the Voice

In her study of Dutch fashion designer Iris van Herpen's work, Anneke Smelik remarks that the intertwining of digital systems and human activity complicates what counts both as material and human. Digital mechanisms are more than simple tools. Rather, they alter how humans relate to their environments and the materials that compose them. DVAs present a valuable opportunity to analyze how digital technologies complicate what of the voice remains human in origin and what becomes an external material.

Returning to Aristotle: humanity's anatomical complexity secured its claim to a certain monopoly of the voice and its metaphysical capacities for meaning production. It is not my claim that the voice's digitization negates this monopoly; rather, it is materialized in a more Marxist sense. The voice becomes part of infrastructures of digital reproduction that impose specific property regimes on humans over their vocal utterances. These regimes, however, need not be total, nor are their infrastructures beyond contestation. As Ochoa Gautier remarks:

> What is particular about the voice is that, as a force that hovers between the world and what humans do with the world, it is particularly poised to be used as a disciplining force and yet it simultaneously easily reveals the limits of such a process. (210)

My short tracing of the vocal and the digital does not aim to provide a complete overview of the voice's disciplining force within a digital context. Instead, like Gautier, it draws attention to the disciplinary potential of the infrastructures behind vocal data, which the tech companies who own them are unwilling to divulge. Amazon's dystopian portrayal of their DVA unwittingly reveals a glimpse of a world of human vocal dispossession brought upon by such a disciplining force.

Once the voice becomes proprietary, its meaning and our interiority become the subject of manipulation and commodification. As data, the echoes of a user's voice, and any artefacts, outcomes, and information resulting from its processing, can become the intellectual property of large tech corporations. The political consequences of this shift are beyond the scope of this chapter. But, as Ingold reminds us, "to know materials, we have to follow them" (437): to know the voice's digital materiality, we must follow its flow. As with any attempt at engaging with materials, this remains an unfinished task.

Works Cited

Barthes, Roland. *Le grain de la voix* [*The Grain of the Voice*]. Seuil, 1999.

Butler, Shane. "What Was the Voice?" *The Oxford Handbook of Voice Studies*, edited by Nina Sun Eidsheim and Katherine Meizel, Oxford UP, 2019, pp. 3–18.

Connor, Steven. *Dumbstruck: A Cultural History of Ventriloquism*. 1st edition, Oxford UP, 2001.

Drazin, Adam. "To Live in a Materials World." Introduction. *The Social Life of Materials: Studies in Materials and Society*, edited by Adam Drazin and Susanne Küchler, Routledge, 2015, pp. 3–28.

Ekman, Ulrik. *The Complexity of Coding Conversational Agents*. Academia.edu. 2019. https://www.academia.edu/37885872/The_Complexity_of_Coding_Conversational_Agents.

Gautier, Ana María Ochoa. *Aurality: Listening and Knowledge in Nineteenth-Century Colombia*. Duke UP, 2014.

Gitelman, Lisa, and Virginia Jackson. Introduction. *"Raw Data" Is an Oxymoron*, edited by Lisa Gitelman, MIT Press, 2013, pp. 1–14.

Ingold, Tim. "Bringing Things Back to Life: Creative Entanglements in a World of Materials." *NCRM Working Paper Series*, July 2010, https://eprints.ncrm.ac.uk/id/eprint/1306/.

Jin, Huafeng, and Shuo Wang. *Voice-Based Determination of Physical and Emotional Characteristics of Users*. US 10,096,319 B1.

Oord, Aaron van den, et al. *WaveNet: A Generative Model for Raw Audio*. arXiv:1609.03499, arXiv, 19 Sept. 2016. *arXiv.org*, http://arxiv.org/abs/1609.03499.

Pieraccini, Roberto. *The Voice in the Machine: Building Computers That Understand Speech*. MIT Press, 2012.

Sigona, Francesco. "Voice Biometrics Technologies and Applications for Healthcare: An Overview." *JDREAM. Journal of InterDisciplinary REsearch Applied to Medicine*, vol. 2, no. 1, 2018, pp. 5–16. siba-ese.unisalento.it, https://doi.org/10.1285/i25327518v2i1p5.

Smelik, Anneke. "Fractal Folds: The Posthuman Fashion of Iris van Herpen." *Fashion Theory*, vol. 26, no. 1, Jan. 2022, pp. 5–26.

Vlahos, James. *Talk to Me: How Voice Computing Will Transform the Way We Live, Work, and Think*. Houghton Mifflin Harcourt, 2019.

Wang, Yuxuan, et al. *Tacotron: Towards End-to-End Speech Synthesis*. arXiv:1703.10135, arXiv, 6 Apr. 2017. *arXiv.org*, https://doi.org/10.48550/arXiv.1703.10135.

"Watch Alexa's 2022 Commercial for the Big Game." *US About Amazon*, 7 Feb. 2022, https://www.aboutamazon.com/news/devices/alexa-2022-commercial-big-game.

Zumthor, Paul. *La Lettre et la Voix : De la "littérature" médiévale* [*The Text and the Voice : On Medieval "literature"*]. Seuil, 1987.

17. Interface

Nishant Shah

The Graphical User Interface (GUI), even in its short-lived history, has been established as the stabilizing principle of contemporary computational practices. The emergence of the GUI allowed us to move away from the human-computer (O'Regan 144), physical-virtual (Ratzer et al. 5), and analog-digital (Keeling 2014) dichotomies that hounded the early years of personal computation, and immediately gave a material visual reference where the human and the computational can be seen to be interacting. From the first deployment of the WIMP (Windows, Icons, Menus, Pointers) elements and interactive functions on Apple's Macintosh machines to the ubiquitous flick, scroll, and pinch interactivity of our multisensory digital devices (Powell 1997), the GUI has been the cornerstone by which the ephemerality of computation could be understood as a material, embodied, and techno-cultural practice.

It is also paradoxically fascinating that the materiality of the GUI is not the surface it is made of. While it would be possible to think through the complexity and technical advancements of the tempered glass that forms the "black mirrored" surfaces of our digital devices, allowing for touch-based haptic and visual interactions to emerge, it is important to emphasize that the technicity of the interface is still opaque and that the GUI merely allows for reification rather than the visualization of that interaction. In this essay, devoted to the materiality of a digital interface, I am suggesting that the need for physical material which is present in our anxieties about ephemeral digitality might have to be suspended as we understand the GUI as an interface that facilitates digital data and information which can only be understood as traffic—something in motion, moving, rather a thing.

It is important to realize that the GUI was not just the site of encounter but also the surface that held computational practices and human perception together. While it is easy to think of the GUI as a thing we see, it has, in fact, two other vision functions: First, the GUI is something we see through. With the establishment of principles like What You See is What You Get (WYSIWYG), the graphical user interface became a porous invitation where we could see the human and the computational bleed and reconfigure (Howard). This reconfiguration responds to and co-constitutes complex tasks through visual rendering. Second, and more intriguingly, the GUI also held a "material agency" (Suchman 363) of witnessing the fleeting and quickly disappearing interactions between the human and the computational. Hence, the GUI has to be framed as a noun as well as a verb—a site where operations happen and an agential space that shapes the very contexts of those operations. The GUI, as Karen Barad would have it, was a space of "inter- and intra-action" (141), where it was making and being made, and also watching the unfolding of the making and being made, all at the same time. It has always encompassed these ambiguities, where it is hyper-visible because of its ubiquity and also invisible because of its multi-touch, natural use characteristics, which continue to shift our attention and focus to the rendered transparency and visual animation of dense and complex computation practices.

We have come to depend on the GUI through visual, haptic, and habitual cues to confirm and affirm our computational interactions through pixelated practice (Hoy). It is safe to propose that the GUI, in all its different consoles to black-mirror avatars, has become the material form through which we understand, analyze, and imagine human-computation engagements (Yue 261). It is the immaterial materiality—the seamless flow of digital information bookended by the physical materials of human touch and computational networks—of the GUI that gives us an ambivalence: It is a border that allows for the crossing and a boundary that contains the entwined transactions in discrete realms. This ambivalence has established the GUI as not just the default of our contemporary computational practices, but also the legitimizing adjudicator of our digitality. The GUI, it might be considered, is the material infrastructure of that moment when the computational and the human become a cyborg unit embedded in ontologies of hybrid fantasies (Nusselder 24).

Despite its centrality, the GUI is often declared obsolescent (Gates), redundant (Sujlana), or replaceable. With every new development in haptic, neural, sound, or immersive computational interaction technology, the bells toll for the passing of the GUI, only to be replaced by even more persuasive, compelling, and attractive visual interfaces that become the next big thing. The GUI is dead; long live the GUI! There is an excitement about prophesizing that this piece of material computational culture shall indeed be replaced or made obsolete because it promises a radical revolution and reimagination of how human-computer practices are described in digital user and design scholarship.

The narrative of a GUI in decline is not merely about technological development, but also about a complete reordering of the world that has been arranged in frameworks of identity, representation, voice, ownership, safety, freedom, rights, and entitlements that are informed by the mechanics, logics, and logistics of the GUI as an unstable stability. The collapse of the GUI as the site of all our actions and the witness of all our transactions, both the processing and the processed, would usher in a paradigm shift that would rewrite the very script of how we live with our computational devices.

Consequently, we see the continued blood-lust for the death of the GUI as a future horizon where we will enter our sci-fi futures of immersive and contextual computation that does not require the materiality of an interface. Concerns about this future shift attention and focus to the new interfaces and their governance, management, containment, and accountability infrastructures to ensure that the hard-won digital rights enshrined in the GUI carry forward to these new interfaces.

However, it is important to realize that the GUI is being replaced, but not because of the emergence of new interfaces. As is seen in most multi-modal, multi-sensory, self-learning, and evolving interfaces, the GUI is not being replaced but being accompanied by multiple modes of engagement which still rely on the GUI as a site of visual reassurance and an affirmation of a completed cybernetic feedback loop that allows for narrative continuity of our digital interactions. The future threat to our digital rights, premised upon a decline of the GUI, is not hypothetical because the real space where the GUI is being made redundant is not in the human and the machine but between the machine and the machine, which is increasingly the most extensive traffic and bandwidth of networked computation.

In her wonderful thesis on *Machine Therapy*, computational artist Kelly Dobson points out that machines do not need interfaces, but surfaces (19). Making a conceptual difference between an interface and a surface, she shows in her prototype robots how the surface is a point of contact. In contrast, an interface is a point of translation. Even when these translations are practices of opaqueness, as demonstrated in Kate Crawford and Vladan Joler's evocative work on *Anatomy of an AI System*, the interface does the work of visualizing, and rendering visible, specific and selected practices of interaction between the two acting agencies. Mercedes Bunz has pointed out that the GUI makes transactions visible and renders them into anthropomorphized, affective, almost juvenile icons and symbols that allow for human actors' ease of usage (194). As Wendy Chun reminds us, these selections are shaped by political decisions and expressions of power, deciding what gets shown and what remains in the nexus of invisible tech-military-governmental powers. The interface performs not just access to a system but access to the mechanics of a system (122). The GUI is fetishized because, in its moment of interaction, it privileges the human watcher as the address of its outputs. Within machine-machine interaction, the human addressee is not needed. With the dispensing of the human user as a destination for the flow of information, there is a new era of ubiquitous computing where machine-machine interaction is the default. The emerging AI-driven, self-learning, computational networks produce a machine intimacy that does not need the mediation of an interface.

We see this machine intimacy—an intimacy between machines (Shah 2)—in the Internet of Things and autonomous neural networks contingent upon massive information shifting rather than in information translation. In such systems, the GUI persists, but only as a secondary appendage that visualizes, abstracts, and graphically renders outputs for consumption rather than offering space for transaction and negotiation with this information. The GUI was a way by which human intention and scale were inserted into computational practices, materially changing the speed and scope of computation and allowing for intervening in the digital circulation circuits through human time. The GUI forced a management, shaping, typifying, and taxonomizing of information sets so that the human could track, trace, shape, interject, object, and modify the information produced in that moment of interaction. The Surface does not follow this logic of the interface. It is shaped by the protocols of computational devices and vectors of information querying and flow. It does not need a visual screen or a moment of humanly readable witnessing of the trace and movement of information.

The emergence of this surface as a replacement of the GUI is a silent process. The GUI is becoming increasingly ubiquitous, from large public signs to wearable computational devices. We see more and more smart devices wearing graphical interfaces inviting us to interact more, often, and with habitual ease. However, the proliferation of the GUI and focusing only on its material presence belies the fact that underneath the visible network of GUIs lurks a larger machinery of connected surfaces that shape the material and informational patterns of how we live, love, and talk with our computational devices.

Once a witness to our conversations, the GUI has been reduced to becoming a silent spectator of our reception—information is just a commodified aesthetic output rather than a malleable and live thing. The GUI stops being an interface and becomes a visual rendering, pretending to be interactive, but largely just communicating informational mandates through cute and accessible graphics. The Interface in the GUI has receded both in form and function, and in this process, it has naturalized a hidden network of surfaces that carry information, perform translations, create archives, and produce meanings that are obfuscated from human knowledge and inquiry. The GUI has stopped being an interface and, in the world of No-UI, has become a reification of power that works through techno-cultural spaces to create an almost sinister network of control and execution of politics. Precisely because the GUI retains the material attention of touch and visualization, it also produces opaque systems that present algorithms as neutral—mere interaction between machines that escapes human detection or oversight—thus making it difficult to counter the algorithmic decision-making hidden under the hypervisual materiality of the GUI.

The demise of the GUI has to be read, not in terms of its invisibility or technological evolution, but in its production as a symbolic space. The new surface of machine-machine interaction becomes the truly material and infrastructural space where information politics will be played out. Material cultures of digital technologies have focused almost exclusively on the GUI and its different manifestations in thinking through tough questions of agency, control, power, ownership, representation, and political economies of living within computational paradigms. I argue that once the materializing force of the human-machine interaction, the GUI has been rendered obsolete, not by its removal, but by being replaced by the surface. This replacement of the interface by surface demands a new critical apparatus, framework, and approach to understand the futures of digital materiality and the material consequences of the GUI as caught in the paradox of being hyper-visible and obsolete simultaneously.

Works Cited

Barad, Karen. *Meeting the Universe Halfway: Quantum Physics and the Entanglement of Matter and Meaning*. Duke UP, 2007.

Bunz, Mercedes. "School Will Never End: On Infantalization in Digital Environments—Amplifying Empowerment or Propagating Stupidity?" *Postdigital Aesthetics: Art, Computation and Design*, edited by David M. Berry and Michael Dieter, Palgrave Macmillan, 2015, pp. 191–202.

Chun, Hui Kyong Wendy. "The Enduring Ephemeral, or the Future Is a Memory." *Critical Inquiry*, vol. 35, no. 1, 2020, pp. 148–71.

Crawford, Kate, and Vladan Joler. "Anatomy of an AI System: The Amazon Echo as an Anatomical Map of Human Labor, Data and Planetary Resources." *AI Now Institute and Share Lab*, 2018, https://anatomyof.ai/.

Dobson, Kelly. *Machine Therapy*. 2007. Massachusetts Institute of Technology. PhD dissertation. https://dspace.mit.edu/handle/1721.1/44329.

Gates, Bill. "The Power of the Natural User Interface." *GatesNotes*, 2011, https://www.gatesnotes.com/about-bill-gates/the-power-of-the-natural-user-interface.

Howard, Scott W. "WYSIWYG Poetics: Reconfiguring the Fields for Creative Writers and Scholars." *The Journal of Electronic Publishing*, vol. 14, no. 2, 2011, https://doi.org/10.3998/3336451.0014.204.

Hoy, Meredith. *From Point to Pixel: A Genealogy of Digital Aesthetics*. Dartmouth College Press, 2017.

Keeling, Kara. "Queer OS." *Cinema Journal*, vol. 53, no. 2, 2014, pp. 152–57.

Nusselder, Andre. *Interface Fantasy: A Lacanian Cyborg Ontology*. MIT Press, 2009.

O'Regan, Gerard. "Graphical User Interface and Human-Computer Interaction." *The Innovation in Computing Companion: A Compendium of Select, Pivotal Inventions*. Springer, 2018, pp. 143–46.

Powel, Adam. "Web 101: A History of the GUI." *Wired*, 1997, https://www.wired.com/1997/12/web-101-a-history-of-the-gui/.

Ratzer, Brigitte, et al. "Bringing Gender into Technology: A Case Study in User-Interface-Design and the Perspectives of Gender Experts." *International Journal of Gender, Science and Technology*, vol. 6, no. 1, 2014, pp. 3–24.

Shah, Nishant. "When Machines Speak to Each Other: Unpacking the 'Social' in 'Social Media.'" *Social Media + Society*, 2015, vol. 1, no. 1, https://doi.org/doi:10.1177/2056305115580338.

Sujlana, Akal. "The Future of User Interface Design (UI)." *QuickReviewer*, 10 April 2020, https://www.quickreviewer.com/what-is-the-future-of-user-interface-ui-design/.

Suchman, Lucy. "Agencies in Technology Design: Feminist Reconfigurations." *Machine Ethics and Robot Ethics*, edited by Wendell Wallach and Peter Asaro, Routledge, 2017, pp. 361–76.

Yue, Audrey. "The Communicative City: Ambient Participation, Place-Making and Urban Screens." *Urban Screen Reader*, edited by Scott McQuire et al., Institute for Network Cultures, 2009, pp. 261–78.

Part VIII: Enfolding the Body

18. Becoming-*with*: On Textile Companions and Fungi Friends

Daniëlle Bruggeman and Lianne Toussaint

Introduction

We wear material things every day. Garments act as a second skin that dresses the physical matter of our bodies. "The magic of cloth," Peter Stallybrass writes, "is that it receives us: receives our smells, our sweat and shapes even" (36). Woven into the fabric, wrinkles, and seams of our clothes are traces of past experiences (Gibson xiv–xv). We engage in intimate material relationships with clothes, which not only carry traces of our past experiences and become material memories (Munteán, Plate, and Smelik) but also traces of how matter becomes clothing. Planting seeds, growing and harvesting cotton or flax, for example, or spinning yarns, weaving textiles, making patterns, designing clothes, cutting and sewing—material pieces of cloth go through a multiplicity of material encounters in the process of coming into being. Clothing carries the material traces of processes of making, of the hands of the workers in the factories or the material traces of the animals and/or non-human living beings—their fur, leather, silk, etc.—that are still present in the garment.[1]

In industrialized processes of making (fast) fashion, human actions have led to the accelerated growth of (mass) production and consumption, which goes hand-in-hand with the systemic exploitation of human beings, non-human animals, and nature's matter. As we wear fashionable clothes that dress our bodies, communicate our identities, and express our cultures, these affective material companions become intricately interconnected with our sense of self. At the same time, the fashion system exemplifies how we as human beings have been mistreating the earth—exhausting and overexploiting natural resources, destroying ecosystems, and creating unhealthy imbalances in biodiversity.

In *Staying with the Trouble*, Donna Haraway reflects on the damaged planet and offers new ways to rethink our relations to the earth and all of its material inhabitants. She proposes to think in terms of "becoming-with," "making-with,"

---

[1] See Femke de Vries's recent artistic research project "Which Animal is Present in your Garment?" (2022), https://practicingsolidarity.artez.nl/contributors/creative-practices/.

"living-with," and even "dying-with" others, including nonhuman "companion species" (2–5, 60) like dogs or monkeys, but also bacteria, fungi, spiders, synthetic hormones, or polymer fibers (Smelik 39). This concept of becoming refers to a process of change and transformation rather than a static "being," as Anneke Smelik explains (45). Becoming-*with*, then, entails the process of transformation evoked by the "intra-action" of (human and non-human) things (Barad 826). The notion of becoming-with offers a productive theoretical lens for thinking through how we could (and should?) live-*with* our fellow material beings, including our textile and nonhuman companions. In addition, this theoretical notion offers another perspective on some of the latest textile and garment design developments. It helps us see how innovative design practices, including textiles made from, or in collaboration with, living matter and technological materials are the concrete materialization of multispecies processes of becoming-with (Haraway 63)—which could potentially also become more sustainable alternatives to the current mass production of clothes and textiles.

Garments created from organisms such as fungi, algae, and bacteria; or from technologies such as solar cells, shape-memory material, and sensors can be understood as objects resulting from the mutually transformative encounter between human designers and nonhuman matter. Entangled in this encounter, the human and the nonhuman are together designing-, growing-, and making-with a whole new generation of garments. Such design practices also demonstrate how "animated" textiles cultivate the capacity for matter to respond (Buso et al.).

This chapter first focuses on new technological wearable companions that strengthen the embodied experiences of wearers and their intimate, physical, sensorial, and material relationship with garments. Here the case of designer Pauline van Dongen's smart jacket *Issho* demonstrates how technology can activate and animate the matter of fashion for therapeutic, emotional, or mnemonic purposes. Secondly, we discuss the recent development of biofabricating textiles and designing-with living organisms such as mycelium—which potentially opens up a radically new perspective on the agentic qualities of the (living) things we wear. Here the case of designer Aniela Hoitink, who works with liquid cultures of mycelium, is interesting because it invites the rethinking of how to make-with and give new life to fungi. In discussing these two cases, we aim to highlight the value of rethinking and affirming alternative ways of designing-, living-, and becoming-with the material things that we wear—our fellow material inhabitants of the earth.

Wearable Companions and the Caress of a Jacket

In *What Things Do*, Peter-Paul Verbeek states that the relation between subject and object is one of mutual constitution: "[n]ot only are they intertwined, but they coshape one another" (112). The relations between humans and the things they wear are a powerful example of such a co-shaping. People and clothes are not separate entities but "hybrid agencies" (Ingold 69) "that constitute one another in the process of becoming" (Smelik 39). Innovative textile designs that integrate technologies radically redefine this process of becoming and what garments can do in contact with the human body. Acting like a wearable companion that actively engages with the wearer, the smart denim jacket *Issho* by Pauline van Dongen offers a thought-provoking case.

Fig. 1: Pauline van Dongen, Issho, 2017. Photograph by Sharon Jane D.

The jacket *Issho* (fig. 1) was designed to encourage a more mindful relationship between the wearer, garment, and environment. The conductive yarns woven into striped areas on the fabric's surface contain multiple sensors that register touch, such as an embrace, stroke, or a pat on the shoulder. After a programmed but slightly variable number of registered interactions, *Issho* responds by giving the wearer haptic feedback through four vibration sensors that simulate the sensation of a gentle caress on the wearer's upper back. Behaving like a close friend, the jacket becomes an active mediator in the social dynamic between wearers and their environment, yet at times also reminds wearers of taking a moment for themselves (Toussaint and Van Dongen). During a small user test with the jacket, wearers reported a heightened awareness of their actions and relation to their immediate surroundings. The jacket affected what wearers experienced (the object of experience itself) and stimulated a more attentive attitude toward their bodies and the world around them (Berentzen). This indicates the potential of designing garments for self-care and well-being. Wearers can *become* more aware of their body and environment *with* the help of a textile companion that actively responds to their embodied actions and interactions.

Issho is an example of how technology can activate and animate the matter of fashion on both a mnemonic and an affective level. First, responsive garments such as *Issho* extend the mnemonic power of clothes. In addition to how garments become imbued with the memories and traces of the places and people they encountered, a smart jacket like Issho also actively produces its own memory and history by sensing, storing, and materializing the sensation of touch. In other words, this jacket can be understood as a thing that records and re-enacts its own social life (Appadurai). In addition, *Issho* acts like a wearable companion that subtly yet actively reminds the wearer of their social interactions as well as of the fact that their body is a *clothed* body (Entwistle). The garment's haptic feedback is a material reminder and animation of "touches from the past." In addition to receiving us (the wearer's smells, shapes, and sweat), it "receives" and even records our intimate interactions with human *and* non-human others.

Second, *Issho* touches upon the affective relationship between humans and the things they wear by reminding wearers to *care* for themselves and be mindful of their bodies and the environment. In times of visual distraction and information overload, this technological garment fosters a non-human type of care for wearers and their bodies, demonstrating that care is not a human-only matter (Puig de la Bellacasa 2). When understanding people and the things they wear as mutually constitutive, it follows that a garment that actively cares for its wearer also creates a wearer that takes better care of the garment.

In sum, *Issho* exemplifies how "becoming-with the practices and artifacts of technoscience" (Haraway 104) can add a new sense of memory, touch, and care to the relationship between nonhuman and other-than-human things, including garments and technologies.

Growing-*with* Fungi Friends

In addition to the new technological material intimacies between wearer and garment, more and more designers have started to grow materials from living organisms, such as fungi or algae, as innovative bio-based alternatives for textiles. This approach of "growing design" originates from advances in biotechnology and enables designers to collaborate with biological organisms (Karana et al. 119). Designing with fungi and fungal mycelium is increasingly popular in the fashion field, allowing for another perspective on new materialisms in fashion (Bruggeman 52).

Fungi live, become and grow underground. As fungal biologist Merlin Sheldrake states in *Entangled Life*, "fungi are everywhere ... They are inside you and around you. ... We all live and breathe fungi" (3–5). Continuously interacting and connecting with plants, trees, and other living beings and organisms—fungi are engaged in complex exchange systems. Exploring the lives of fungi, Sheldrake shows how they can be seen as "odes to other ways of being" —as they can assume dozens of different sexes, transform nonlife into life, and force us to question where one organism stops and another begins (Dunn 722). Mycelium is the vegetative lower part of fungi and consists of a network of interwoven hyphae, which are its long, tubular branching structures. Mycelium has been identified as the largest living organism on earth and grows due to its symbiotic relationship with the materials that feed it (Haneef et al.). Mycelium-based materials can be biofabricated into organic composites. However, pure mycelium materials can also be grown by harvesting a liquid culture of mycelium, which is the "liquid fermentation of fungal micro-organisms" (Karana et al. 121). Once it has dried, mycelium cultivation results in materials resembling leather, paper, or plastic.

Dutch fashion designer Aniela Hoitink experiments with growing mycelium-based materials, which she has called MycoTEX. In this design practice, materials are directly grown from a natural, living organism. This fundamentally changes the process of designing and making clothes and the relationship between the designer/maker and the living matter that is becoming a piece of clothing. Design here is transformed into biofabrication, activating and giving new life to organisms with new materialities. She developed a 3D manufacturing method that allows for seamless, on-demand produced and custom-made clothes grown from compostable mushroom roots – without the need to cut and sew. After using these materials or once these designs are worn out, the biodegradable garments can be buried in the ground to decompose. In this sense, Hoitink mimics the closed loops and wasteless regenerative life cycles that can be found in nature.

Since Hoitink uses 3D molds instead of flat pattern making, the mycelium could directly grow into any desired shape and wearable design to fit the human body. In doing so, this case of "growing design" explores the relationship between the biological matter of living organisms and the bodily matter of the wearer. Allowing the mycelium to act like a second skin on the human body brings human and fungi matter into dialogue—an innovative process of collaborating with the living matter of fungal companions. In starting from the potential of how living organisms grow and become, this design process embraces the "material agency" of the biological matter of fungi while creating new material(ist) intimacies and relations. Indeed, in this case, "matter is not just passive and inert stuff, but should be considered as an active and meaningful actor in the world" (Smelik 42). This requires the designer to open up to working with matter and materiality as "more than 'mere' matter: an excess, force, vitality, relationality, or difference that renders matter active, self-creative, productive, unpredictable" (Coole and Frost 9; see also Smelik 47). Even though the designer remains one of the main actants in the case of MycoTEX, creating the conditions for growing the mycelium, this design practice does express another way of designing-*with* biological matter. This opens up a path to reconsidering how people engage with the material things of this world and the "apparent capacity of things to act back" (Ingold 69)—a process of collaborating with living matter in the "nature-culture continuum" (Braidotti 31).

These new interspecies interactions in fashion and design practices help to think through the material capacities of the things and living matter that we wear and continuously become-*with*, which increases our understanding of how we live- and die-with non-human beings and other companion species.

A Matter of Care

In our times of exploitation and exhaustion of nature, it is a matter of care to stay with the trouble in order to learn to embody the daily practice of making kin with the more-than-human world, respecting planetary boundaries as well as all of earth's material inhabitants (Haraway 2–5). The destructive practices of the fashion industry have helped fashion theorists and practitioners to realize that it is ever more urgent to rethink the relationships between wearer and garment and between human and non-human matter in terms of the active matter that we are all living- and dying-with. From human beings, this requires an attitude of humbling, an awareness of the different temporalities of other human or non-human materialities, a politics of care for ourselves and others; an interspecies approach, creating space for all living beings, living matter, and other species to enact their agency—allowing all material inhabitants of the earth to grow, become, transform, and create new connections and relationships while nourishing each other. This also means approaching fashion differently, starting from an affirmative ethics in order to move beyond its industry's destructive forces while opening up fashion's potential to connect, make, and become-*with* new materialities—embracing the possibilities of life. Let's try to see garments as companions to become (friends) with, to touch and be touched by, to make memories with, allowing us to grow and thrive with—in a way that those people that matter most in our lives do.

Works Cited

Appadurai, Arjun, editor. *The Social Life of Things: Commodities in Cultural Perspective*. Cambridge UP, 1986.

Barad, Karen. "Posthumanist Performativity: Toward an Understanding of How Matter Comes to Matter." *Signs*, vol. 28, no. 3, 2003, pp. 801–31.

Berentzen, Isabel. *Issho: An Intelligent Denim Jacket*. Delft University of Technology, M.A. Thesis in Integrated Product Design, 2016.

Braidotti, Rosi. "A Theoretical Framework for the Critical Posthumanities." *Theory, Culture and Society*, vol. 36, no. 6, 2019, pp. 31–61.

Bruggeman, Daniëlle. *Dissolving the Ego of Fashion: Engaging with Human Matters*. ArtEZ Press, 2018.

Buso, Alice, et al. "The Unfolding of Textileness in Animated Textiles: An Exploration of Woven Textile-Forms." DRS2022, Summer 2022, Bilbao, Spain.

Coole, Diana, and Simone Frost, editors. *New Materialisms: Ontology, Agency, and Politics*, Durham: Duke UP, 2010.

Dunn, Rob. "The Fantastical Lives of Fungi." *Science*, vol. 368, no. 6492, Spring 2020, p. 722.

Entwistle, Joanne. *The Fashioned Body: Fashion, Dress and Modern Social Theory*. 2nd ed., Polity Press, 2015.

Gibson, Robyn. *The Memory of Clothes*. Sense Publishers, 2015.

Haneef, Muhammad, et al. "Advanced Materials from Fungal Mycelium: Fabrication and Tuning of Physical Properties." *Scientific Reports*, vol. 7, no. 41292, January 2017.

Haraway, Donna. *Staying With the Trouble: Making Kin in the Chthulucene*. Duke UP, 2016.

Ingold, Tim. *The Life of Lines*. Routledge, 2015.

Karana, Elvin, et al. "When the Material Grows: A Case Study on Designing (with) Mycelium-Based Materials." *International Journal of Design*, vol. 12, no. 2, 2018, pp. 119–36.

Munteán, László, Liedeke Plate, and Anneke Smelik, editors. *Materializing Memory in Art and Popular Culture*. Routledge, 2017.

Sheldrake, Merlin. *Entangled Life: How Fungi Make Our World, Change Our Minds and Shape Our Futures*. Random House, 2020.

Smelik, Anneke. "New Materialism: A Theoretical Framework for Fashion in the Age of Technological Innovation." *International Journal of Fashion Studies*, vol. 5, no. 1, 2018, pp. 33–54.

Stallybrass, Peter. "Worn Worlds: Clothes, Mourning, and the Life of Things." *The Yale Review*, vol. 81, no. 2, 1993, pp. 35–50.

Toussaint, Lianne, and Pauline van Dongen. "In Touch with the Now: Stimulating Mindfulness through a Smart Denim Jacket." *APRIA*, vol. 1, no. 0, 2019.

Van Dongen, Pauline. *A Designer's Material Aesthetics Reflections on Fashion and Technology*. ArtEZ Press, 2019.

19. Clothing For/Against Walking

Anna P.H. Geurts

This chapter is about happy and less happy collaborations between people and (other) materials. In particular, it is about how people and materials work together in the act of walking. What happens when stuff does not operate as expected, and the walking breaks down? This is a phenomenological question that cannot be answered in the abstract. People in different times and places, with different physical and social make-ups, perform and experience walking and its breakdowns in very different ways. Our question, therefore, deserves historically, culturally, socially, and somatically sensitive analyses. This chapter makes a plea for such analyses and offers suggestions on how they might be performed, especially in historical cases, because these are arguably the hardest to retrieve. I offer two tools for such analyses. First, I will propose to distinguish between "helpful" *materials* and "unhelpful" *matter*. I suggest that when, in the experience of walkers, materials turn into matter, this has at least four phenomenological consequences: for the materials themselves, for the walker's body, the activity of walking, and the walking space. Second, I will suggest that we cannot discover what happens in these four phenomenological transitions from material to matter by looking at materials/matter only, but that we need to listen to humans' stories, too.

Let me start with two examples from my own mobility history.

A teenager on a school day, traversing a western-European town on foot. I am wearing new shoes: leather ballet flats. They look best without socks, and the weather is too warm for socks, anyhow. In the afternoon, I notice a sharp pain. The heels of my shoes have filled up with blood, and I need to go barefoot for the rest of the day. This has several consequences. That day, the city for me is reduced to pavement and asphalt: it is all I can see because I have to ensure I do not tread on broken glass or dog mess. At the same time, as I will explore in a moment, going barefoot feels liberating that afternoon, initiating new interactions between my skin, flesh, and bones and the materials surrounding me.

A second example. I am visiting a European city, wearing a new coat. It is long and wide, made of fairly thick woolen cloth lined with viscose. The lining is not attached at the hem, and both pieces of fabric have a deep split at the back and the front. They hang freely from my waist down, being fastened with only two buttons at the height of my chest and stomach. I like how they dance about my legs and drape around my ankle when I climb the stairs at the station. The next moment, I fall flat on my face. From then on, I start discovering how much effort it takes me to walk safely in the coat. Obstacles at foot level are easily missed and tripped over because of its length and the movement of its fabrics. I need to pick up all the different strands of the coat whenever I take a step up. In addition, rain makes the coat even heavier than it already is.

These examples illustrate literary scholar Bill Brown's distinction between objects and things. This is a phenomenological distinction rather than an ontological one: it pertains to how humans *experience* physical entities. Brown calls physical entities objects when they have meaning to humans: when humans see their point, their use. Things, in contrast, comprise all physical entities in their undomesticated appearance. They do not need to be intelligible or useful to humans to exist. A specific subset of "things" consists of those things humans emphatically perceive as obstructive. They form so many obstacles to the ways people expect or hope to run their lives. This subset is pertinent to this chapter: when I tripped over my coat, it turned from an object into a thing, and this mattered for my walking.

In fact, this had a range of consequences for me as a human user of the coat. To understand these consequences, however, we need to look not only at things but also at materials. In the humanities, there is a renewed interest in phenomenology. Phenomenology entails the examination of experience, not in the sense of the store of knowledge a person gains over time, but in the sense of their feelings and thoughts about the world around them *as they occur*. In trying to learn more about these experiences, looking at materials is vital because materials form such a significant factor in creating them. Before I continue this argument, a clarification on how I conceptualize materials. Tim Ingold has rightly questioned the focus on artifacts in material culture studies. This privileges the self-contained, human-made object and its consumption to the neglect of non-object materials ("Toward an Ecology" 435). However, there is a more fundamental reason to focus not just on artifacts when we investigate experience. As anthropologists Adam Drazin and Susanne Küchler have shown, it is not always possible to distinguish between finished objects and materials. For one, the distinction depends partly on the history of these physical entities, a history not always known and also not always relevant to the person interacting with them. It does not always make sense to distinguish between, for instance, a rock in the landscape—a natural material—and a stone monument—a human-made object. For another, many entities are called a material in one professional discipline (for instance, design) but not in another (for example, engineering): Drazin calls these "thing-manifested materials" (xx–xxiv). In short, it does not always make sense to distinguish between form and substance, or object and material, especially when focusing on human experiences of them.

My own experience confirms this. The stiffness of the shoes that caused my feet to bleed was not simply part of the material, leather. The once supple hide from which my shoes were made was already stiffened in the production of the leather but only became so hard as to hurt my skin when they were turned into shoes. The leather thus assumed new properties once shaped as a shoe. Nor was this stiffness simply part of the form "shoe:" my cotton shoes are not stiff in the same way, for example. Moreover, my *old* leather shoes are no longer so stiff, either. So, the stiffness was part of a particular stage and form in the life of the material: my new-shoes-of-leather. It makes more sense, therefore, to regard both groups, objects *and* materials, as part of the same analytical category. This does not need to lead back to studying these materials-in-form only as cultural symbols or objects of economic exchange: my focus is still firmly on their physically experienced properties, such as their roughness/smoothness, their malleability/stiffness, or their insulative properties. These properties matter tremendously to their human users, and they are part and parcel of what users commonly perceive to be the materials of their tools, which is why we need to pay close attention to these.

Adding this insight to Brown's plea to distinguish objects from things, we might similarly distinguish materials from other matter. Drazin and Küchler reserve the term "materials" for categories of matter that have meaning to humans: when I put on my new shoes, the shiny leather appeared to me as beautiful and protective. "Matter," in contrast, is "material stuff in general," in Drazin's words (xxvi). In light of Brown's distinction, though, I would like to use the term "matter" in this essay more specifically for physical entities in their undomesticated, seemingly meaningless or useless appearance; entities that occasionally seem even to work against people's aims actively. This highlights the dramatically different relations that can exist between walkers and the materials with which they surround themselves. The leather that was a material to me when I put on my shoes suddenly became "matter" when it started hurting so much that I had to take the shoes off. The leather stopped playing the role I had wished, even forced it to play. This distinction between materials and matter should help us analyze what feels smooth and natural to people when they walk, and what does not. *Materials* are their taken-for-granted helpers. *Matter* is what resists their will or understanding. It is what they encounter when walking goes awry.

Studying this process of going awry is vital in current phenomenological endeavors. When, for walkers, elegant cloth and protective leather turn into obstinate matter, this profoundly impacts their mobility: where they can go, how much effort this takes, and *how* they walk, observe, and are in space. But why should we want to know exactly how this impact differs across time and between different people(s)? For one, the new phenomenology differs from the old in acknowledging the diversity of human experiences and no longer taking the present-day, privileged researcher as a model for all experience. Second, historical and anthropological claims about the distinction between materials and matter need testing, for instance, the idea that people used to be more familiar with the materials they encountered in their day-to-day life and that their work therefore used to be easier than it has become since the start of the present revolution in materials (Drazin xxi). Materials were not necessarily more familiar to their users in the past, however, because labor specialization and leisured classes are both long-standing social phenomena. Eighteenth-century porters, for instance, treated their soles with wax and rosin in order not to slip (Dolan 134). Meanwhile, the wealthy travelers they carried around in their sedan chairs did not practice this technique and would therefore have had a harder time climbing steep rocky terrain. This is no isolated example: materials have always had their secrets, depending on their users' occupation or socioeconomic class (Geurts, "Travel"). A third reason for this kind of study lies outside the academy. Assumptions about mobility form the basis of governments' plans for future material landscapes. Such assumptions, like academic assumptions, have long started from "model" citizens. Mobility, however, comes about in the interplay of nonhuman and human physical, financial, and ideological possibilities and therefore works differently for different humans living in different environments. There is no one-size-fits-all solution to mobility obstacles. Nor—to emphasize the positive side—does an obstacle always need to be an obstacle, as my coat will soon show.

Experiments and Stories

First, however: how to research these different impacts that materials-turning-into-matter may have? Our initial impulse may be to reach for texts that create and reflect on the cultural meaning of materials: from news items about mobility to cultural commentaries or advertorials for hiking equipment. Yet most of these offer only armchair analyses. Instead, Ingold suggests "engaging quite directly with the stuff we want to understand: by sawing logs, building a wall, knapping a stone or rowing a boat" ("Materials" 2–3). Cultural and historical researchers might thus observe and experiment with items they buy in a shop, find in an archive or museum depot, or reconstruct themselves—and they have been doing so in abundance, especially archaeologists and anthropologists. One advantage is the richness of information collected this way; another is that it circumvents the usual bias for literate people. The coat in which I stumbled on the stairs, for example, which is of a fairly nineteenth-century European cut, might say something about the urban walking practices of many nineteenth-century Europeans: that these practices were slower, more laborious, and more physically risky than their twenty-first-century equivalents, perhaps.

When I discussed this possibility with a friend, however, they told me how pleasant their hiking in the Crimean Mountains had been, despite wearing long and mid-length A-line skirts of a fluid to moderate drape (rather than stiffer fabrics that stand out more from the body), comparable in effect to my coat. They had developed a habit of kicking the fabric ahead at each step before landing their foot on the ground, and, to them, this was no effort at all. Our respective interactions with comparable fabrics thus differed significantly. A plausible explanation for this difference would be my friend's lifelong skirt-wearing experience. Both of my own experiences of walking-gone-wrong, narrated above, involved purchases of a type of item to which I was unaccustomed. Perhaps only the inexperienced are hindered by long garments or painful shoes.

In nineteenth-century travel accounts, for instance, many skirt wearers—their skirts made of cloth, linen, cotton, or silk—indeed make nothing of their costume. However, my explanation fell apart when considering the accounts of some of the travelers who have become famous for wearing both skirts and trousers. These individuals frequently cite the impracticality of skirts, and globetrotter Ida Pfeiffer, for instance, tucked up their skirts on travel days (Heidhues 290). Their preferences, bodily capabilities, or (others') expectations about how to walk apparently led to different ways of experiencing fabrics from my friend's, despite their shared life-long experience. This means there is no necessary correlation between a material-in-form and the experiences a person can have with it: the material and cut of a piece of travel clothing do not, on their own, determine travel experiences, and scholars' experiments with these materials can therefore offer only partial insights into specific people's experiences (see Corn 43). For if we were to argue exclusively from our own material observations and experiments, that would automatically also mean arguing only from our own standpoint, which may lead to cultural myopia and anachronism. Even if materials have certain tendencies, as Drazin writes, the properties noticed or employed by humans differ from use to use, from person to person. Different cultures or industries may even classify chemically and physically identical stuff as different materials altogether (xviii, xxvi). We, therefore, need to supplement their direct study with other sources.

Ingold offers a key to what these sources may be: "the properties of materials [...] are neither objectively determined nor subjectively imagined but practically experienced [by humans]. In that sense, every property is a condensed story" ("Materials" 14). So, to find when, for walkers, materials turn into renegade matter, we have to find their stories. Elizabeth Shove and their colleagues have modeled such work from a sociological perspective. They collected interviews about, for instance, whether kitchens in British households "work" for those who have to live with them and which tools and materials are coveted and why—leading indeed to different degrees and forms of (dis)satisfaction (22–39). Historians can find similar stories by examining first-person writing, for instance, travel diaries.

What we find there is an astounding range of preferences. An example: while present-day Europeans may find it perfectly obvious that different left- and right-hand shoes are best for walking on foot, nineteenth-century European women often wore straights: pairs of identically shaped shoes (Swallow). Nothing in the diaries of Dorothy Wordsworth, to name one avid walker, has suggested to me so far that this hindered their 30-kilometer day treks. Of course, when feet bleed, as mine did, this may be taken as an obvious sign of discomfort, but the body does not always speak so clearly or independently. That is, the influence of cultural normality is enormous, both on the body and the mind. People tend to prefer the familiar (Geurts, *Travel and Space*), and differently cultured limbs are also literally shaped differently because they have been wearing different clothing or doing different work. For example, feet are partly shaped by the shoes in which they have been enclosed. The same goes for the other body parts people use to walk: legs, arms, hands, and so on, depending on one's way of walking, on wheels, hands, feet, or knees. Discomfort and pain are culturally and individually specific as well: they can be ignored, overpowered by distractions, or dealt with in various more positive ways (Andrews), all of which mechanisms are culturally inflected. As a result, uncomfortable clothes can still take people on euphoric hikes. These examples show the importance of finding the sources that speak of this rich variety in human interactions with clothing. Once we have found them, what kinds of discoveries can we make?

What Matter Reveals

We discover that when walkers see material turn into matter, this has a surprisingly wide range of consequences. Brown writes that objects—in our case: materials—form a window onto life, nonintrusive and faithful to human intentions as they are, and therefore, as it were, transparent (4). I want to argue that matter forms a possibly even bigger "window": it offers a view onto at least four things.

First, it offers a view onto materials and matter themselves. Precisely because matter is untransparent, visible, and noticeable (Brown 4), it forces humans to look at it. That is, the breakdowns of my ordinary walking practice foregrounded the stiff leather of my shoes and the unpredictably flowing wool of my coat. In a sense, these breakdowns even *created* these matters for me because I ascribed different properties to them while I was still happy with them (that is, when they were still materials to me). Simultaneously, such stories about breakdowns help humans recognize what materials, in their more faithful guise, are doing for them. Therefore, by detailing specific people's estrangement from materials as these turn into matter, these stories enable both their protagonists and researchers to see the cultural meanings that these materials typically had at a given time and place.

Yet this window does not only offer a view onto material and matter, but onto other important aspects of walking as well. For, second, matter turns people's attention to their bodies while changing them at the same time. As philosopher Drew

Leder writes, people tend not to notice most of their body until part of it seems to dysfunction: then, they suddenly become aware of it. This "dys-appearance" of the body has been analyzed through a cultural lens by Madeleine Akrich and Bernike Pasveer, among others, but much work is yet to be done, especially historically. When a body part "dys-appears"—the skin on my heel, for example—this may be due to a faulty interface between materials—as caused by my failure to wear stockings or soften the leather first—and this may transform the material leather into matter. However, I also feel pained and perhaps annoyed by or alienated from the skin on my heel itself. The dys-appearance of my skin can thus be strong enough for the skin to turn from a material into matter (this is akin to but not the same as Ingold's argument that organic beings are also materials: "Materials" 4).

Third, these stories can teach us a great amount about the activity of walking. A first thing they can tell us is what walking with material-turned-matter feels like. My new coat and shoes turned my usually easy walking practice into an effort: I had to keep a constant eye on the ground, raising the fabric of my coat when needed, avoiding too-sharp objects while accepting stepping on others, and I moved along more slowly than usual. However, observing the effects of these breakdowns in walking also reveals positive transformations. Going barefoot added several welcome aspects to my walking experience. It was fun for me to shake this everyday necessity up a little. I felt like I was boiling walking down to its essentials, learning that this was feasible even in a busy European city, both socially and physically. This gave me, at that moment, a sense of freedom. These two observations raise important questions about the relationship between normality and discomfort or pain. What forms of routine discomfort, whether having always been normal or normalized over time, are accepted by the people who suffer from them or even cease to hurt altogether? And what forms remain painful or a cause for complaint? For me, a temporary lack of shoes had positive as well as negative effects. Some people prefer permanently to forgo shoes. For many others, however, a lack of shoes is not a choice at all but a source of pain. For many others again, wearing no shoes is only normal: they have different ways of making the interface between skin and ground workable and unobtrusive. Ironically, this is similar to how, for many of the dwellers of the European town in which I was walking, the unquestioned norm was *always* to wear shoes. And so, a final form of knowledge that matter can offer us about walking is to make explicit how specific groups of people usually do it and with what rationale. Breakdowns reveal what people take for granted. Many routinely expect their bodies and the materials around them to cooperate in smooth human-nonhuman assemblages. Moments of breakdown show how complicated these assemblages are and how interdependent human bodies and other materials are. Each is adapted to the others. Moreover, how they are adapted differs tremendously between individuals with different bodies and material means and between different cultures. The rubber-soled shoes that I wear are only worn in some places. *My* skin and *my* city's littered pavements usually work together well because I have learned to put these rubber soles between them. I do not know whether my skin and feet would have been capable of this experiment in wintertime or in a city without separate pavements for pedestrians. Also, on a social level, my going barefoot raised some eyebrows—though no more than that. Had, say, a police officer done the same thing, the social effects would have been far greater.

Fourth and last, materials-turned-matter change walkers' relationship to the surrounding space. Sociologist Mike Michael already wrote about how painful boots can disturb the connection that hikers try to establish with nature. My own walking had a similarly significant impact on my relationship with the city. It redirected my attention from the events at eye level—people, traffic, shopfronts: the things I usually pay the most attention to—to what was happening on the pavement. Again, the effects were a mixture of discomfort and pleasure. I was on the lookout for broken glass, another material-turned-matter, but I saw much more than that: different makes of pavement or maintenance-hole cover, urban plants, and animals. In addition, I could not only see but also feel more. The paving slabs were of a smooth texture, while the asphalt I had to cross every now and then was more porous, though still pleasant to my feet. The slabs also transferred the heat of the sun to my feet. Furthermore, as a seeing person, I was reminded more than usual of the tactile paving put in place to guide walkers with partial or no sight, with my soles perceiving its shapes as sharp ridges and troughs.

Thus, materials turning into matter may cause hindrance to walkers and so reveal what they expect their walking to be like, but it may also bring about new experiences, including positive ones: of the material or matter itself, the activity of walking, the walker's body, and the world around them, depending on who, when, and where they are. Next to engaging deeply with mobility-related materials and matter themselves, researchers interested in these questions, therefore, need to listen to the stories people across human history have to tell about what happens to them when an activity such as walking breaks down.

Works Cited

Akrich, Madeleine, and Bernike Pasveer. "Embodiment and Disembodiment in Childbirth Narratives." *Body and Society*, vol. 10, no. 2–3, 2004, pp. 63–84.
Andrews, Kerri. *Wanderers: A History of Women Walking*. Reaktion, 2021.
Brown, Bill. "Thing Theory." *Critical Inquiry*, vol. 28, no. 1, 2001, pp. 1–22.
Corn, Joseph J. "Object Lessons/Object Myths? What Historians of Technology Learn from Things." *Learning from Things: Method and Theory of Material Culture Studies*, edited by W. David Kingery, Smithsonian Institution, 1996, pp. 35–54.
Dolan, Brian. *Ladies of the Grand Tour*. HarperCollins, 2001.

Drazin, Adam. "Material Transformations." Preface. *The Social Life of Materials: Studies in Materials and Society*, edited by Adam Drazin and Susanne Küchler, Bloomsbury, 2015, pp. xvi–xxviii.

Geurts, Anna P.H. "Travel in Nineteenth-Century Europe: Modern Technology and Freedom of Movement." Forthcoming.

———. *Travel and Space in Nineteenth-Century Europe*. Routledge, forthcoming.

Heidhues, Mary Somers. "Woman on the Road: Ida Pfeiffer in the Indies." *Archipel*, no. 68, 2004, pp. 289–313.

Ingold, Tim, "Materials against Materiality." *Archaeological Dialogues*, vol. 14, no. 1, 2007, pp. 1–16.

———. "Toward an Ecology of Materials." *Annual Review of Anthropology*, vol. 41, 2012, pp. 427–42.

Michael, Mike. "These Boots Are Made for Walking …: Mundane Technology, the Body and Human-Environment Relations." *Body and Society*, vol. 6, no. 3–4, 2000, pp. 107–26.

Shove, Elizabeth, et al. *The Design of Everyday Life*. Berg, 2007.

Swallow, A. "The History of Shoes." *Baillière's Clinical Rheumatology*, vol. 1, no. 2, 1987, pp. 413–29.

20. Mylar Foil: Blankets of Silver and Gold

Jeroen Boom

Within the endless circulation of contemporary media images, a common visual trope has emerged in which refugees arriving on European beaches are covered in blankets of silver and gold. Besides materials such as rubber (life vests, rafts), wood (boats, shelters), and paper (invalid passports, washed-up photographs), these sheets of mylar heat foil belong to an ecology of circulating matter within the Mediterranean border zones, being wrapped around bodies, used to cover the roofs of tents, or left behind as litter shimmering on the shores.[1] In this chapter, I will look at several images and video artworks as temporary semiotic fixations of this flow of meaning and matter in the context of what has come to be known as the European "refugee crisis." My focus lies with the materiality of the mylar foil, which, as new materialist thinkers such as Karen Barad and Jane Bennett claim, is not inert or passive, neither permanent nor determinate, but produced in performative materializations, in material enactments of boundaries and fixations. Starting from this realization, and following Arjun Appadurai and Igor Kopytoff's call to trace the cultural biographies of things and materials "as they move through hands, contexts, and different uses" (Appadurai 34) and are "classified and reclassified into culturally constituted categories" (Kopytoff 68), I will attend to the different ways in which photographers, video artists, and filmmakers use the material aesthetics of mylar—its shimmering texture, its wavy movements, its non-translucent qualities, among other things—to create different meanings and associations. The reflective thermal material, as my argument goes, apart from its compression of different plastic and metallic materials, also consists of conflicting layers of signification. In pulling apart these different layers, zooming in on images of crisis, one can trace the tensions between various connotations and affects that stick to this material, from its hopeful humanitarian promises to its dehumanizing threats.

Named after its most well-known production brand, mylar foil is made of an artificially manufactured composition, or a meshwork, as Tim Ingold would claim, of different material layers compressed into a low-weight sheeting. It contains a thin plastic film with a reflective aluminum coating, known as metalized polyethylene

---

1   See also Bridle.

terephthalate, which grants it its gold and silver color, and is made to be highly heat reflective. The thermal emergency blanket has its roots in space exploration, as a technology invented by NASA to protect spacecrafts against extreme temperatures. Soon after its invention, going beyond the scope of space aeronautics, mylar foil has been widely used to cover human bodies to protect them from hypothermia. When worn, in its organic-metallic symbiosis and biological-technological coupling, the polyester film becomes an extension of the human skin, allowing bodies to protect themselves from thermal radiation and recover their core temperature. One of the essential properties of the mylar material is its ability to isolate heat, shielding not only from radiation but also from the gaze of heat-sensitive infrared surveillance cameras, which cannot sense and detect what is underneath the heat-reflective foil. This secretive thermal aspect of the mylar blanket is made explicit in Richard Mosse's video installation *Incoming* (2014–17), in which long-range heat-sensitive surveillance cameras were used—those designed to trace "enemies" and "intruders" in war and border zones—to visualize the heat radiation of refugees on the sea and in the camps, reducing them to different gradations of body heat captured in monochrome images. At one moment, when the thermal camera fixates its gaze on a figure wearing a thermal blanket, which moves softly in the wind, the figure underneath the foil starts to become formless.

Because of the isolating properties of the polyester film and because higher heat values translate into darker pixels, the heat-sensitive camera marks out this material in blurry white shades, obstructing the filmmaker's attempts to focus, often to the point of abstraction. The figure, therefore, appears ghostly, deprived of distinctness, almost like a blank canvas. The heat reflection of mylar thus protects bodies from the violent controlling gaze of surveillance drones but at the same time deprives them of definition as human individuals.

Whereas its initial purpose was tied to technological optimism and human progress, heat sheets, at least in the context of forced and clandestine migration, now bear a strong connection to notions of survival and bare life. The blanket covers those bodies which, in the terminological framework of Giorgio Agamben, have been reduced to naked biological existence, deprived of political status and vulnerable to external sovereign powers. In Ai Wei Wei's critically acclaimed documentary *Human Flow* from 2016, sheets of heat foil figure as a visual trope to stress the large scope and multitude of migrants reduced to this bare condition of life, marked by the same golden blankets, morphing bodies into masses, crowds, and streams of migration. The film is consistent with the proliferation of media images depicting the tragedies on the maritime borders of the European continent, in which emergency sheets have become an important symbolic trope of humanitarianism. At the same time, while keeping their bodies safe from hypothermia, within the realms of representation, the reflective and opaque material qualities of these sheets tend to have a dehumanizing effect on refugees, homogenizing them into masses without faces, contributing to a systematic erosion of difference. In one of its staggering scenes, viewers see how the generous hands of aid workers cover refugees in these blankets, putting them in long lines to get into busses in which the shimmering reflection of the mylar material blurs the edges and contours of these bodies. In this sense, the film fits within a larger tradition of artworks and media discourses that zoom out to focus on the scale of the emergency by dwelling either on the high numbers of refugees arriving or on the numerous piles of material remains they leave behind.

Gianfranco Rosi's documentary *Fuocoammare* [*Fire at Sea*] from 2016 draws on similar visual tropes. At the same time, it is self-aware of its own framing mechanisms insofar as it also turns its gaze to the processes and technologies of control to which refugees are subjugated as they arrive on the island of Lampedusa. Rosi opens his documentary with dense clusters of noise infiltrating a radar system from which disembodied and desperate-sounding voices emerge. After some moments, these distanced voices materialize into the bodies of refugees, crammed together in rafts or standing in line to be registered and photographed by Italian authorities. They are framed as an anonymous and homogenous collective, represented in long shots on the open sea or mediated through monitors and screens, always locked within controlled confines. Migrant boats are portrayed as small dots on the empty horizon, deprived of their broader geopolitical context, while upon arrival, their passengers are homogenized into indistinguishable bodies covered with the same golden mylar blankets. In a few medium long shots, these reflective blankets stick out among the more muted and darkened skins of the bodies that wear them, shining bright but obscuring faces and personal features (fig. 1).

Fig. 1: *Still from Fuocoammare [Fire at Sea], 2016, Gianfranco Rosi, courtesy of Cinéart Nederland BV.*

These so-called mass images reduce refugees to what Allen Feldman calls "anonymous corporeality," a form of "pervasive depersonalization" in which "generalities of bodies—dead, wounded, starving, diseased, and homeless—are pressed against the [screen] as mass articles" (407). Liisa H. Malkki connects this description to the specific context of refugee representations, in which "no names, no funny faces, no distinguishing marks, no esoteric details of personal style enter, as a rule, into the frame of pictures of refugees when they are being imagined as a sea of humanity" (388). The texture and the wavy movements of the mylar material, especially when wrapped around human bodies, look like a visual literalization of this "sea of humanity." For all its pleasant shimmering properties, or precisely because of its amorphous rendering of the human figure, it also robs individual refugees of their singular characteristics, as they are universalized into a stream of objectified bodies and muted masses.

Fig. 2 and Fig. 3: Migration as Avant-Garde, 2008–2017, Michael Danner, permission granted by the artist.

It is with the work of Michael Danner that I want to close this chapter, as he makes the aesthetic connection between the wrinkling material of mylar and the rippling textures of the sea explicit in his photo series *Migration as Avant-Garde* (2008–17) by inserting a golden filter over an image of ocean tides and juxtaposing this image with a photograph of a piece of mylar left behind (figs. 2 and 3). The latter picture shows the mylar material with a cluttered background, outside its conventional and preordained function in the material-semiotic order, as disposable waste. Via the spectral logic of the trace, images of dispossessed and displaced refugees still haunt the image, filling in the pressing absent presence at the center of the composition. However, the photograph here also goes beyond its metonymic relation to migrant bodies and exposes the thingness of the mylar material itself as existing outside of objecthood. Because of its arrangement next to an image of a shimmering golden sea, besides its connotation with migrants making oceanic crossings, the depiction of the mylar material here also enters geological and anthropo/scenic terrain, being converted into an emblem of ecological devastation.

There lies a certain sardonic cynicism in the fact that, as video artist James Bridle also hints at it, this material technology that is born from extra-terrestrial colonialism and opportunism now casts a long shadow over notions of human progress, symbolizing one of the largest humanitarian refugee crises in decades. This conflation of connotations shows once again how meaning flows in and out of matter and how materials acquire different significations over time, in different contexts, and for different people. My argument above attests to a range of shifting identities and meanings that attach themselves to the mylar foil as part of different affective-material-discursive practices. From matter to metaphor, in the specific context of images of migration, the golden foil goes from a tool of humanitarian help to a trope of massification and desubjectification to a symbol of plastic pollution and ecological debris. Tracing the different cultural lives and representational modes of mylar foil allows one to traverse different worlds of crisis and concern, reflecting on conflicting connotations and establishing transversal relations, bringing together hope and despair, the promises of the future, and the harsh realities of survival.

Works Cited

Agamben, Giorgio. *Homo Sacer: Sovereign Power and Bare Life*. Translated by Daniel Heller-Roazen, Stanford UP, 1998.

Appadurai, Arjun, editor. *The Social Life of Things: Commodities in Cultural Perspective*. Cambridge UP, 1986.

Barad, Karen. *Meeting the Universe Halfway: Quantum Physics and the Entanglement of Matter and Meaning*. Duke UP, 2007.

Bennett, Jane. *Vibrant Matter: A Political Ecology of Things*. Duke UP, 2010.

Bridle, James. "A Flag for No Nations." *Booktwo.org*, 19 Jan. 2016, http://booktwo.org/notebook/a-flag-for-no-nations/.

Danner, Michael. *Migration as Avant-Garde*. Verlag Kettler, 2018.
Feldman, Allen. "On Cultural Anesthesia: From Desert Storm to Rodney King." *American Ethnologist*, vol. 21, no. 2, 1994, pp. 404–18.
Fuocoammare [Fire at Sea]. Directed by Gianfranco Rosi, Cinéart Nederland, 2016.
Human Flow. Directed by Ai Wei Wei, Independent Films, 2017.
Incoming. Directed by Richard Mosse, 2014–17.
Ingold, Tim. *Being Alive: Essays on Movement, Knowledge and Description*. Routledge, 2011.
Kopytoff, Igor. "The Cultural Biography of Things: Commoditization as Process." *The Social Life of Things: Commodities in Cultural Perspective*, edited by Arjun Appadurai, Cambridge UP, 1986, pp. 64–92.
Malkki, Liisa H. "Speechless Emissaries: Refugees, Humanitarianism, and Dehistoricization." *Cultural Anthropology*, vol. 11, no. 3, 1996, pp. 377–404.

Part IX: Touching Texts

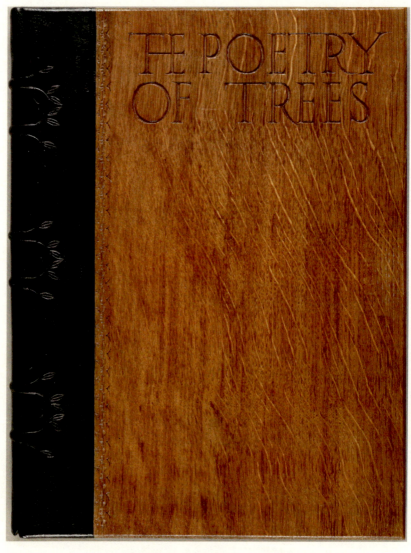

Fig. 1: The cover of Thomas Pitfield's The Poetry of Trees (1942). Copyright of the Pitfield Trust. Reproduced with the permission of the Pitfield Trust.

21. An Archive of the Future: Wood in Thomas Pitfield's *The Poetry of Trees*

Frederik Van Dam and Ghidy de Koning

> Wood finished in glistening black lacquer is the very best; but even unfinished wood, as it darkens and the grain grows more subtle with the years, acquires an inexplicable power to calm and soothe. (Tanizaki 12)

In the opening pages of his celebrated essay on Japanese aesthetics, *In Praise of Shadows* (1933), the Japanese novelist Junichirō Tanizaki pauses to consider the qualities of toilet fixtures made from wood. Whereas materials such as porcelain and nickel earn his opprobrium for their garish glitter, wood is praised for its patina; as it ages, its texture thickens, allowing holder and beholder to discover beauty in its darkness. Although Tanizaki's reflections on this dusky kind of beauty stem from a consideration of Japanese culture, they also indicate how wood, as a material, is marked by time. Once a tree has been felled, wood will rot and disintegrate; skilled woodworkers can halt and reverse this process, however, thus, like necromancers, giving the tree a second life. To the artisans working with wood, the precise moment in the process of decomposition is vital: craftsmen engaged in carving wooden utensils, such as spoons, will generally prefer wood that is still fresh and slightly "wet," while those engaged in making chairs will ensure that their wood is sufficiently dry. Artisans' decisions about when to carve and how to chisel are, of course, also influenced by the type of wood (say, ash versus walnut), not to mention the way in which the tree was chopped down and the wood was stored; as the famous Japanese-American woodworker George Nakashima writes in praise of the burly oak, for instance, "this species should be cut when the last of its life juices are ebbing, when its only future is decay.... Sawing this 'treasure' calls for the precision of a diamond cutter" (91). With proper treatment and proper use, in short, wooden objects may extend the tree's existence beyond its original lifespan. This new life, moreover, is not immutable. As many a musician knows, wood contracts and expands according to the moods of the season; it breathes. In every work of wood, then, the spirit of the tree may be said to linger; hovering in the twilight, no longer alive yet not quite dead, wood is a material with ghostly, undead qualities.

Perhaps as a result of the material's association with temporality, artists have long recognized wood's power to induce a state of contemplation. One might consider the almost painterly use of wood in the wall paneling of Federico da Montefeltro's *studioli* in the ducal palaces of Urbino and Gubbio. Through the wood-inlay technique known as intarsia, the paneling creates optical illusions that heighten these rooms' function as a place for meditation and study. In the hands of a major craftsman and designer like George Nakashima, to give a more contemporary example, wooden objects like coffee tables attain the status of a sculpture. Indeed, the way in which Nakashima's work aims to get in touch with a tree's soul is not unlike the way in which premodern artists crafted wooden effigies of gods and magical creatures. As these examples suggest, wood can be transformed into myriad forms and shapes, which is probably why Aristotle's mind, "when he sat down to think about materials—his was arguably the first systematic attempt to do so, at least in European philosophy— . . . drifted naturally to the forest" and he adopted the Greek word for wood (ὕλη) for his thinking about materiality (Adamson 2–3). The artist on which we will focus, Thomas Pitfield, has not—or, at least, not yet—attained the canonical status of these different thinkers and makers; as such, one of his works in and on wood, *The Poetry of Trees* (1942), has some untapped potential for an exploration into the kind of reflections that wooden works of art may produce. Taking our cue from Ann-Sophie Lehmann's reminder that materials in art "are embedded in a web of language on a cultural level, and it is through textual references in inventories, recipes, anecdotes, pamphlets, and poems that their meaning-making becomes most obvious to us" (18), we will be paying attention to the interplay between wood's material affordances and its historico-cultural context. Pitfield's fascination with wood's ghostly qualities, we aim to show, was partly a response to the horrors of industrial warfare.

The first and arguably most striking way in which Pitfield's "book" uses wood is its cover (fig. 1). In the original version, created in 1942, the work is bound in thin panels of English brown oak (15"x11") that have been sanded, beveled, and varnished, with the title engraved on the front. From the moment that one holds this work, then, one is touching the remains of its subject matter, one of the eponymous trees. On the inside of the work (which has no page numbers), the reader first encounters a beautiful endpaper made from a woodcut of two interlocking waves, one with trees in bloom and one with their withered counterparts. This interleaving of life and death strikingly captures the eerie feelings that wood may inspire. The following pages contain ten prose sketches and ten images printed on a thick yellow paper—paper which, of course, was made from wood shavings that were boiled, washed, bleached, and mixed with water before being pressed into sheets. Each of the ten two-page "chapters" revolves around a tree native to Britain: the common elm, beech, Scots pine, Lombardy poplar, horse chestnut, silver birch, wych elm, willow, oak, and yew. The accompanying images of the trees are linocuts, a method of relief printing that uses a sheet of linoleum (which is itself made of linseed oil, derived from flax) as a relief surface. Pitfield's choice for linoleum (especially in contrast to steel engraving) is significant. Originally developed in the 1860s as a deck covering for battleships, linoleum soon began to replace wood as a material for hand-pulled prints. As such, linocuts are made with the same tools—chisels, gouges, carving knives, and burins—and techniques as the woodcut (Amann 9). Like the woodcut, moreover, the linocut does not lend itself to mass reproduction: to print the linocut, ink or paint is applied manually with a dabber or a roller.

The use of wood in the creation of *The Poetry of Trees* has its roots in the author's youthful years in Bolton, which he ironically describes as "a forest of [chimney-stacks], spreading a black foliage, branching into one immense canopy of smoke" (Pitfield, *A Cotton-Town Boyhood* 9). Yearning to escape the cotton mills and weaving sheds, Pitfield imagined trees wherever he could; at one point, he planted a lime sapling where the privy used to be. Pitfield's love of the forest and his interest in craftmanship—inherited from his father, a joiner—were heightened by the onset of World War II: his dislike of industrial production segued into a loathing of industrial warfare. As a committed pacifist, Pitfield translated his opposition to the war into linocuts with an overtly pacifist message. In *The Poetry of Trees*, this pacifist dimension is somewhat veiled but becomes apparent when we consider the work's particular concern with the oak. The oak occupies a special place in the book's catalog of trees. In most of his descriptions, Pitfield is keen to explore the ways in which trees' personalities express moods that humans cannot put into words. "On a still, moonless night," for instance, "the very air creeps eerily about [the yew], whispering things too ghostly for the language of living men" (*The Poetry of Trees*). Only in his sketch of the oak, his subjective portrayal moves into a more detached, historical register. Since the oak "has been claimed as a national hero," Pitfield argues, the English have "accommodated its characteristics into [their] own versions of [themselves]." Instead of being swayed by the oak's aura, he continues, "we must try to disentangle [the oak] from the old history-book associations that cling to it, populous as gnats by summer streams." Pitfield's injunction to strip the oak of its ideological cortex can be understood more clearly when we take stock of its historical and cultural significance.

The oak has a long-standing role in English culture. Rather than planting oaks in large forests, as in France, the English prioritized their appearance, which resulted in the planting of oak trees in smaller clusters (Thirgood 7) and thus associating them with the picturesque (Burton 17). At the same time, these aesthetic qualities seeped into a particular ideology. With its large crown and typically thick branches, the oak became a symbol of the nation's strength (Cosgrove 48; Fulford 164). This symbolism acquired a material dimension during the Napoleonic Wars (1803–1815) when oak provided one of the primary resources for constructing battleships (Cosgrove 51). More so than its Baltic and French cousins, the English oak was known for its solidity and played a vital role in parts of the ship where the combined force of water and wind usually resulted in weaker spots (Thirgood 9). As a result, many naval ballads put the oak in service of a patriotic message (Fulford 164). Given these ideological mystifications, it bears reminding that ships constructed with English oak were also "crucial to the brutal operations of the slave trade" (Adamson 4). Pitfield's choice for oak in his cover, then, may be understood as a provocative gesture: he reclaims this material from its military and imperialist connotations. His uncanny linocut of the oak extends his critique: suffused with darkness and shadows, it goes against the grain of the picturesque quality that the oak is supposed to have.

Pitfield's critique of industrial warfare also intersects with what may be considered the archetype of the book's form, the xylotheque. The xylotheque is a particular kind of arboreal herbarium: rather than describing the plants that it documents, it consists of books that were "made out of a particular type of wood, the spine covered with the corresponding bark and decorated with associated moss and lichens. Once opened, the book would reveal samples of dried leaves, flowers, seedlings, roots, and branches, with a special compartment in the spine holding a written description of the species' biology and use" (Lovejoy). This way of documenting trees originated in the seventeenth century, became popular as a cabinet of curiosities in the Enlightenment, morphed into an important taxonomic method of nineteenth-century biology, and was disregarded for a major part of the twentieth century. Intriguingly, there are some nineteenth-century Japanese collections that consist of wood blocks decorated with painted illustrations of twigs, leaves, flowers, fruits, and seeds (Lack). Pitfield's work is a creative echo of the xylotheque: its oak cover corresponds to the outside of a xylothetic volume, while its prose and pictures resemble the contents of such a collection. Although we cannot assess Pitfield's intentions, it is tempting to argue that he was one of the first to reassess these collections. In recent years, indeed, xylotheques have been rediscovered: responding to the ongoing mass extinction of species and deforestation, artists are creatively engaging with the form, and scientists are rediscovering their use as a means of conservation (Figueroa et al.; Vásquez-Correa). Looking at Pitfield's work as a xylotheque implies that it has an archival function. The archive that Pitfield creates is very different from the totalizing vision of nineteenth-century biologists: it is a personal and emotional archive, not a scientific collection. The sentiments that Pitfield's descriptions and images express are akin to Tanizaki's vision of a premodern world in which natural materials allow one to reflect on the passing of time.

Pitfield is not alone in choosing wood to reflect on the transience of our existence. His art dovetails with other works in wood. George Nakashima's "Altars for Peace," huge walnut tables with free edges that preserve the tree's natural outline, use the ancient device of the butterfly key not only as a practical joint but also as a metaphor: they "remind us of the brevity of human lives and of the fragility of the environments in which we—humans, animals, and trees—exist" (Duarte-Gray 121). In his famous *7000 Eichen: Stadtverwaldung statt Stadtverwaltung* (*7000 Oaks: City Forestation Instead of City Administration*), begun in 1982, Joseph Beuys invites reflection on the change of nature through time: by planting oaks that grow next to basalt stones that remain unchanged, Beuys argued for "an ecopolitical and spiritual transformation of society through art, in its relationship to living beings in general" (Arnaud 261). In a similar vein, Katie Patterson's *Future Library* project, "in which a forest of trees will become an anthology of books to be printed in 100 years . . . unfolds concurrently over long, slow time—a century—and the present moment—the diurnal, daily cycles of the trees, the seasons, and the author's yearly contributions and handover events" (Harris et al. 39; cf. Bronstein). Like these more modern artists, we feel, Pitfield was considering the deep time of nature as opposed to the mechanical time of human history. In Pitfield's case, the seeds for his articulation of an arboreal kind of temporality might be traced to the threat of the atomic bomb. As Paul K. Saint-Amour has recently argued, the foundations for fear of total annihilation were laid during the interwar period, as the practice of air-raid alerts turned "cities and towns into spaces of rending anticipation . . . amounting to a proleptic mass traumatization" (7–8). Even though Pitfield does not explicitly refer to the experience of a collective pre-traumatic stress syndrome, it is not too far-fetched to see his love of the countryside as a response to such a condition. From this perspective, the backward-looking temporality of *The Poetry of Trees* might be interpreted as a form of topiary therapy.

In a paradoxical way, which matches wood's ghostly qualities, *The Poetry of Trees* reached a larger audience only after the demise of its creator. At a recent exhibition at the Atkinson in Southport (2022–2023), which owes its title to Pitfield's work, *The Poetry of Trees* enters into a dialogue with such works as Ibrahim El-Salahi's "Meditation Tree" (2018), an aluminium sculpture, and Heywood and Condie's "Nil By Root" (2022), a laminated pine tree that was choked with sand and washed out to sea in the 1970s. This sense of belated acknowledgment seems to be the fate of artworks in wood. Beuys's project is continuing after his death, as in Heather Ackroyd and Dan Harvey's *Beuys' Acorns*. Patterson's library will be completed only in 2114. Nakashima's peace project, too, did not reach its conclusion during his lifetime. Only in 2001 did Nakashima's Russian Altar reach its destination; it now sits in the Tsereteli Gallery at the Russian Academy of Arts. At a time in history when the threat of nuclear war seems stronger than ever, except for the Cuban Missile Crisis, one wonders whether it would be possible to have Nakashima's American and Russian Altars moved to the offices of the presidents of the US and Russia. That way, these leaders might be prompted to redirect their attention to the climate catastrophe that surrounds us before we humans, too, become the ghosts of our future. While the exhibition at the Atkinson may not have been intended to make its visitors reflect on our own geopolitical and ecological moment, we hope that our examination of the role of wood in Pitfield's *The Poetry of Trees* shows that attention to the material history and the material affordances of wood is vital to grasp the significance of this work of art fully: through his use of wood Pitfield prompts us to think about a different future, one in which a consideration of the natural world ensures that we do not willingly consign ourselves to the archive of our planet's history.

Acknowledgments

We would like to thank Esther Folkersma for traveling to and reporting on the exhibition on *The Poetry of Trees* at the Atkinson in Southport; Bente Faaij for enlightening us on the nature of the woodcut; and Stephen Whittle for sharing his article on Thomas Pitfield as artist and printmaker, which will shortly be published by the Thomas Pitfield Trust.

Works Cited

Adamson, Glenn. "Oak." *Material Intelligence*, vol. 1, 2021, pp. 1–12.

Arnaud, Jean. "Confused Forces: The Tree, Living Memory in Twenty-First Century Art." *Interdisciplinary Literary Studies*, vol. 24, no. 2, 2022, pp. 254–91.

Amann, Per. *Woodcuts*. Artline, 1989.

Bronstein, Michaela. "Taking the Future into Account: Today's Novels for Tomorrow's Readers." *PMLA*, vol. 134, no. 1, 2019, pp. 121–35.

Burton, Anna. *Trees in Nineteenth-Century English Fiction: The Silvicultural Novel*. Routledge, 2021.

Cosgrove, Denis, and Stephen Daniels. *The Iconography of Landscape: Essays on the Symbolic Representation, Design and Use of Past Environments*. Cambridge UP, 1988.

Duarte-Gray, Isabel. "The Tree as Archive: George Nakashima and the Nuclear Age." *Close Reading the Anthropocene*, edited by Helena Feder, Routledge, 2021, pp. 116–30.

Figueroa-Mata, Geovanni, et al. "Automated Image-based Identification of Forest Species: Challenges and Opportunities for 21st Century Xylotheques." *IEEE International Work Conference on Bioinspired Intelligence*, 2018, pp. 1–8. DOI: 10.1109/IWOBI.2018.8464206.

Fulford, Tim. "Romanticizing the Empire: The Naval Heroes of Southey, Coleridge, Austen, and Marryat." *Modern Language Quarterly*, vol. 60, no. 2, 1999, pp. 161–96.

Harris, Paul, et al. "Archivists of the Future." *Time's Urgency*, edited by Carlos Montemayor and Robert Daniel, Brill, 2019, pp. 37–43.

Lack, H. Walter. "Plant Illustration on Wood Blocks: A Magnificent Japanese Xylotheque of the Early Meji Period." *Curtis's Botanical Magazine*, vol. 16, no. 2, 1999, pp. 124–34.

Lehmann, Ann-Sophie. "How Materials Make Meaning." *Netherlands Yearbook for History of Art / Nederlands Kunsthistorisch Jaarboek Online*, vol. 62, no. 1, Jan. 2012, pp. 6–27.

Lovejoy, Bess. "Xylotheks: Wondrous Wooden Books That Hold Wooden Collections." *Atlas Obscura*, 2014. https://www.atlasobscura.com/articles/xylothek.

Nakashima, George. *The Soul of a Tree: A Woodworker's Reflections*. Introduction by Dr. George Wald, Kodansha International Ltd, 1981.

Pitfield, Thomas. *A Cotton-Town Boyhood*. Kall Kwik, 1993.

———. *The Poetry of Trees*. Knights Press, 1944.

Saint-Amour, Paul K. *Tense Future: Modernism, Total War, Encyclopedic Form*. Oxford UP, 2015.

Tanizaki, Junichirō. *In Praise of Shadows*. Translated from the Japanese by Thomas J. Harper and Edward G. Seidensticker, Vintage, 2001.

Thirgood, J. V. "The Historical Significance of Oak." *Oak Symposium Proceedings*, USDA Forest Service, Northeastern Forestry Experimental Station, pp. 1–18.

Vásquez Correa, Ángela María. "Xilotecas, importantes colecciones de referencia." *Columbia Forestal*, vol. 20, no. 2, 2017, pp. 192–201.

22. Soft Leather, Wounded Buttons, and a Silk Ribbon: Clothing a Birgittine Rule Manuscript

Kathryn M. Rudy

Saint Birgitta of Sweden (circa 1303–1373) founded an order that attracted the attention of several European rulers, who then established Birgittine convents. The new convents required copies of the Rule of Saint Augustine, used in Birgittine convents alongside the Constitutions of Saint Birgitta. This chapter considers one such copy (now Ghent, University Library, MS 607) and, most importantly, its binding: a soft leather envelope binding edged in silk ribbon. I will consider the various skills and crafts required to manufacture such a binding and relate those to their counterparts in producing the Birgittine habit. By applying materials and techniques from the domain of sartorial textiles, nuns fed their creativity in the separate field of manuscript binding. Reflecting on the materials in this binding, one can see how Birgittine nuns forged a relationship between their own bodies and the "body" of their Rule book. In the acts of selecting materials and crafting those materials into a binding, not only did they imitate Mary—to whom all Birgittine convents were dedicated—but they also forged connections between and among the various Birgittine convents, which similarly "clothed" their Rule books with home-spun and hand-crafted materials. By paying close attention to the materials they selected, in both their habits and their bindings, we can see how they asserted their Birgittine group identity.

The Manuscript and Its Contents

Ghent, University Library, MS 607 comprises only 90 parchment folios, each measuring circa 295 x 215 (text block: circa 180 x circa 141–146) millimeters.[1] This is significant because the large size and grand white margins support the book's ceremonial role in displaying a foundational document for the convent. One can imagine that the manuscript was used for reading aloud in the Chapter House or for new sisters to ceremonially profess their faith by reciting the formulas, copied in Dutch

---

1   A basic description of the manuscript and all the images are available at https://lib.ugent.b e/en/catalog/rug01:000990667.

and Latin within its folios. The manuscript has not, however, been used extensively. This is because the Reformation came decades after the manuscript was produced, marking its sudden obsolescence. Stylistic considerations set its date of production around 1500.

The manuscript contains the bull issued by Pope Martin confirming the Constitutions of Saint Brigitta, the Rule of Saint Augustine, and a profession of faith. These texts are each given twice, in Latin and Dutch. It also contains two full-page miniatures. The first depicts Saint Birgitta writing her visions as an angel whispers to her, flanked by two Birgittine nuns. This image shows the genesis of the saint's Revelations. The second image depicts Saint Augustine standing before a cloth of honor and holding his attribute, the heart, while two diminutive Birgittine nuns venerate him. The image of Saint Augustine prefaces the Latin version of his Rule. The manuscript was written by one hand in the *bâtarde* script fashionable at Southern Netherlandish courts. Instead of assuming that MS 607 was copied in the convent of Dendermonde, it is more plausible that it was copied by a professional scribe connected to the Burgundian court in Ghent, Bruges, or Mechelen.[2]

After Napoleon closed the convents in the French-occupied territories, French officials removed the church goods, including the manuscripts. For the next few decades, many were sold, some entered regional secular collections, and some changed hands, singularly or in small groups. In 1850, M. Van Oosthuyzen, the pastor at Zele, donated Ghent, UL MS 607—together with MSS 603, 604, 605, 606, and 608—to the Ghent University Library. This group of manuscripts had come from the convent at Dendermonde, dedicated to Onze-Lieve-Vrouw-ten-Troon (Our Dear Lady of the Throne), also known as Mariëntroon.[3] Soon after it

---

[2] The manuscript also has what may be an early use of the parenthesis (MS 607, fol. 5v, col 1). Willem de Vreese and Edward Gailliard posit that MS 607 was written by the same scribe as a luxurious Birgittine prayer book (Ghent University, MS 205), also written in decorous Burgundian *bâtarde*, and that both manuscripts were made in the Birgittine Abbey of Maria Troon, Dendermonde (25–26). However, I do not agree that the same hand copied the two manuscripts: the scribe of MS 205 exaggerates the differences between thick and thin, emphasize the slant of tall letters in comparison with the rather upright spines of the tall letters in MS 607, and the scribe of MS 205 makes the letters float midway between the heavily ruled lines. Furthermore, I do not think that either manuscript was copied in Dendermonde. Connection with the court and its resources, however, can be explained by the fact that the Dendermonde convent had been founded by nobles: Isabella of Portugal, the Duchess of Burgundy, laid the first stone on 30 January 1466. Subsequently, the convent grew with the support of various Burgundian nobles until it had 67 members in 1499. The convent retained strong ties with individuals at courts, who supported the abbey financially, until Napoleon's armies closed it in 1797. Among the people mentioned in the convent's necrology were Charles the Bold; Mary of Burgundy; Isabelle of Portugal; and Margaret of York. See Reynaert and de Vlaminck.

[3] For manuscripts from this monastery, see Sander Olsen.

was founded as a double monastery in 1466, the men moved out, turning it into an all-female convent. Whereas most prayerbooks were bound in boards, this group of manuscripts donated to the Ghent UL, MSS 603–608, were all Birgittine administrative manuscripts, each bound in a limp binding.

One of those manuscripts was an English cartulary (MS 604) containing all of the papal bulls, confirmations, and privileges relevant to the Birgittine monastery of Syon outside London. MS 604 also contains a separate charter dated 1471 from Thomas, bishop of Canterbury, as well as two English wax seals that have been attached by cords to the limp vellum binding. This English manuscript, in possession of the nuns at Dendermonde, attests to the network among the various Birgittine houses in England, the Low Countries, Germany, and the motherhouse in Vadstena. They clearly shared manuscripts and knowledge about, among other things, bookbinding techniques. The seals on MS 604 reveal an important reason the Birgittines chose limp bindings for their administrative documents.

Binding and Embellishment

Shortly after MS 607 entered the Ghent University Library collection in 1850, it received a brief description in French pasted to the first folio, which describes the binding as "reliure primitive en cuir de Russie" ("original binding in Russian leather"). The manuscript is in a large, soft leather envelope binding, which is similar to a limp vellum binding in that it wraps around the cut edge of the book block with a flap (fig. 1). Whereas limp vellum bindings may have been considered a no-frills, low-cost solution to protecting the leaves, here the soft leather serves as a substrate for rich and symbolically-charged embellishment.

Fig. 1: *Binding of the Rule from Mariëntroon. Dendermond, ca. 1500.* Ghent, University Library, MS 607, binding.

Fig. 2. *Inner flap of the binding of the Rule from Mariëntroon. Dendermond, ca. 1500.* Ghent, University Library, MS 607, Blue linen paste-down.

The decision to bind the Rule in a limp leather binding stood in opposition to the more expected choice, a binding made of boards covered in tooled leather. In fact, the convent of Dendermonde had its own metal stamps for making stamped leather bindings, at least three of which survived (Verheyden). However, I have no evidence that the Birgittines themselves made the panel-stamped bindings, nor that they had access to the necessary woodworking skills and equipment to do so, such as a saw to size the boards correctly for the book block, a plane, a bore to make the channels in the oak planks. The bespoke stamp may have been used by a non-monastic professional. I believe two important material reasons lay behind the Birgittines' choice to use a limp binding. First, the soft leather could be sliced into, meaning that such a binding could be affixed with cords bearing seals, which would declare its contents authorized, as with the case of MS 604. Second, this type of binding could be made and embellished by the sisters themselves, even if they had not copied the manuscript. It allowed them to work the binding with multiple crafts that would certainly have been within the nuns' skill set. For the first reason, Birgittines in Mariëntroon and elsewhere bound administrative manuscripts in limp leather. However, they only embellished prize manuscripts.

The leather is the wrong texture to be tooled—it is too spongy—and instead has been embellished with various textiles. First, the leather has been lined with blue-dyed linen, made with a plain weave (fig. 2).[4] The binding required some 63 x 31 centimeters of soft leather and the same amount of linen, which has been glued to the leather. The linen is the same material the nuns wore on their bodies, and the soft leather would have been of the same kind as one would use to make a satchel, such as the one depicted in the miniature as Birgitta's attribute: the pilgrim's scrip. According to their Rule, the "mantle shall not be on the outside gathered nor pleated, nor curiously made, but straight and plain" (108; ch. 3). In lining the book with plain fabric, tightly cropped, they were following aspects of their own prescribed habit: plain, with no excess. Perhaps if they had not had this Rule in mind, they would have given the manuscript a floppy chemise binding that extended far beyond the book block.

The Birgittines have further embellished the book with veils: inside that flap and before the first folio is a guard of very fine brown silk.[5] This fabric, constructed in plain weave, has a woven-in embellishment consisting of pairs of thicker threads in the warp, to give the fabric a subtle texture stripe along its length. Hemmed on all four sides to prevent fraying, the silk is not attached at the gutter, and it is doubtful that it is currently in its original intended location. Rather, it was probably used as

---

4 I have assessed the fiber content and weave structure of the textiles by visual and auditory inspection and have not confirmed my assessments with a lab analysis.

5 In my estimation, the silk threads are about 2/120-weight, i.e., 60 km/kg. For a full discussion of veiling images, see Sciacca.

a veil above one of the miniatures. That would explain the needle holes at the upper corners of miniatures as well as the frayed holes at the corresponding upper corners of the veil. By sewing in veils, the nuns dressed both the book itself and the images within it. Of course, they also veiled themselves: to "take the veil" was synonymous with taking a vow of religious profession, the very ceremony whose instructions are enshrined in the book. The book authenticates the veiling of the nun, while the nun, in a reciprocal action, veils the book.

Fig. 3: The Virgin weaving at a band loom. Paris, ca. 1410. The Hague, Royal Library, MS 76 F 21, fol. 14r.

The other textile embellishments are also charged with meaning. The entire periphery of the cut leather has been edged with a narrow, woven band of green, red, and gold silk passementerie.[6] While it is possible that the Birgittines purchased the woven ribbon from an outside source, it is more likely that they produced it themselves. Firstly, a Birgittine nun could imitate Mary, who is sometimes depicted as a young virgin weaving in the temple, as in an early fifteenth-century manuscript illumination (fig. 3). In this image, Mary is weaving a band loom, the same type of loom used to create the silk ribbons embellishing the binding.

Fig. 4: Detail of the binding showing the types of passementerie. Ghent, University Library, MS 607.

Further evidence that the Birgittines received the raw material—green, red, and gold silk thread—is that they worked it into several different products, including the woven ribbon just discussed and the braided cord. If this hypothesis is correct, then they used long strands of the green silk thread, plus thrums, to produce radially braided cord terminating in textile knobs with tassels (fig. 4). The two kinds of passementerie have been made for different roles in the book. The flat ribbon, which bends best along one axis, has been applied to stay flush with the planar edge of the leather, while the braided cord, which bends in every direction and is thick rather

---

6 Robin Fleming demonstrates that medieval England was awash with silk. For example, silk bands woven with tablets (or with band looms) appeared in England in the eleventh century. Other silk textiles were recycled from larger garments, such as ecclesiastical robes.

than flat, has been used as a lace to secure the button. Further testimony to their access to raw materials, and further support for my hypothesis that the nuns crafted the binding themselves, they used the same green and red silk thread to sew the head and tail end bands to the book block.

The flat woven silk ribbon reappears for another function: as bookmarks, fastened at the head of the spine (fig. 5). Although the bookmarks are similar to the bands embellishing the book's cover, the bookmarks have no gold thread, and the warp of the bookmarks consists only of ten green and one red thread. The red edge is created by passing an opposing pair of red silk threads through the shed as a weft. These twist at the edge in a rhythmic way to create a pattern. The subtle differences between the various bits of ribbon throughout the book suggest that they were homemade and constructed with thrums by the nuns rather than made by some larger commercial enterprise that would have had large supplies of silk thread at hand and not depended on thrums.

Fig. 5: Detail with bookmark made of woven silk band. Ghent, University Library, MS 607, fol. 9r.

The braided cord slips around (horn?) buttons, the crowning achievement of the binding. According to their Rule, the nuns were to fasten their mantles with buttons. Here they have transferred the technology of veiling to their binding rather than using, say, a brass fastener. Each button has been affixed to the envelope flap with red and white silk threads in a specific pattern that exploits the buttons' four holes. Revealing the thought process of the maker, the red and white crossed threads draw upon the pattern on a Birgittine nun's headwear, as specified in the Rule:

> Upon the veil must be set a crown of white linen cloth, to which must be sewed five small particles of red cloth, as five drops, the first particle on the forehead, another behind, the third and fourth about the ears, and the fifth in the middle of the head, in the manner of a cross; this crown shall be made fast in the middle of the head with one pin, and this crown shall both widows and virgins wear in token of continence and chastity. (109; ch. 3)

Whereas the buttons could have stayed perfectly secure with two holes, the Birgittines used buttons with four. (Whether they made these buttons themselves or commissioned them is uncertain.) They then chose thread colors and stitching patterns that would introduce the motif from their distinctive headgear to the elaborate binding of their most important foundational documents. In effect, they have crowned the manuscript with the same strategy with which they were crowned themselves: with red and white textiles that symbolized Christ's sacrifice. In this process, woman and book have been reciprocally crowned.[7]

A Broader Context

That books, people, and ideas flowed between the houses is apparent when one compares the binding of Ghent MS 607 with Birgittine bindings made elsewhere.[8] Clearly, it shares a basic form with the cartulary from the English Birgittine house called Syon (Ghent UL, MS 604), mentioned above. It even more closely resembles Stockholm, Royal Library, MS A 24, which contains the Rule for the monastery of Vadstena.[9] Written in Swedish, dated 1451 and attested by the Bishop of Vadstena on 6 May 1452, it was made for, and presumably bound by, the sisters at the original

---

7 Bynum shows that the crown itself was more important than the formal vows for nuns to feel themselves as professed and recognize each other as professed (97–128).

8 In addition to the soft vellum and leather bindings in the Ghent University Library, mentioned above, one should also consider a copy of the Rule now in the Society of Antiquaries of London. As a small quarto of only thirty-one folios, this manuscript is smaller than Ghent MS 607; however, it is also bound in a limp leather brown "chemise." For the Society of Antiquaries of London, inv. SAL/MS/339, see https://discovery.nationalarchives.gov.uk/details/r/bcf06f97-c9b9-4b3f-a94e-88688f19ffb9.

9 For a description and basic bibliography, see https://www.manuscripta.se/ms/100214. For highly crafted photos of the binding, see the National Library of Sweden's Flickr feed: https://www.flickr.com/photos/25300312@N08/5061907761/in/set-72157625120216684/

Birgittine monastery in Vadstena (fig. 6). The binding is an inversion of that around Ghent MS 607. The Vadstena binding consists of dyed linen over soft leather, padded with parchment waste. Whereas the sisters in Dendermonde used the materials and techniques they had at hand—red and white silk thread, and a stitching technique—the sisters in Vadstena, using linen, have exploited a radially looped thread technique to cover their buttons, resulting in red and white wound-like designs to imbue their binding with Christological meaning.

Fig. 6: *Binding of the Rule of Saint Birgitta from Vadstena, with wax seals. Vadstena, 1451/52. Stockholm, Royal Library, MS A 24.*

It is unlikely that the mother house in Vadstena would have sent this manuscript to the house in Dendermonde, for the sisters there would not have been able to read the Swedish text. More likely is that the motherhouse sent instructions to the daughter house to order a cartulary from the best scribe they could find and then bind it as if the book itself were taking a profession of faith and needed to be dressed appropriately. It is as if Vadstena exported the general idea of clothing the book but left it up to the daughter houses to interpret the instructions with the materials and techniques at hand.

In conclusion, some of the prescriptions for dressing sisters have been transferred to dressing the manuscript. It is possible that the Birgittine nuns bound Ghent MS 607, Stockholm A24, and other manuscripts themselves, and that they chose a soft leather binding because it exploited skills and crafts they already possessed, those they could transfer from sewing their own habits. Rather than outsource this work to male professionals, they used materials at hand, including recycled silk fabric, dying, weaving, sewing, and stitching techniques, and other skills necessary to make their habits, possibly including button making. They also used several passementerie techniques, including using a band loom to make a warp-faced woven ribbon. They would have possessed sufficient tools and skills to make soft leather bindings to protect, embellish, and display their most important manuscripts, which were dressed as a reflexive reference to the instructions they contained.

Acknowledgments

In 2018–19, Anneke Smelik and I were fellows together at the Netherlands Institute for Advanced Study. During those intellectually engaging months, she encouraged me to think more broadly about the role of textiles in the late Middle Ages. I am grateful to her as both a colleague and a friend. For their helpful comments on an earlier draft of this paper, I thank Julia Faiers, Cecilia Mazzocchio, Irene van Renswoude, Elizabeth Sandoval, and the volume editors. The reading room staff at the Ghent University Library kindly provided access and images. Patrik Granholm kindly brought me the conservation file for MS A 24 at the Kungliga biblioteket in Stockholm. The writing of this essay was funded by the Deutsche Forschungsgemeinschaft (DFG, German Research Foundation) under Germany's Excellence Strategy in the context of the Cluster of Excellence Temporal Communities: Doing Literature in a Global Perspective – EXC 2020 – Project ID 390608380.

Works Cited

Bynum, Caroline Walker. *Dissimilar Similitudes: Devotional Objects in Late Medieval Europe*, Zone Books, 2020.

Fleming, Robin. "Acquiring, flaunting and destroying silk in late Anglo-Saxon England." *Early Medieval Europe*, vol. 15, no. 2, 2007, pp 127–58.

Reynaert, Joris. "Het Middelnederlandse gebedenboek van de Brigittinessen te Dendermonde (Hs. Gent, Universiteitsbibliotheek 205)." *Jaarboek De Fonteine 32*, vol. 24, 1980–1981, pp. 29–48. Part 2. *Opstellen voor A. van Elslander [Essays for A. van Elslander]*.

Rule of Our Most Holy Saviour and the Additions of the Monastery of Saint Saviour and St. Bridget of Syon, Plymouth, 1914. PIMS, University of Toronto, https://archive.org/details/ruleofourmostholoobriduoft/page/n9/mode/2up.

Sander Olsen, Ulla. "Handschriften en boeken uit het Birgittinessenklooster Maria Troon te Dendermonde." *Ons geestelijk erf*, vol. 63–4, 1989–90, pp. 89–106.

———. "Handschriften en boeken uit het Birgittinessenklooster Maria Troon te Dendermonde: Supplement." *Ons geestelijk erf*, vol. 71, no. 3, 1997, pp. 215–27.

Sciacca, Christine. "Raising the Curtain on the Use of Textiles in Manuscripts." *Weaving, Veiling, and Dressing: Textiles and Their Metaphors in the Late Middle Ages*, edited by Kathryn M. Rudy and Barbara Baert. Brepols, 2007, pp. 161–90. Medieval Church Studies.

Verheyden, Prosper. "De paneelstempel Onze-Lieve-Vrouw-ten-Troon." *De Gulden Passer*, vol. 24, 1946, pp. 19–32. DBNL, www.dbnl.org/tekst/_gul005194601_01/_gul005194601_01_0002.php

Vlaminck, A., de. "Nécrologie du double monastère de Sainte-Brigitte à Termonde." *Gedenkschriften Oudheidkundige Kring van Dendermonde*, 1901, pp. 3–64.

Vreese, Willem de, and Edward Gailliard. "Dietsche kalenders." *Jaarboek der Koninklijke Vlaamsche Academie voor Taal- en Letterkunde*, vol. 27, 1913, pp. 17–115.

Part X: Materials of Scholarly Performance

Fig. 1: Corridor leading to arts classrooms in school 1. Photograph by the author.

23. The Arts Classroom

Edwin van Meerkerk

Introduction

The school is a modernist building on the edge of a former country estate, some fifteen minutes walking from the town center. Its grounds are separated from the street by four-foot-high hedges. It is exam time, the premises are quiet, and pupils walk the corridors talking only in suppressed whispers. Turning left from the entrance, my guide leads me to a semi-detached wing of the building that houses the visual arts and gymnastics classrooms. This annex used to be a swimming pool, its dark-brown tiled staircases and corridors reminding me of a long-forgotten past. We have taken a dead-end turn: pupils only come here with a specific purpose, there is none of the regular traffic in these corridors, no pupils looking at their phones seated on benches. A series of doors—locked and without any sign of a function; are they former dressing rooms? Showers?—have been spray-painted with Super Mario in a run, jumping from one door to the next (fig. 1).

The smell of school paint, that distinct odor that is not quite acrylic, mixed with the scent of sawdust washes toward me even before I enter the classroom. At first, all I see are artworks: statues, paintings, a desk chair with a seat consisting of large spikes, their aggressive feel compensated by two angel wings protruding from the back. The chair stands next to a mobile whiteboard that seems beyond cleaning after years of student graffiti. The walls and the doors of cupboards have received a similar treatment with a mixture of figures, abstract lines, obscenities, and political messages. The result is a messy whole of shapes and colors that are simultaneously ugly and intriguing. It invites one to look for details, make connections, take up a bucket, and clean up the mess. A rumble from above gives the feeling that the room is alive. The gym, one floor up, creates a permanent soundscape of a-rhythmic pounding.

The classroom is a maze. My walking becomes a staggering movement, trying not to step on anything. The profusion of colors and materials draws my eyes everywhere at once, further slowing my pace. Is that a...? Is that thing hanging upside down? Surfaces challenge me to decipher their writing; faceless statues stare at me, questioning, thought-provoking, maybe welcoming. Carefully navigating the meandering paths through the classroom, I am forced to focus on every detail of shape, color, texture, and smell. All objects are unique, even the tools, each broken or bent in their own way. In a state of decomposition, artworks tell a story of their afterlife, their makers having left the school long ago.

Post-Qualitative Inquiry

This chapter takes an approach that has recently emerged in the humanities and social sciences: Post-Qualitative Inquiry (PQI). The relation between PQI and other qualitative research (I will explain the use of the term inquiry below) is slightly problematic. While taking a turn from traditional approaches, many seek to remain within the broad domain of the social sciences. David Roussel, who has tried to carve out a niche within PQI that he calls "immersive cartography," writes that "Perhaps it is immersive cartography's continued attention to the wildness of data, to its mutant proliferation through lively experimentation, that maintains its most overt connection with what might be termed a "social science" (80).

PQI tries to break away from traditional western notions of science and research. Elizabeth St. Pierre, one of the most outspoken advocates of PQI, stresses that earlier qualitative research has never been able to break out of the confines of positivist, quantitative norms and values. For St. Pierre, PQI needs to rid qualitative research of this burden (Lather and St. Pierre; St. Pierre, "Post Qualitative Inquiry"). The PQI perspective is ecological in the sense that Ingold ("Materials") uses the term to foreground the processual and interactive aspect of engaging with the world and materiality. Le Grange calls this the "(re)turn to realism(s):" "a return to critical realism; a turn to speculative realism and matter-realism (new materialism) because existing philosophies (phenomenology, critical theory and poststructuralism) are no longer adequate for responding to current challenges" (4).

PQI scholars prefer the term inquiry to method(ology), to stress the unfolding of research while it is taking place. Research is performative (Le Grange 8), and method is refused (St. Pierre, "Post Qualitative Inquiry") in order to overcome the "language/material binary" (St. Pierre, "The Posts" 650). This line of thought is akin to many elements of philosophies of the South (Ubuntu) and East (Taoism, 道家). By recognizing this connection and provincializing Western thought, Wu et al. argue, we can become aware of the value of the paradoxical thinking of Taoism and the need to see all aspects of research (writing, thinking, observing, and philosophizing) as one. The same is true for Ubuntu, which has been described as "philosopraxis" (Wu et al. 516) and a "generous ontology" (Forster), namely one that allows for both objective and subjective, individual and collective perspectives.

Thus, I have let myself be guided by the materials in the arts classroom, letting the structure of the research follow the connections that unfolded before me, listening to what it told me through its texture, smell, and color. It is an open and, for me, a first exploration in "un/doing" research (Wu et al. 515).

The Arts Classroom

The classroom is square-shaped, with slit-like windows high up the walls. What happens here stays here, it seems to say. For the pupils, the room is a free zone where school rules do not apply. Amid their own graffiti (and that of their predecessors), they sit listening to a radio at high volume. They do their schoolwork, but also walk in and out as they please. The three adjacent arts classrooms invite similar un-school-like behavior: the materials a pupil might be looking for could be anywhere in this outburst of raw materials and artworks (fig. 2). They might want to store their unfinished project on one of the stuffed shelves in a forgotten corner or in the storeroom that is officially forbidden to them, but which is never locked and thus claimed as their territory.

The footloose behavior is the result of the studio atmosphere in the rooms. This is further reinforced by the fact that one of the teachers uses his classroom as his own studio, not just after hours but during classes. The statue he is currently working on has a prominent place in front of the classroom. It is impossible to work according to plan, not least as any kind of material one might want to work with will be hard to find. Even if it can be found, it will be oddly shaped, bent, or part of another piece. While searching for one thing, a pupil will find another. Thus, the stuff in the classroom dictates what is being made and what it can be made with. Who, then, is the artist? It is the materials just as much as the pupils or the teacher; that much is clear.

However, this free state on the fringes of the school is under constant threat from the system. Cleaning staff must regularly be denied entrance, lest they remove stuff and bring order. Sometimes, however, the pressure becomes too strong. Just before my visit, the exam pieces were on display, to be judged by external examiners. One of the three art classrooms had to be brought into a presentable state for this; an annual ritual wherein the art teachers grudgingly allow normalcy into their domain. Now, only a few days later, the works are still standing on the tables, but kipple has already started to take over. The exam objects have become gatherings of materials as they evolve or disintegrate into new objects. Some works have toppled, cards with captions are lying on the floor, and tools and materials are returning to the tables. Pretty soon, some of the artworks will have merged with other objects to engage in new assemblages.

Fig. 2: Bent and incomplete tools in arts classroom of school 1. Photograph by the author.

Another school, on a sunny day, located right outside the city, next to a regional highway along which cars and trucks roll night and day, creating a monotonous buzz. After passing through the gate, a brick wall blocks the traffic noise, and I enter arcadia: trees, fields, ponds, and birds—lots of birds. The school building is only a decade old and thus still recognizable as a school. It breathes peace and quiet. The entrance curves into the building, luring me inside. As I step in, I notice a large poster on my left spelling the rules of proper behavior with the school's name as an acronym. I walk into a spacious hall with an open stairway that allows a view outside through the glass wall beyond, showing lush green nature. To the right, an open space invites me to sit, whereupon the janitor welcomes me and, after hearing of my quest, guides me to the arts classroom. From the corridor, nothing distinguishes it from the other classrooms: the same wooden door, the same side window with the same translucent lilac strip showing the room number.

Fig. 3: Storeroom in school 2. Photograph by the author.

I enter an open, orderly room smelling of linoleum and soap. Two walls have windows from floor to ceiling, again revealing the nature outside. The natural light shines on rows of white tables still being cleaned by the pupils who have just finished the final class of the day. Others are washing their materials in one of the sinks. Cleansed materials are then put in their proper places. Linocuts sit in the drying racks, paint with the paint, paper with the paper, and spoons with the spoons. One of the spoons was bent double as a prank by one of the classmates and is immediately restored to its proper form. As I tour the room, I pass cupboards and drawers labeled with their contents. The storeroom is open, with a yellow sign "entry to the storeroom for teachers only" on the steel sliding door (fig. 3). No pupils enter. Above my head, an electrical conduit circles the room, with fold-out arms with sockets. The gutter itself is used as a display for a row of artworks.

Everything in the classroom seems to have been arranged by its material properties—glass, paint, paper, wood, and metal. Pots are kept on shelves by size, and tools hang neatly on a board, ordered by shape and size. I only touch cupboard doors and tables for fear of disturbing something so deliberately arranged. However, the neatness of the classroom does not make it sterile. There is a pot of tea with paper cups on one of the tables for the pupils that took the class this late in the day. The artworks all have a happy, colorful character. The linocuts are all inspired by a poem, most of them of a flower. In the far corner of the classroom, a series of painted portraits stand in a row. They are all the same size: canvas on a wooden frame, with remarkably similar portraits in school paint and bright colors. Friendly faces, each of them.

Coda

Faceless statues in creative chaos. Friendly, familiar faces in a neat and orderly classroom. One can feel a correlation, but is there causality? Do the things in the classroom influence the pupils' work, or is it a result of the pedagogy? My feeling is that it is dialogical, at the very least. A conversation between the wood, the paint, the paper, the tools, the teacher, the pupils, and the curriculum. Embodying different relations to materials, the two classrooms teach different ways of engaging with materials, allowing them to be alive or seeking to contain or constrain them. Illustrating Ingold's distinction between art made in correspondence with the materials and the hylomorphic imposition of form onto matter (Ingold, "Toward an Ecology" 435), the two classrooms ultimately demonstrate that the materials' use and re-use in the art classroom is not a form of recycling; instead, it is a part of life.

Works Cited

Forster, Dion A. "A Generous Ontology: Identity as a Process of Intersubjective Discovery—an African Theological Contribution." *HTS Teologiese Studies/ Theological Studies*, vol. 66, no. 1, 2010. https://hts.org.za/index.php/hts/article/view/731.

Ingold, Tim. "Materials against Materiality." *Archaeological Dialogues*, vol. 14, nr. 1, 2007, pp. 1–16.

———. "Toward and Ecology of Materials." *Annual Review of Anthropology*, vol. 41, 2012, pp. 427–42.

Lather, Patti, and Elizabeth A. St. Pierre. "Post-Qualitative Research." *International Journal of Qualitative Studies in Education*, vol. 26, no. 6, 2013, pp. 629–33.
Le Grange, Leslie. "What is (Post)Qualitative Research?" *South African Journal of Higher Education*, vol. 32, no. 5, 2018, pp. 1–14.
Roussel, David. *Immersive Cartography and Post-Qualitative Inquiry*. Routledge, 2021.
St. Pierre, Elizabeth A. "The Posts Continue: Becoming." *International Journal of Qualitative Studies in Education*, vol. 26, no. 6, 2013, pp. 646–57.
———. "Post Qualitative Inquiry, the Refusal of Method, and the Risk of the New." *Qualitative Inquiry*, vol. 27, no. 1, 2021, pp. 3–9.
Wu, Jinting, et al. "Perturbing Possibilities in the Postqualitative Turn: Lessons from Taoism and Ubuntu." *International Journal of Qualitative Studies in Education*, vol. 31, no. 6, 2018, pp. 504–19.

24. Ink on Paper

Carlijn Cober

Introduction

What materials mark the life of the intellectual? As I write this chapter at my desk at the university, I have my laptop in front of me. A white rectangle digitally mimics a piece of paper. The words I type appear in black, in a font my handwriting could never equal. If I'm lucky, these sentences will someday materialize as ink on paper. For me, the work does not take on meaning or feel "real" until it is printed. However, the ink itself is not tangible once it is dry—my fingers touch the paper, but they cannot feel its contents. This does not mean there is no ink spillage before the work reaches its final stage in print. During the writing process, my hands are often marked by the involuntary traces of a blue ballpoint pen. I wear them as a badge of honor, for they signify my work. Academics deal with ink constantly. As researchers and teachers, we are pen-pushers, ink-slingers, *scribouillards*; endlessly scribbling notes in the margins of books; grading papers with plastic red ballpoints; editing articles by drawing big black crosses over the freshly printed pages we no longer find necessary. Pencil can be erased too easily; it does not have the same gravity.

It is only when words are inked on paper that they become tangible texts. What does it mean for a text to be tangible? How does ink's material effect of tangibility—a particular effect that only surfaces in its "social life"—relate to the material qualities of ink itself (Drazin xxvi)? I will propose that ink offers a point of connection between the material and the affective elements of academic culture by exploring this material through Barthes's notion of *tangibilia* (*The Preparation of the Novel* 56). In the first half of this chapter, I will explore "tangibility" as one of ink's most interesting material properties. The second part will focus on Roland Barthes's affective description of writing with ink to explore the relationship between writing materials and style. The last part of this chapter will evoke Barthes's concept of the *tangibile* to draw a parallel between ink's ability to attach itself onto paper on the one hand and readers' experience of attachment to the words on the page on the other.

Material Properties of Ink

For over three thousand years, ink has been paramount for recording and disseminating knowledge. It was discovered by several ancient civilizations roughly around the same time, as some of the earliest known examples stem from Egypt, China, and Greece (Britannica). Early types of ink were made from soot and water and, in some cases, a binding agent such as gum Arabic, egg whites, or glue. This mixture resulted in a black substance that was either liquid or solid and would lend itself well to be transferred onto flat surfaces made from natural fiber, such as wood, cloth, silk, paper, and papyrus (Needham 3).[1] Different materials were used for the black pigmentation, such as lampblack, bone black, or carbon black. While blue pigments such as Han Blue, Egyptian Blue, or Maya Blue were already used in dyes for fabrics, blue ink was developed later by the incorporation of indigo made from plants or by incorporating minerals such as azurite and lapis lazuli.[2]

Tim Ingold uses the example of pen and ink to highlight the historical process of production, rather than consumption, of material culture ("Materials" 8–9). For far too long, he argues, the focus has been on the "thingliness" of objects instead of the raw materials they are made of (9).[3] From this perspective, the material turn has overlooked the materials themselves by privileging reflections on their materiality on a metalevel (3). Ingold aims to rectify this by offering a brief history of the production of gallnut ink—a type of ink made from the oak apple, which became especially popular in Europe from the twelfth century onwards but is still used today (9). Unlike types of ink that do not have strong binding agents and would cause the liquid to sit on top of the parchment, gallnut ink sinks into the fibers of the parchment and is absorbed by it. As the ink attaches itself to paper, it gains in longevity. Inversely, this type of ink could not easily be erased and wiped out and would, in some cases, even burn through parchment because of its high levels of acidity (Gilbert Redman). Even though methods of writing and printing have since taken on many different forms, ink remains the dominant material for the written word worldwide. Inventions such as Gutenberg's printing device (1440), the fountain pen (1827), the biro (1931), and inkjet printers (1976) have also had an impact on the consistency of ink, as these different tools require different levels of viscosity and fluidity.

---

1   While ink may have been discovered simultaneously in ancient Egypt and ancient China, Tsien Tsuen-Hsuin and Joseph Needham argue in their book dedicated to paper and printing in Chinese civilization that "there is no doubt that paper-making originated in China" (3).
2   Many different plants were used to make indigo, such as the *Indigofera tinctoria* in parts of Asia, *Polygonum tinctorum* in East Asia, *anil* in Central and South America, *Natal Indigo* in India, and *woad* in Europe (Paul et al.).
3   Also known as "thingness," following Bill Brown's "Thing Theory" (4).

Ink is something of a shapeshifter, as it can be both fluid and solid. By adding water to the solid substance, ink can be turned into a liquid with varying degrees of thickness. By letting the ink dry, it becomes a solid, fixed agent again. Ink flows; it follows the movements of my hands and reveals the deeply personal aspect of my writing—my body has determined its shape. Ink spills; it is tangible only in its fluid form, either at the moment of production, when tragedy strikes and water hits the paper, the ink pots fall, or the pen bursts.[4] Several phenomenologists have drawn attention to the tangible material quality of ink. Martin Heidegger and Jacques Derrida have both explored ink's fluidity as a metaphor to liquefy meaning by placing words "under erasure" (*sous rature*), that is to say, by crossing out certain words ~~like so~~. The thin line indicates a removal or revision but paradoxically allows the words to remain on the page. This practice has therefore been used to emphasize a certain aporia in a text, highlight the inadequacy of language or concepts to convey knowledge (Heidegger), or question the distinction between absence and presence and the system of signification as a whole (Derrida). In cases like these, an extra layer of ink drawn through a word or sentence is used to point toward the limits of language and signification. It is a thin line between the spillage of ink and the slippage of meaning.

Thinking From the Materials

A thinker who has described his physical engagement with ink and pens in great detail was Roland Barthes. His love of blue ink and fountain pens is well-documented. Many of his handwritten notes and manuscripts have been exhibited in the 2015 retrospective *Les écritures de Roland Barthes* at the Bibliothèque National de France in Paris (Badmington 48; Budelis; Gallix). The following ink-related anecdote will serve as a brief case study of writing as an affective practice. When, in September 1973, an interviewer for *Le Monde* asked Barthes whether he had a "method of working," Barthes gave him an intimate description of his preparation for writing and the act of writing by hand (*The Grain of the Voice* 177). He details how the consumption of pens has become something of an addiction for him, an act not just of habit but of *craving*:

> Take the gesture, the action of writing. I would say, for example, that I have an almost obsessive relation to writing instruments. I often switch from one pen to another just for the pleasure of it. I try out new ones. I have far too many pens—I don't know what to do with all of them! And yet, as soon as I see a new one, I start craving it. I cannot keep myself from buying them. . . . In short, I've tried everything . . . except Bics, with which I feel absolutely

---

4   Neil Badmington has written extensively about several "Inkidents" (61), most notably the anecdote Barthes tells in his courses on "The Neutral" of knocking over a bottle of pigment in the shade "Neutral."

> no affinity. I would even say, a bit nastily, that there is a "Bic style," which is really just for churning out copy, writing that merely transcribes thought. In the end, I always return to fine fountain pens. The essential thing is that they can produce that soft, smooth writing I absolutely require. (178)

Barthes's affectionate description of fountain pens versus Bics reveals a particular kind of pleasure connected to the act of writing, as is signaled by the words he uses that are all connected to *jouissance*: "almost obsessive," "pleasure," "craving," and a lack of inhibition ("I cannot keep myself from buying them"). The last ambiguous phrase emphasizes the relation Barthes observes between tool and style, as "that soft, smooth writing" refers to the touch of the pen, the paper, and the style of prose he aspires to. The fountain pen's agency is particularly poignant compared to his musings on the ballpoint pen, or Bic. For if the ballpoint "merely transcribes thought," the fountain pen apparently does more than record information. The particular distribution of ink through a fountain pen adds a surplus value for Barthes, as handwriting is part of the writer's style. *Style* is a technical term in Barthes's oeuvre connected to the bodily and cognitive act of writing and to writing as a personal signature. As it is intimately connected both to the body and to personal style on the one hand and to the language system on the other, *writing* can never be completely neutral or objective (*Writing Degree Zero* 12). Even typewriting, an ostensibly "neutral" movement of the body, generates a certain type of text: "Every day I practice typing for half an hour, in the fond hope of acquiring a more 'typewriterly' writing . . . (with two fingers, because I don't know how to type)" (*The Grain of the Voice* 179).

In short, Barthes theorizes that different writing tools produce different types of writing—in terms of style and content. His affectionate description of writing tools is a testament to the approach that Deleuze and Guattari have advanced, namely "to follow the materials." Ingold refers to this as "thinking *from* the materials, not *about* them," akin to how Merleau-Ponty viewed the entanglement of subjects and objects through his concepts such as "flesh" and "intertwinement" (Ingold "Toward an Ecology" 437; Merleau-Ponty lxxxiv). In line with Heidegger and Derrida, Barthes speculates that different writing tools and how they distribute ink impact how we think. Barthes's reflections on his "almost obsessive relation with writing instruments" (*The Grain of the Voice* 178) reveal that the objects that are used as writing tools, as well as their materiality, "matter" more to his conceptual framework and the production of his critical thinking than has been acknowledged so far.[5]

---

5 A notable exception is Liedeke Plate's "New Materialisms," which discusses the material context of the publication of Barthes's "The Death of the Author": the experimental, multimedia issue of *Aspen 5+6*, which consisted of white boxes filled with all kinds of different objects—such as texts, photographs, film, records, artworks, etc. De Pourcq further discusses the implications of the multimedial context of Barthes's essay (344).

Tangibilia

Barthes's interest in the sensual aspects of reading and writing in later works such as *The Preparation of the Novel* (2010) and *The Neutral* (2007) increasingly reveal a phenomenological stance. In his lectures and seminars for the Collège de France from 1978 to 1980, published posthumously as *The Preparation of the Novel* (2010), Barthes unfolds the concept of *tangibilia*:

> In narrative or intellectual texts, I've long been alert to the presence of words with concrete things, objects as referents—let's say, broadly: things you could touch, *tangibilia*, cf. Plates in an Encyclopaedia. Succession of sensual objects—it's rare to find tangibilia in classical texts (*Dangerous Liaisons*, for example); they play an important role in the *Life of Rancé* (orange trees, gloves). (Personally, I always put them in [...]). (56)

In this example, Barthes does not distinguish objects, things, or matter, as would be the case in a more Heideggerian approach (and subsequent fields such as object-oriented philosophy or thing theory). We can gather that Barthes's concept of the tangibile refers to literary descriptions of the material world, to stuff that can be touched. In this sense, *tangibilia* are "micro hypotyposes" (57), referring to the rhetorical practice of elaborate visual descriptions of a thing, event, or phenomenon. Within the figure of hypotyposis, something is depicted so vividly that the reader almost feels its presence and imagines they could almost touch it (Sintobin 20). Etymologically, tangibility refers to two qualities: firstly, it is "easy to see or recognize," and secondly, it is "able to be touched or felt." In its first meaning, tangibility refers both to visual perception in a strict sense and to recognition as a cognitive process. In its second meaning, the tangible refers both to the sense of touch and to emotional receptivity. Barthes also refers to this double meaning when he connects the materiality of objects described in literature to the sensual impact they make on him as a reader. This double meaning becomes apparent when Barthes describes an example of a "failed" haiku that fails precisely because it does not include a sensual object: "it doesn't take, it doesn't come together, it doesn't cut into me: no *Tangibile*, no hypotyposis" (*Preparation* 58). Tying in with the second meaning of tangibility, the *tangibile* thus also refers to the ability of literature or poetry to "touch" or affect its reader, in this case, to "cut into" him.

This inherent potential of texts to wound their readers is described as the key feature of the work of art that manages to create a "Moment of Truth" (*Preparation* 106–07), the phenomenon when a textual fragment captivates the reader, absorbs them, and engenders a strong attachment based on its emotional force. It is "the conjunction of an overwhelming emotion (to the point of tears, to the point of distress) and a self-evident truth giving rise, within us, to the certainty that what we're reading is the truth (has been the truth)" (104). A truth that "we can neither interpret nor transcend nor transgress," it is a matter of acute *presence*, captured best by the realization that "Love and Death *are here*, that's all that can be said" (107). In his analysis of the grandmother's death as a Moment of Truth, Barthes stresses again that the concrete elements in this description contribute to this affective experience. He praises Proust for the fact that "he always adds in something concrete, as if he were going to the root of the concrete":

> The little attack on the Champs-Elysées: the flushes, her hand in front of her mouth; during her illness: it hurting when Françoise combs hair, etc. Why is this *true* (and not just *real* or *realistic*? Because the more concrete it is, the more it is alive, and the more alive it is, the more it will die; this is the Japanese *utsuroi* a kind of enigmatic surplus value bestowed by writing. (105–06)

The descriptions of objects, things, and materials make them present and reveal their transient nature. This tangible quality of the text, in turn, determines its "aliveness," pointing to its equal footing with other subjects and objects in the world. In this sense, these concrete details serve as "impressions" in multiple ways.

In *The Cultural Politics of Emotion* (2004), Sara Ahmed uses "impression" as an analytical tool to describe how "emotions are shaped by contact with objects" (6). I feel this term is very useful to explain the multifaceted nature of Barthes's notion of *tangibilia* as a similar analytical tool that describes the circulation of emotion, in this case, between reader, writer, text, pen, and paper. I will directly relate the several different meanings of the term "impression" Ahmed describes Barthes's notion of the *tangibile* to reveal some striking similarities: first, *Tangibilia* convey the impressions of a character or author of a specific phenomenon, revealing their cognitive and bodily experiences; second, they allow their readers to form an impression of a particular scene, to imagine a reality; and third, they make an *impression on* readers, leave a mark on them, as these *tangibilia* both convey an affective value and can have an affective impact on readers. As ink presses on paper, it, in turn, leaves its mark on us. As Ahmed states, "We need to remember the 'press' in an impression. It allows us to associate the experience of having an emotion with the very affect of one surface upon another, an affect that leaves its mark or trace" (6). Barthes's notion of the *tangibile* hints at a similar theory of emotion through his discussion of the importance of material qualities as markers for a circulation of affect.

Final Thoughts

Ink is a "sticky" substance. As it flows through the pen I wield, ink follows the movements of my hand. My movements determine its shape, but the instrument I hold, in turn, determines my movements. Together, the writing instrument and I create a style and produce a personal signature. As ink attaches itself to the fibers of paper or the skin of our hands, its stickiness becomes more than a material property; it becomes an effect of "a relation of 'doing'" (Ahmed 90). This sticky quality of ink can be viewed as an "effect of the histories between bodies, objects and signs," blurring the distinction between active and passive, subject and object. What remains is the touching of different surfaces (91). Barthes's obsession with ink and pens reveals the personal significance of these materials. The practice of writing by hand informed a large part of Barthes's identity as an academic and author. Following his own notion that the way we write impacts the way we think, we could speculate that the ideas he formed later in life—after having tried and failed to substitute writing his works by hand with writing them directly on a typewriter—were a spillover from his obsession with ink in a most literal sense. A few of these late insights include ideas about the intimate act of notation as the beginning of writing; the importance of the personal signature of the writer; the writer as a private person rather than a public textual figure; and the idea that reading and writing are part of an affective practice (*Preparation* xxvi). There, in his blue, slightly tilted handwriting, we discern something decidedly not "Neutral."

In Barthes's affectionate description of trying out pens and different types of ink, we as readers find *tangibilia*. As emblems of stuff that can be touched and stuff that touches us, they denote touch in a literal, haptic sense and a metaphorical sense, through pathos or affect. These *tangibilia* reveal a connection between the academic and the affective within the life and work of Roland Barthes. On a metalevel, they cause the same intermingling of the academic and affective for me, as his reader. I am touched by these concrete examples because they reveal an affective relation toward the act of writing itself. After all, the material practice of academic work has largely remained the same. It is there in the root of concrete materials, combined with the tone of affectionate reminiscence over these writing materials, that I find a "concision of affect and writing . . . the last degree of meaning"; the surplus value of writing (*Preparation* 107). By describing materials that can be touched through a medium that he feels an affective relation with, the medium of ink has the ability to leave an impression on its reader. Like the ink in which his text was written, it has made its mark on me.

Acknowledgments

I want to thank the editors and my colleagues Jeroen Boom, Mirte Liebregts, and Tom Sintobin for their valuable ideas and suggestions for this chapter.

Works Cited

Ahmed, Sara. *The Cultural Politics of Emotion*. 2nd ed., Edinburgh UP, 2014.
Badmington, Neill. *The Afterlives of Roland Barthes*. Bloomsbury Academic, 2016.
Barthes, Roland. *The Grain of the Voice: Interviews 1962–1980*. 1981. Translated by Linda Coverdale, Vintage Books, 2010.
———. *The Neutral: Lecture Courses at the Collège de France (1977–1978)*. Translated by Rosalind E. Krauss and Dennis Hollier, Columbia UP, 2005.
———. *The Preparation of the Novel: Lecture Courses and Seminars at the Collège de France (1978–1979 and 1979–1980)*. Translated by Kate Briggs, Columbia UP, 2011.
———. *Writing Degree Zero*. 1953. Translated by Annette Lavers and Colin Smith, Hill and Wang, 2012.
Britannica, The Editors of Encyclopaedia. "Ink." *Encyclopedia Britannica*, 1 Apr. 2021, https://www.britannica.com/topic/ink-writing-medium.
Brown, Bill. "Thing Theory." *Critical Inquiry*, vol. 28, no. 1, 2001, pp. 1–22.
Budelis, Kristina. "Barthes's Hand." *The New Yorker*, 8 Sept. 2010. https://www.newyorker.com/books/page-turner/barthess-hand.
De Pourcq, Maarten. "'De Auteur is Dood', zeggen de auteurs: het essay van Barthes in zijn context." ["'The Author is Dead', Say the Authors: Barthes's Essay in Its Context."] *Lampas*, vol. 55, no. 4, 2022, pp. 337–55.
Drazin, Adam. "Materials Transformations." Preface. *The Social Life of Materials: Studies in Materials and Society*, edited by Adam Drazin and Susanne Küchler, Bloomsbury Academic, 2015, pp. xvi–xxviii.
Gallix, Andrew. "The Writer Postponed: Barthes at the BnF." *Los Angeles Review of Books*, 23 Aug. 2015. https://lareviewofbooks.org/article/barthes-panorama/.
Gilbert Redman, Jessica. *Scriptorium: Inks*. Medieval Manuscripts, 2015. https://gilbertredman.com/medievalmanuscripts/codicology/scriptorium-inks/.
Ingold, Tim. *Knowing from the Inside: Cross-Disciplinary Experiments with Matters of Pedagogy*. Bloomsbury Academic, 2022.
———. "Materials against Materiality." *Archaeological Dialogues*, vol. 14, no. 1, 2007, pp. 1–16.
———. "Toward an Ecology of Materials." *Annual Review of Anthropology*, vol. 41, 2012, pp. 427–42.
Merleau-Ponty, Maurice. *Phenomenology of Perception*. 1945. Translated by Donald E. Landes, Routledge, 2012.
Needham, Joseph, and Tsien Tsuen-Hsuin. *Science and Civilisation in China. Volume 5: Chemistry and Technology. Part 1: Paper and Printing*. Cambridge UP, 1985.
Paul, Roshan, et al. *Indigo and Indigo Colorants*, 31 Mar. 2021. Wiley Online Library. https://onlinelibrary.wiley.com/doi/10.1002/14356007.a14_149.pub3.

Plate, Liedeke. "New Materialisms." *Oxford Research Encyclopedia of Literature*, edited by John Frow et al., Oxford UP, 2020. https://doi.org/10.1093/acrefore/9780190201098.013.1013.

Sintobin, Tom. "'En toch meen ik, heb ik overal vermeden in de pure en eigenlijke beschrijving te vallen': Het probleem van de beschrijving bij Stijn Streuvels" ["'And yet I believe I have avoided pure descriptions everywhere': the problem of descriptions within the works of Stijn Streuvels"]. *Handelingen*, vol. 55, 2001, pp. 19–37.

25. The Scholar's Coffee

Liedeke Plate

In the debate about materiality, the human body has a special place. On the one hand, as "a gathering together of materials in movement," the body is "a thing" (Ingold, "Toward an Ecology" 437) and, as such, an object of study for the emergent field of cultural materials studies. On the other hand, as theorists of embodied knowledge—and embodied subjectivity, embodied cognition, "embodied this and that, embodied everything" (St. Pierre 139); in short, of embodiment—have pointed out, the site from which the body as a thing is approached is itself such a dynamic center of unfolding activity. We, scholars, are things as well; and we should, therefore, be wary not to reproduce the subject/object, self/other, (embodied) mind/body dichotomies that the new ontologies of new empiricisms and new materialisms are at pains to undo in their quest for a more ethical understanding of the entanglement of things in the world. As a feminist scholar, a former ballet dancer, and a woman in academia, I know how deeply Cartesian dualism's ontological gap is ingrained in academic life and thinking. In this chapter, I seek to circumvent this reflex by focusing on the "bodymind" or "mindbody" of the (cultural studies') scholar at work. The brevity of the chapter requires that I limit my subject. I will therefore center my discussion on a specific moment in its life: the coffee break. In this way, thinking from the materials that gather in the "intra-action" (Barad) of scholar and coffee and foregrounding the material and biochemical dimensions of the embodied subject of academic scholarship, I break a lance for materializing theories of embodied subjectivity.

The Scholar as Thing

"[P]eople are things too," Tim Ingold remarks in his essay "Toward an Ecology of Materials" (437). His observation that "the body . . . is a dynamic center of unfolding activity" (437), while banal in stating the obvious, also reminds us of how much a recognition of this has been left out of sites of knowledge production such as the lab, the lecture hall, and the office. To be sure, omnipresent coffee and snacks vending machines, adjustable desks in the office, food courts, and sports centers are nods to the bodies of twenty-first-century universities' employees and students. Nevertheless, rarely is the thinking, reading, writing, discussing, debating, and arguing that form the core of the life of the humanities scholar thought from the materials in movement that is the scholar's body. While the number of popular science books on the influence of food on the brain and the brain-gut connection is growing (e.g., Enders; Mayer; Naidoo), these neuroscientific insights are rarely part of the humanities scholar's regimen. Unlike in professions like dance or sports, where much attention is devoted to the body and how to optimize its performance, no culture of the body exists in academia. And whereas magazines and websites for amateur cyclists, for instance, abound in advice on what and when to eat and drink for best performance on each ride, there are no such nutritional or lifestyle guides for academics.[1]

There are different ways of understanding materials. One is to think of them in terms of properties and attributes. Another is to know a material "not by what it is but what it does" (Ingold, "Toward an Ecology" 434). This performative, alchemical approach to materials accords well with my proposed inquiry into the academic's coffee break. While there is virtually no literature on nutrition and academics, the same cannot be said of coffee. Widely acknowledged as integral to many an academic life, with the central nervous system stimulating substance being called "almost a life source" for graduate students (on phdstudent.com) and a staple of most academics' experience of writing (e.g., Collini ix), coffee is nevertheless rarely thought about as part of the scholar's "gathering of materials."[2] Whereas one of my colleagues regularly dons his T-shirt that says: "Instant human: just add coffee," another received and followed her coach's advice to take a cappuccino break halfway through the morning as a moment for herself: a time-out for rest and reflection. A

---

[1] My remarks here are inspired by a talk by Rosemary G. Feal at the 2007 Modern Languages Association of American (MLA) annual convention in Chicago. Feal, then executive director of the organization, spoke about "What I learned from running," discussing how food impacted her marathon-running performance. Delivered at a Sunday 8.30 AM conference session entitled "Strategies for Success: Autobiographical Meditations," the talk was not only inspirational. It was also ground-breaking: the first time a scholar of languages and literature delivered a talk at the premiere conference about the body in such a material way. On the one hand, the talk, which listed "Seven habits of highly successful athletes," was about mindset: the advocated "strategies" for a successful academic career, with advice such as to "carry your own water" and that "every run is different." While meant as metaphors for the academic "runs" (projects, grant applications, etc.) of the university scholar, the constant references to the foods, drinks, and their effects on the runner's performance made clear that in the (daily) life and performance of the academic, the materiality of the body and the composition of the foodstuffs that affect its biological activities also contribute to their performance in a significant but theoretically largely underrecognized way. The metaphor, however, is also fraught and has been under fire in the context of Dutch academics for a while now; see Levi and Young Academy Leiden.

[2] For a notable exception, see Johnson and Mullen 55–56.

moment of "slow food" that is also a moment of "slow science" (Stengers) for a "slow professor" (Berg and Seeber), this cappuccino break not only forms an interruption of the culture of speed in the academy that ironically serves to sustain it, enabling the scholar to cope with it. It also disrupts deeply ingrained conceptions of being, knowing, relating, subjectivity, and agency.

The Scholar's Coffee Break

Let us follow the scholar on her coffee break. Having ordered her cappuccino and retired to a quiet place, she sits and lifts the cup to her lips. It is an industrial ceramic cup, hard to the touch. The heat of the coffee brew prepared with steamed milk foam has barely spread to the cup primed for heat retention. As her lips touch the microfoam that gives the cappuccino its distinct texture, a sensation of well-being spreads through the body. The moment she has been longing for is happening; it is taking place in the incorporation of the drink. As the coffee and milk foam make their way along the gastrointestinal tract and interact with the different bacteria that inhabit it, hormones are released. Though not the focus of her thought, which may already wander toward the class she will soon be teaching or still linger with the meeting she has just left, the internal transformation is not going unnoticed. After all, she deliberately takes this break to attend to her inward feeling.

Using it as a "technique of the body" (Mauss) that enables her to grapple with the outside world, for the scholar, the coffee break becomes a situated and embodied moment of being, knowing, doing, and relating. In her book *Eating in Theory*, the anthropologist of the body Annemarie Mol describes how the transformative entanglements of eating, tasting, chewing, swallowing, digesting, and excreting invite us to rethink what it is to be human. Taking her cue not from "'the human's' cognitive reflections *about* the world" but from "human metabolic engagements *with* the world" (3), the shift Mol proposes "interfere[s] in vested understandings of 'the human'" (24). It interferes in the hierarchy of the senses that governs the university as an institution and "western thought" more broadly, valuing sight and hearing above smell, taste, and touch (52–53; see also Howes; Fiore). It also interferes in the subject/object dichotomy and the worldview it sustains. "Here is the bottom line," Mol explains: "as an eater I do not first and foremost apprehend my surroundings, but become mixed up with them" (30).

Telling the Materials' Histories

"To understand materials is to be able to tell their histories," Ingold writes (434). Indebted to Karen Barad's notion of matter as "ongoing historicity" (821) and to Deleuze and Guattari's philosophy of "becoming," Ingold's conception of the historicity of materials and his injunction that we follow the life of materials is central to a cultural studies approach to materials of culture. The focus on materials in itself is a critical shift, providing a necessary counterpoint to the genesis amnesia that has come to dominate the Global North's consumer culture. As Karl Marx already knew, forgetting how things were made stands at the heart of the commodity.[3] This forgetfulness extends to the materials of which things are made. Inviting us to attend to the "meshwork" of "entangled lines, of bodily movement and of material flow" (435), Ingold's admonition furthermore directs our attention to the journeys of materials, of where they have been and where they go.

"The living body," Ingold writes, "is sustained thanks only to the continual taking in of materials from its surroundings and, in turn, the discharge into them, in the processes of respiration and metabolism" ("Toward an Ecology" 438). In *Bodies of Water*, Astrida Neimanis offers a posthumanist feminist approach to this material entanglement of self and other/world by focusing on the material "water" and how our "watery embodiment" implicates us in other animal, vegetable, and planetary bodies through various hydrological cycles. As she writes, "the flow and flush of waters sustain our own bodies, but also connect them to other bodies, to other worlds beyond our human selves" (2). In *Eating in Theory*, Mol similarly comments on the entanglement of the self with its surrounds, noting how, as an "internally differentiated being"—since "distinct body parts relate to foodstuff in different ways"—she is continually "getting enmeshed in intricate ways with pieces of my surroundings" (36). These surroundings are not limited to her immediate vicinity. Indeed, in our era of globalization, we need to acknowledge the materials' journeys not just through time but also across the globe, which make the human body a gathering of materials in movement from very different and distant places.

The coffee break entangles the scholar in the world and in complex histories. Roasted, ground, and percolated into the cappuccino, the coffee bean traveled to the scholar's coffee distributor from places around the globe, where it was grown and

---

3   As I write in "Amnesiology," the commodity is to be understood as suppressing the memory of its production process and, consequently, as having lost its capacity to remind people of where it has been, its history, and its travels (Plate 148–49). In "Orientalism's Genesis Amnesia," Mohamad Tavakoli-Targhi builds on Bourdieu's concept of genesis amnesia to argue that the formation of Orientalism as an area of European academic inquiry systematically obliterated the dialogic conditions of its emergence and the production of its linguistic and textual tools.

harvested under poor labor conditions (Wild). The emergence and development of coffee drinking as central to Western Culture in general, and Dutch culture in particular, is part and parcel of its colonial history.[4] In *Black Gold: The Dark History of Coffee*, Anthony Wild describes how the drink became popular in seventeenth-century Holland, as the Dutch managed to obtain coffee seedlings from Yemen and started coffee plantations in their new tropical colonies. These became very lucrative businesses for the plantation owners, enabling Dutch wealth in the ensuing centuries and the culture of coffee drinking that continues to play an important role in Dutch everyday life to this day.[5] Thus, as she savors her cappuccino, traces of the travels and encounters of the coffee plant make their way into and through the scholar's body. And as they become part of her, mixing and becoming-with other materials' histories, including those of milk and her genes, they connect her in a very material way to other bodies, other times, and other worlds, both human and nonhuman.

"Materials are not *in* time; they are the stuff of time itself," Ingold writes (439), inviting us to think of time and temporality as in themselves material, as well as of the different times that gather at the moment. Giving us pause to think, sense, feel, taste, swallow, ingest, and digest, the coffee-drinking break thus becomes a starting point for a more ethical understanding of being, knowing, and relating, to ourselves and others, human and nonhuman, in the present and from the past.

Works Cited

Barad, Karen. "Posthumanist Performativity: Toward an Understanding of How Matter Comes to Matter." *Signs*, vol. 28, no. 3, 2003, pp. 801–31.

Berg, Maggie, and Barbara K. Seeber. *The Slow Professor: Challenging the Culture of Speed in the Academy*. U of Toronto P, 2017.

---

4   My use of the term "Western Culture" here is meant to refer to the geopolitical formation formerly known as such while resonating with the quip attributed to Gandhi, who allegedly responded to a journalist's question, "What do you think of Western civilization?," by saying: "I think it would be a good idea."

5   Tea, chocolate, and sugar have parallel and intersecting histories; the latter's uses include sweetening and mitigating the bitterness of coffee. The Rijksmuseum in Amsterdam recently exhibited Rembrandt's portraits of Marten and Oopjen accompanied by the following explanatory wall text: "Marten and Oopjen's wealth had everything to do with the money that Marten's father, and later the couple themselves, made processing raw sugar from Brazil in Amsterdam. It was sugar grown, harvested, and processed by enslaved Africans. Much money was made in Europe from sugar, which had quickly become very popular. The Amsterdam sugar industry supplied much of Europe's demand. This huge production could only take place through large-scale use of people in slavery" (trans. Deepl.com). See also Stam, which discusses coffee drinking and its connotation of homeliness and coziness (in Dutch, "gezelligheid") as contested Dutch immaterial heritage (23–32).

Bourdieu, Pierre. *Outline of a Theory of Practice*. Translated by Richard Nice, Cambridge UP, 1977.

Collini, Stefan. Foreword. *The Slow Professor: Challenging the Culture of Speed in the Academy*, by Maggie Berg and Barbara K. Seeber, U of Toronto P, 2017, pp. ix–xiii.

Enders, Giulia. *Gut: The Inside Story of Our Body's Most Underrated Organ*. Rev. ed., Greystone Books, 2018.

Feal, Rosemary G. "Strategies for Success: Autobiographical Meditations," MLA Annual Convention, 30 Dec. 2007, Sheraton Hotel, Chicago.

Fiore, Elisa. *Gentrification, Race, and the Senses: A Sensory Ethnography of Amsterdam's Indische Buurt and Rome's Tor Pignattara*. 2021. Radboud U, PhD dissertation.

Howes, David, editor. *Empire of the Senses: The Sensual Culture Reader*. Routledge, 2004.

Ingold, Tim. "Toward an Ecology of Materials." *Annual Review of Anthropology*, vol. 41, no. 1, 2012, pp. 427–42.

Johnson, Brad W., and Carol A. Mullen. *Write to the Top! How to Become a Prolific Academic*. Palgrave Macmillan, 2007.

Leiden Young Academy. "Science is NOT like competitive sports." Voices of Young Academics, 22 July 2021. https://www.voicesyoungacademics.nl/articles/science-is-not-like-competitive-sports.

Levi, Marcel. "Wetenschap is topsport" ["Science is Top Sports"]. *Onderzoek* [Research]. NWO [Dutch Research Council], 2021. https://www.nwo.nl/wetenschap-topsport.

Mauss, Marcel. "Les techniques du corps" ["Techniques of the Body"]. *Sociologie et anthropologie*, 9th ed., PU de France, 1985, pp. 363–86.

Mayer, Emeran. *The Mind-Gut Connection: How the Hidden Conversation Within Our Bodies Impacts Our Mood, Our Choices, and Our Overall Health*. HarperCollins Publishers, 2016.

Mol, Annemarie. *Eating in Theory*. Duke UP, 2021.

Naidoo, Uma. *This Is Your Brain on Food*. Little, Brown Spark, 2020.

Neimanis, Astrida. *Bodies of Water: Posthuman Feminist Phenomenology*. Bloomsbury, 2017.

Plate, Liedeke. "Amnesiology: Towards the Study of Cultural Oblivion." *Memory Studies*, vol. 9, no. 2, 2016, pp. 143–55.

Rijksmuseum & Slavernij: 1500–1650. 1 July 2020, Rijksmuseum, Amsterdam. https://www.rijksmuseum.nl/en/rijksstudio/20160--rijksmuseum/collections/rijksmuseum-slavernij-1500-1650?ii=0&p=0

Stam, Dineke. *Immaterieel erfgoed in Nederland* [*Immaterial Heritage in the Netherlands*]. Den Haag, Nationale UNESCO Commissie, 2006.

Stengers, Isabelle. *Another Science is Possible: A Manifesto for Slow Science*. Translated by Stephen Muecke, Polity Press, 2018.

St. Pierre, Elizabeth A. "Troubles with Embodiment." Afterword. *Methodologies of Embodiment: Inscribing Bodies in Qualitative Research*, edited by Mia Perry and Carmen Liliana Medina, Routledge, 2020, pp. 138–48.

Tavakoli-Targhi, Mohamad. "Orientalism's Genesis Amnesia." *Antinomies of Modernity: Essays on Race, Orient, Nation*, edited by Vasant Kaiwar and Sucheta Mazumdar, Duke UP, 2003, pp. 98–125.

Wild, Anthony. *Black Gold: The Dark History of Coffee*. Harper Perennial, 2010.

List of Contributors

Brigitte Adriaensen is Professor of Hispanic Studies at Radboud University. She is the principal investigator of the NWO Vici research project "Poison, Medicine or Magic Potion? Shifting Perspectives on Drugs in Latin America (1820–2020)." Earlier, she directed the NWO Vidi research project "The Politics of Irony in Contemporary Latin American Literature on Violence." Her publications are situated in the fields of humor studies, violence studies, and environmental studies.

Nuno Atalaia is a Portuguese researcher, teacher, and musician residing in the Netherlands. His work explores the intersections of new media, performance, and the history of human vocality. He has a double MA from The Hague Royal Conservatory and Leiden University and is currently finishing his Ph.D. at Radboud University. He is also co-director of the ensemble Seconda Prat!ca, with which he has performed and taught around the world.

Jeroen Boom is a doctoral candidate in the Department of Modern Languages and Cultures at Radboud University, working on essay films and the role of moving images as nodes of resistance in processes of social and political stigmatization. He also coordinates the research group Critical Humanities at the Radboud Institute for Culture and History (RICH) and teaches courses on film and visual culture.

Daniëlle Bruggeman is a cultural theorist and Professor of Fashion at ArtEZ University of the Arts in the Netherlands. She teaches at the MA Critical Fashion Practices and leads the ArtEZ Centre of Expertise Future Makers. Bruggeman holds a Ph.D. in Cultural Studies and has published on topics including the fluid, performative, and embodied dimensions of identity, and fashion as a new materialist aesthetics. The publication *Dissolving the Ego of Fashion: Engaging with Human Matters* (2018, published by ArtEZ Press) presents the current research themes of the ArtEZ Fashion Professorship. Bruggeman's current research focuses on an emerging practice-based critical fashion discourse, developing alternative systemic approaches, and thinking through the issues of (non-)human agency and material agency from a post-anthropocentric perspective.

Carlijn Cober is a Ph.D. candidate at the Radboud Institute for Culture and History (RICH) and in Radboud University's Department of Modern Languages and Cultures. Her dissertation, *Reading for Feelings*, examines postcritical elements in the works of "critical" theoreticians such as Roland Barthes and aims to provide a theoretical foundation for affective reading experiences. She is interested in the connection between literature and emotion, "the personal" in relation to literary theory, and the social use of texts.

Maarten De Pourcq is Professor of Literary and Cultural Studies at Radboud University. He researches receptions of Greco-Roman antiquity in twentieth- and twenty-first-century culture, which he studies in relation to artistic practices and cultural criticism, ideas and debates on cultural heritage, and processes of social and cultural change. Among his recent publications is the co-edited volume *Framing Classical Reception Studies* (Brill, 2020).

Oscar Ekkelboom is a Ph.D. candidate at the Radboud Institute for Culture and History (RICH) at Radboud University. His work focuses on the presence of colonial structures and ideas in museum displays today. Taking decoloniality as a starting point for thinking and doing, he engages in a process of listening to those who have been denied access to the canons of art.

Airin Farahmand is a Ph.D. student at the Radboud Institute for Culture and History (RICH) at Radboud University, where she also obtained her BA in Arts and Culture Studies (cum laude) and her Research Master's in Art and Visual Culture. Her dissertation project focuses on artworks engaging with the plastic crisis. Before moving to the Netherlands, she completed a BSc in Mechanical Engineering at Tabriz University. In a broader sense, her research interests include questions of agency, representation, body politics, and feminist future-making.

Anna P.H. Geurts is a historian and works as an Assistant Professor at the Radboud Institute for Culture and History (RICH). Geurts publishes on everyday experiences of space and time in interaction with changing technologies, is the Dutch translator of Neel Doff's autobiographical novel *Keetje trottin* (translated as *Keetje op straat*), and is under contract with Routledge for a study of travelers' experiences of European spaces in the nineteenth century.

Mette Gieskes is Assistant Professor of Modern and Contemporary Art at Radboud University. She received a Ph.D. from the University of Texas at Austin, with a dissertation on the use of systems in American art of the 1960s and 1970s. She has published articles on artists including Philip Guston, Sol LeWitt, Tamara Muller, and Francis Alÿs, and is currently writing texts on Simon Hantaï and Moniek Toebosch. She is co-editor of *Retrospection and Revision in Modern and Contemporary Art, Literature and Film* (Palgrave 2023, with Mathilde Roza) and *Humor in Global Contemporary Art* (Bloomsbury 2023, with Gregory Williams).

Hanneke Grootenboer is Professor of the History of Art at Radboud University. Her scholarship examines early modern visual and material culture through the lens of contemporary art and theory. She focuses on the relationship between art and thought, in particular around topics such as touch, intimacy, interiority, and miniaturization. Her latest monograph is entitled *The Pensive Image: Art as a Form of Thinking* (U of Chicago P, 2021).

Ghidy de Koning holds a BA in English (2021) and is currently completing an MA in Literary Studies at Radboud University.

Vincent Meelberg is senior lecturer and researcher at Radboud University's Department of Modern Languages and Cultures and the Radboud Institute for Culture and History (RICH), and at the Academy for Creative and Performing Arts in Leiden and The Hague. He is a founding editor of the online *Journal of Sonic Studies*. His current research focuses on the relationship between sonic practices, technology, and creativity. Besides his academic activities, he is active as a double bassist in several jazz groups, as well as a sound designer.

Edwin van Meerkerk is Associate Professor in the Department of Modern Languages and Cultures and the Radboud Institute for Culture and History (RICH) of Radboud University. He specializes in arts education, cultural policy, and sustainability. He also works as an endowed professor of Creating Connected Commons at ArtEZ University of the Arts. He is one of the editors of the forthcoming third *Yearbook of the European Network of Observatories in the Field of Arts and Cultural Education* (ENO), which is devoted to Arts and Cultural Education in a Challenging and Changing World.

László Munteán is Assistant Professor of Cultural Studies and American Studies at Radboud University. At the Radboud Institute for Culture and History (RICH) he leads the research group *Memory, Materiality, and Affect*. His publications have focused on the memorialization of 9/11 in literature and the visual arts, as well as on photography, urban culture, architecture, and cultural heritage. In a broader sense, his scholarly work revolves around the intersections of literature, visual culture, and cultural memory in American and Eastern European contexts. With Anneke Smelik and Liedeke Plate he co-edited the volume *Materializing Memory in Art and Popular Culture* (Routledge 2017).

Niels Niessen holds a Ph.D. (2013) from the University of Minnesota. He is a Researcher of Cultural Studies at Radboud University. At the Radboud Institute for Culture and History (RICH) he leads the research group *Platform Discourses: A Critical Humanities Approach to Tech Companies* (funded by the European Research Council). His book *Miraculous Realism: The French-Walloon Cinéma du Nord* (2020) appeared with SUNY Press. Currently, he works on the book *The End of Everyday Life: Resisting Technofeudalism*.

Liedeke Plate is Professor of Culture and Inclusivity at Radboud University and the director of Radboud Institute for Culture and History (RICH). She frequently collaborated with Anneke Smelik, publishing on issues of cultural memory and forgetting and inquiring into the material turn in literary and cultural studies. Together, they edited *Stof en as. De neerslag van 11 september in kunst en populaire cultuur* [*Dust and Ashes: Remembering 9/11 in Art and Popular Culture*] (Van Gennep, 2006), *Technologies of Memory in Art and Popular Culture* (Palgrave, 2009), *Performances of Memory in Art and Popular Culture* (Routledge, 2013), and, with László Munteán, *Materializing Memory in Art and Popular Culture* (Routledge, 2017).

Tess J. Post is a Ph.D. candidate at Radboud Institute for Culture and History (RICH). Her research focuses on the mythology of milk in the Netherlands. She is interested in tackling the complexities of seemingly banal objects. Coming from a comparative literary background, her work combines postcolonialism, critical animal studies, and ecofeminism.

Rianne Riemens is a Ph.D. candidate at Radboud Institute for Culture and History (RICH), working on a dissertation about the role of tech companies in the climate crisis, as part of the ERC project "Platform Discourses" led by Niels Niessen. Her research takes place at the intersection of media studies and the environmental humanities, with a special interest in internet and energy infrastructures and Big Tech discourse.

Kathryn Rudy (Kate) is Bishop Wardlaw Professor of Art History at the University of St Andrews, a member of the St Andrews Institute of Medieval Studies, and the Director of the Centre for the Study of Medieval Manuscripts and Technology (CeMManT). She is also Excellence Professor at Radboud University. She holds degrees in English literature, art history, and medieval studies and completed a post-doc at Utrecht in Middle Dutch Literature.

Michiel Scheffer studied geography and international economics at Utrecht University, Erasmus University Rotterdam, and the London School of Economics. He holds a Ph.D. from Utrecht University (1992). He has been teaching at the Amsterdam Fashion Institute, Saxion Hogescholen, and Institut Français de la Mode. Besides an academic career, he held several management positions in the fashion and textile industry and in politics. He wrote his chapter in this book as Program Manager of Sustainable Textiles at Wageningen University and Research.

Nishant Shah is Professor of Global Media at the Chinese University of Hong Kong, a Faculty Associate at the Berkman Klein Centre for Internet and Society, and a knowledge partner with the Digital Asia Hub and Point of View. His interests are at the intersections of digital technologies, feminist practice, and social movements.

Tom Sintobin is Assistant Professor of Literature and Tourism Studies at Radboud University. His research interests include Dutch and Belgian literature (1890–1970) with a special emphasis on travel literature and local color fiction, tourist cultures in coastal cities in the low countries, and online travel accounts.

Lianne Toussaint is Assistant Professor in Media, Arts and Society at Utrecht University. Her research focuses on fashion and wearable technology, particularly the relations between the human body, technology, and clothing. She defended her dissertation *Wearing Technology: When Fashion and Technology Entwine* in 2018. Toussaint recently participated in a collaborative project on developing reusable protective garments for hospital staff and is currently developing a research project on innovative protective clothing.

Frederik Van Dam is Assistant Professor of European Literature at Radboud University. His scholarship is situated at the intersection of intellectual history and literary criticism, with a focus on the long nineteenth century. He is the author of *Anthony Trollope's Late Style: Victorian Liberalism and Literary Form* (2016) and the co-editor of *The Edinburgh Companion to Anthony Trollope* (2019). His articles have appeared in journals such as *English Literary History*, *Studies in Romanticism*, and *Partial Answers*. His most recent work revolves around art and cultural diplomacy in the interwar period, with particular attention to Hungarian literature. He is the book review editor of the *European Journal of English Studies* and a member of the Radboud Young Academy. In 2015, he interviewed the éminence grise J. Hillis Miller for a documentary, *The Pleasure of that Obstinacy*.

Astrid Van Oyen is Professor of Roman Archaeology at Radboud University. Her research focuses on the archaeology of Roman Italy and the Western provinces, with a particular interest in the socio-economic history of non-elites, craft, rural economies, and human-thing relations. She is the author of *How Things Make History: The Roman Empire and its Terra Sigillata Pottery* (Amsterdam UP, 2016) and *The Socio-Economics of Roman Storage: Agriculture, Trade, and Family* (Cambridge UP, 2020).

Timotheus Vermeulen is Professor of Media, Culture and Society at the University of Oslo. He has published widely on screen media, contemporary art, and cultural theory, including books on metamodernism, suburban culture, and most recently (with Kim Wilkins) the oeuvre of Richard Linklater. He is currently finishing a manuscript for SUNY Press with the working title *Gesture and Time: Screen Performance as Temporal Form*. Vermeulen is a contributor to *Art Forum* and *Frieze*.

Wilco Versteeg is a teacher and researcher at Radboud University and St. Joost School of Art and Design in Breda. He obtained his Ph.D. from Université Paris Diderot, with a study on documentary photography in contemporary wars and conflicts. He specializes in the history and theory of photography and cinema. He is also a professional conflict photographer, with a deep interest in European protest movements.

Social Sciences

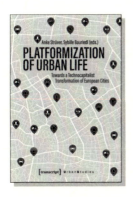

Anke Strüver, Sybille Bauriedl (eds.)
Platformization of Urban Life
Towards a Technocapitalist Transformation of European Cities

September 2022, 304 p., pb.
29,50 € (DE), 978-3-8376-5964-1
E-Book: available as free open access publication
PDF: ISBN 978-3-8394-5964-5

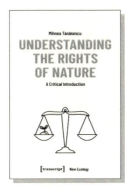

Mihnea Tanasescu
Understanding the Rights of Nature
A Critical Introduction

February 2022, 168 p., pb.
40,00 € (DE), 978-3-8376-5431-8
E-Book: available as free open access publication
PDF: ISBN 978-3-8394-5431-2

Oliver Krüger
**Virtual Immortality –
God, Evolution, and the Singularity
in Post- and Transhumanism**

2021, 356 p., pb., ill.
35,00 € (DE), 978-3-8376-5059-4
E-Book:
PDF: 34,99 € (DE), ISBN 978-3-8394-5059-8

**All print, e-book and open access versions of the titles in our list
are available in our online shop www.transcript-publishing.com**

Social Sciences

Dean Caivano, Sarah Naumes
The Sublime of the Political
Narrative and Autoethnography as Theory

2021, 162 p., hardcover
100,00 € (DE), 978-3-8376-4772-3
E-Book:
PDF: 99,99 € (DE), ISBN 978-3-8394-4772-7

Friederike Landau, Lucas Pohl, Nikolai Roskamm (eds.)
[Un]Grounding
Post-Foundational Geographies

2021, 348 p., pb., col. ill.
50,00 € (DE), 978-3-8376-5073-0
E-Book:
PDF: 49,99 € (DE), ISBN 978-3-8394-5073-4

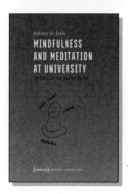

Andreas de Bruin
Mindfulness and Meditation at University
10 Years of the Munich Model

2021, 216 p., pb.
25,00 € (DE), 978-3-8376-5696-1
E-Book: available as free open access publication
PDF: ISBN 978-3-8394-5696-5

All print, e-book and open access versions of the titles in our list are available in our online shop www.transcript-publishing.com